Organizing
the
Breathless

Organizing
the
Breathless

Cotton Dust,
Southern Politics,
& the
Brown Lung
Association

ROBERT E. BOTSCH

THE UNIVERSITY PRESS OF KENTUCKY

Copyright © 1993 by The University Press of Kentucky

Scholarly publisher for the Commonwealth,
serving Bellarmine College, Berea College, Centre
College of Kentucky, Eastern Kentucky University,
The Filson Club, Georgetown College, Kentucky
Historical Society, Kentucky State University,
Morehead State University, Murray State University,
Northern Kentucky University, Transylvania University,
University of Kentucky, University of Louisville,
and Western Kentucky University.

Editorial and Sales Offices: Lexington, Kentucky 40508-4008

Library of Congress Cataloging-in-Publication Data

Botsch, Robert Emil, 1947–
    Organizing the breathless : cotton dust, southern politics, and
the Brown Lung Association / Robert E. Botsch.
        p.   cm.
    Includes bibliographical references and index.
    ISBN 0–8131–1818–2 (alk. paper)
        1. Cotton manufacture—Health aspects—Southern States.
2. Byssinosis—Social aspects—Southern States.   3. Brown Lung
Association—History.   4. Cotton dust—Health aspects—Southern
States.   5. Textile workers—Health and hygiene—Southern States.
I. Title.
RC965.C77B68   1993
363.11'967721'0975—dc20   92–42053

This book is printed on recycled acid-free paper meeting
the requirements of the American National Standard
for Permanence of Paper for Printed Library Materials.

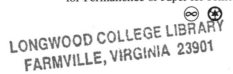

To my mother and father

CONTENTS

ABBREVIATIONS

ACGIH   American Conference of Governmental Industrial Hygienists
ACTWU   Amalgamated Clothing and Textile Workers Union
AFL–CIO   American Federation of Labor–Congress of Industrial Organizations
ATMI   American Textile Manufacturers Institute
BCPP   Birmingham Citizen Participation Program
BLA   Brown Lung Association
BLOC   Breath of Life Organizing Campaign
B–WAC   Brooklyn Welfare Action Council
CETA   Comprehensive Employment and Training Act
COLD   Chronic Obstructive Lung Disease
COPD   Chronic Obstructive Pulmonary Disease
CWP   Communist Workers Party
EPA   Environmental Protection Agency
IUD   Industrial Union Department
LCHA   Love Canal Homeowners Association
NIOSH   National Institute for Occupational Safety and Health
OCS   Officer Candidate School
OSHA   Occupational Safety and Health Administration
PIRG   Public Interest Research Groups
SIOH   Southern Institute for Occupational Health
SNCC   Student Nonviolent Coordinating Committee
SSDI   Social Security Disability Income
TWUA   Textile Workers Union of America
UMW   United Mine Workers
VISTA   Volunteers in Service to America
WHO   World Health Organization

ACKNOWLEDGMENTS

This book, like any book, would not have been possible without the help and assistance of many people. Members and former members of the Brown Lung Association were kind, courteous, and generous in sharing their thoughts and feelings over more than a decade. They continued to talk to me even after reading early versions of papers I wrote that were not entirely complimentary. Former staffers were willing to talk to me both on and off the record at odd hours and odd places and sometimes drove considerable distances to meet me. They went beyond facts to share their own thoughtful insights and evaluations.

Dr. Robert Castellan of the National Institute of Occupational Safety and Health was most patient. He helped me understand the current state of research on the subject of byssinosis and pointed me to sources that do not show up in normal bibliographical searches.

I am particularly grateful to the textile executives and managers who gave me their time and perspectives, knowing full well that the story was not one that would heap praise on the industry. Openness and tolerance of criticism are important steps in creating a more positive vision of some future South.

Paul Cimbala, who left the South to study it from the safe distance of Fordham University, gave this ahistorical political scientist significant help with historical context patiently reading early drafts sent to him in bits and pieces. Tom E. Terrill, another scholar of the South, offered a number of constructive criticisms in his reading of an early draft. Ben Judkins deserves my thanks in several ways. This book builds on his pioneering sociological study (1986) of the Brown Lung Association. In addition to providing a foundation, he generously gave of his time, reading a late draft of the manuscript and making helpful and supportive suggestions.

I am grateful to Val Lumans and the rest of the administrators at the University of South Carolina, Aiken, for allowing me a semester's sabbatical. The five months they gave me, thought it seemed like five weeks, allowed me to get the bulk of the writing accomplished.

My best critic and helpmate, Carol Sears Botsch, taught extra classes to help support our family while I was laboring on this project. Beyond that, she listened and encouraged me when I had doubts, vastly improved my prose with her suggestions, and quieted the children when I was doing telephone interviews. Far from least important, she reminded me to save computer files frequently when spring thunderstorms rumbled across the midlands of South Carolina. I also thank my children, David and Matthew, who are far too old and full of energy to take naps, as David did when I wrote my first book, but were quiet and understanding when I needed extra time.

I could just about feel something inside that told me all the things he said were true. He used to sit here and tell me how strong men were in the Valley when they were young and how weak they were when they grew up breathing cotton lint into their lungs and dying with blood on their lips.

— Erskine Caldwell
God's Little Acre, 1933

INTRODUCTION.
A SOUTHERN TRAGEDY

"The Valley" is a series of small mill towns that lie along Horse Creek between Aiken, South Carolina, and Augusta, Georgia. When I came to South Carolina in 1978, I learned that this was the same valley Erskine Caldwell had described in *God's Little Acre*. In this tale of eccentric and fiercely romantic individualists, Caldwell made several references to weak old workers who were "spitting their lungs into the yellow dust" (1933, 123). Some forty years later novelist Pat Conroy described the same area in a biting indictment of worker exploitation by local mills:

For twenty miles America has a savage and well preserved vision of what was wrong with the industrial revolution. . . . The Valley shelters a grim and fiercely proud native . . . . The mill is in his blood. . . . History has trapped him. . . . The only organization they have is The Mill. The Mill cares for them, entertains them, takes care of their sick, and is always ready to perform fatherly duties if emergencies arise. No one can convince the people of the Valley that the reason they are so buried in this miasma of hopelessness is directly due to the benign shepherding of the Mill. No one has told these people along the long sad highway that the Mill is guilty of high crimes, unforgivable crimes, crimes for which they would fiercely deny responsibility. [1974, 52–54]

Reading these literary references about a place and people so near my new home sparked my interest. Both novelists were alluding to "brown lung," the popular name given to the occupational disease byssinosis, which is associated with exposure to cotton dust. I heard about a new organization of retired mill workers in the Valley who were fighting for workers' compensation and trying to force the mills to reduce dust exposure. The retired workers and the organizers who helped them called it the Brown Lung Association.

If successful, this organization would be a remarkable historical precedent. As historian David Carlton argues, southern workers have tenaciously and stubbornly resisted almost all forms of organization in the past, even when it was in their own self-interest. "Deeply suspicious of all forms of organization, the operatives were never much more than a group of individuals facing a well-organized opposition. Not only were their social attitudes inappropriate to the complex society they had entered by moving to the mills, but those very attitudes provided them with few means of protesting" (Carlton 1982, 314). For more than the next decade I observed the group to see if they would succeed where so many others had failed.

The story of this small organization and its near-complete demise is worth telling for several reasons. First, it is a profoundly human story that raises eternal moral questions of right and wrong, but with some shades of gray as well. One can see the heroic struggle of people who rose above their physical, educational, and cultural constraints for a short period of time in the twilight years of their prematurely shortened lives. There is tragedy. They inevitably succumbed to these weaknesses and to external forces over which they had no control. Through their heroic and tragic efforts some of them—though far from all—gained a measure of human dignity in the self-conscious awareness of both struggle and inevitable defeat.

As is the case with most human stories, there is no clear ending. The protagonists won partial victories and endured many defeats. Their actions will have ripple effects for generations to come. They contributed to changes that will forever alter the lives of working people who will have no knowledge of what these sick and dying victims of the New South accomplished.

The antagonists in this human story were the managers and owners. They are usually type-cast in the role of greedy villains who epitomize the worst tendencies of southern-style laissez-faire capitalism. Some fit that role, just as some of the thousands of would-be claimants were malingerers. But in a larger sense, both the mill operators and the workers were trapped in a political, economic, and social system that very few understood and even fewer could control. In addition to being prisoners of southern history and economics, they found that realities external to the South limited their options.

King Cotton placed tyrannical demands on both his nobles and their millhand serfs. Long after he was unable to provide prosperity to any but a few, he was kept in power at the expense of the many.

To keep him in power, those who ran the mills ignored the problems of workers that were so obvious to outsiders. They absolved themselves of blame by passing the responsibility to others and by claiming ignorance. Much of that ignorance was self-imposed—a characteristic all too frequently found in southern history.

When King Cotton was finally forced off the throne, many of his former subjects were left unprepared to deal with the new realities of world competition in the information age. The greatest villains in this southern tragedy were the economic and political leaders. They failed in their most fundamental task—leadership. Instead, they blindly served the status quo. They failed to provide any realistic vision of an alternative future.

The story of the Brown Lung Association is valuable for a second reason. The rise and fall of this small group tells us quite a bit about southern politics, culture, interest groups, union organizing efforts, the making and implementation of policy, and economics. It certainly does not tell us everything about the south. I have been teaching southern politics long enough to know that the South is far too complex for any one story to encompass all its mysteries and contradictions. Since the burning experience of the Civil War created the American South as a self-conscious separate nation (Woodward 1960, 19), two related central questions have shaped its political history (Key 1949, 5). What role would blacks play in southern society? How would the South deal with the severe economic problems left by the war and a subsistence agricultural economy in an industrializing world? The story of the Brown Lung Association tells us relatively little about race relations, although race does play a minor role in the life of the organization. On the other hand, the story tells us a great deal about how the South attempted to deal with its economic problems. It tells us about the winners and the losers in the long campaign to industrialize the region.

Southerners have lived under a great deal of pressure for generations. The unique mixture of race (or caste) politics and economic class politics creates much of the pressure in southern political life. The recipe involves explosive contradictions: civility and insult, loyalty and rebellion, community conformity and exaggerated individualism, neighborliness and individual isolation, family-centered love and family-directed violence, high church attendance and high prison populations, and love of politics combined with low political participation. Cash (1941) and Key (1949) suggest reasons for and results of these opposing forces. Many actively stirred the mixture: redeemers, planters, bourbons, demagogues, all too often fraudulent populists, and even middle-class advocates of the industrial new

South. They did so for their own benefit. But though they often did benefit, the mixture frequently exploded, sometimes harming them but almost always harming those below them. Even when it did not explode, it had a constant corrosive effect on the people of the region wearing them down both physically and mentally. Southerners are like characters in an ongoing Greek tragedy, nobly flailing away in a losing fight. We marvel that they last as long as they do. Our own spirits are buoyed by the fact that they struggle at all.

This story tells us about the lives and place of those who labored in textiles. The mill workers of the South were so separated a a class that they nearly approached caste status (Carlton 1982; Hall et al. 1987). That is, they were marked by birth as members of a group from which they could not easily escape. We can't understand this little band of disabled workers without understanding something about how they were seen by those who regarded themselves as superior.

Ever since V.O. Key (1949) equated southern politics with one-party factional politics, political scientists have focused on the role of political parties in the South. We have been looking for change in this arrangement. We have been seeking a "new" southern politics. To this end we have studied the voting rights movement, the reactionary Republican "southern strategy"—which plays a role in the story of this small group—and the changing demography of the South. All of this is quite important. One cannot understand southern politics without understanding the failures of party politics.

We have not done enough, however, to understand interest-group politics, which replaced parties in the making of public policy in the South. One explanation is that interest groups are a little more difficult to study; less empirical data are readily available. Whatever the reason, too little emphasis has been placed on how public policy actually is made in the South. With few exceptions, relatively little has been written about the central role of interest groups in southern politics (Hrebener and Thomas 1992, ix).[1] The story of the Brown Lung Association is the story of southern interest groups in action. It is the story of power, as are all political stories. It involves the power to make things happen and prevent them from happening (Gaventa 1980). The great political sociologist C. Wright Mills described organization as the mobilization of bias. The Brown Lung Association is the story of southern bias in organizational mobilization.

The rise and fall of the Brown Lung Association illustrates the importance of what historians call context. Political scientists tend to use the term "external environment" to describe the same kinds of factors. The larger political, economic, and social environment played an important role in this conflict. The title and content of the widely heralded study by Earl and Merle Black, *Politics and Society in the South* (1987), asserts the importance of internal and external context. What the protagonists did was important, but environmental forces are at least as important in explaining the final policy outcome in this struggle over workers' compensation and working conditions in textile mills.

Finally, I hope this case study will prove to be a worthwhile addition to a growing literature on grassroots activism. At the end of the book I compare the brown lung movement with others, such as the black lung movement, neighborhood organizations, and the Welfare Rights Movement.

A word on methodology. Between the late 1970s and the writing of this book I have periodically followed both one local chapter of the association and the larger organization in a number of ways. When the group was most active, I was a participant-observer. I attended more than a dozen meetings, cover-dish suppers, and other events, such as a training session for the breathing clinics it operated. At those sessions I took notes and talked to members and organizers. In addition to short, informal conversations, I completed over sixty hours of formal interviews: twenty five hours with some fifteen former staff and organizers (several of whom were interviewed two or three times), twenty-five hours with about thirty members both in person and on the telephone, five hours with half a dozen textile officials representing several companies, and at least another six hours with a variety of lawyers, legislators at state and national levels, state officials responsible for the enforcement of safety laws, and medical researchers. One of my most valuable sources was the diary of a student intern. He worked on a daily basis with the local chapter for the last six months of 1981, a critical period when the organization peaked and began to decline. His logs were invaluable in extending my own eyes and ears to understand how the organization actually functioned.

Persons interviewed whom I cite by name gave me permission to do so. All those interviewed who did not want to be quoted by name are listed in the references and cited simply as "Interviews." In a very few cases I unilaterally chose to omit names when I thought a quotation or incident might cause needless embarrassment. That may not be in the best scholarly tradition, but it reflect my own southern background.

In addition to the usual library research, I consulted organization records that are housed in the Southern Historical Collection,

Southern Folklife Collection of the Manuscripts Department at the University of North Carolina, Chapel Hill (BLA Papers). The collection includes about 3,500 items filling almost nine feet of shelf space, in addition to some audiovisual materials. They were donated in the mid-1970s by the staff lawyer, Candice Carraway, who ran the association's legal office, by long-time staff member Betty Bailey, and Florence Sandlin, who was the last president of the Greensboro, North Carolina, chapter. Finally a number of former members and staff gave me either their own papers or copies of them.

I have tried to make the story readable for undergraduate students. To that end, I have purposely minimized academic jargon (most theoretical commentary has been relegated to notes). The first three chapters focus on the cultural, political, public policy, and scientific settings in which this struggle took place. My assumption is that one cannot fully understand what happened without understanding all these parts of the environment. Those interested in reading only the story of the Brown Lung Association should begin with chapter four. The book concludes with what I think to be the most significant comparative lessons of this struggle.

1

THE CULTURAL AND POLITICAL SETTING

They came from the failed farms and the hollows of the Appalachian Mountains. They came because they saw no other alternative, bringing with them their families, their broken dreams, and their habits of mind and behavior. Although they stubbornly resisted the changes mills demanded of them and maintained as best they could the things they held dear (Hall et al. 1987, 43; Newby 1989), milltown life altered their physical being, their family relationships, and their habits and beliefs.

THE SOUTHERN MILLTOWN

The building of textile mills and the accompanying mill villages around the turn of the century gave rise to a new culture across the rolling hills of the piedmont of the South, the milltown culture. To understand the Brown Lung Association, we must first examine the cultural setting in which it was born. We must understand the political and socioeconomic values that its members inherited from their grandparents. These values serve as an important explanatory factor—though certainly not the only factor—in the birth, life, and passing of the Brown Lung Association.

In the years surrounding the turn of the century, the advocates of the New South began making significant headway in transforming the region from an agrarian society to an industrial society. As David Carlton makes clear in his insightful analysis of the 1880–1920 period, the mill villages built to serve as housing and as social control mechanisms for the mill operatives created a new culture. The townspeople who ran the mills, invested in the mills, and did business with the mills soon regarded that culture as "the mill problem" (Carlton 1982, 129). This new culture, created by conflicting forces, ambitions, and visions of society, proved to be a problem not only for those who wanted control over and stability in the new industrializing South but also for the workers. The values and habits of the milltown culture posed nearly insurmountable obstacles to the organization necessary to share in profits or to guarantee a safe and healthy workplace (Newby 1989; Griffith 1988, 161–76).[1]

Middle-class entrepreneurs saw the textile mills of the New South as the key to their rise to economic dominance (McLaurin 1971, 15) and social prominence. Their success required a large number of dependent and reliable workers (Carlton 1982, 10; Luebke 1990, 3). Although owners justified the creation of mill villages in philanthropic terms—providing work for displaced white farmers—this was little more than an advertising gimmick used by industrial promoters who were willing to try any labor source in order to turn a profit (McLaurin, 1971, 43; Carlton 1982; 72–78). Some mill owners attempted to use black labor so that there would be "no more trouble about labor—no strikes, labor unions, etc. among the whites" (quoted in Carlton 1982, 158). Others tried to import immigrant labor from the North, but that effort failed because of low wages and because it ran against traditional southern xenophobia. Southerners perceived the immigrants to be "filled with socialistic ideas" (Carlton 1982, 113–14), likely to form groups and make organized demands when reality did not match what they had been promised.[2]

Mill owners' only alternative was to utilize the whites of their own region. This had been their natural inclination in the first place, because the culture of white supremacy and southern regionalism led them to believe that southern whites would provide optimal labor. Although mill owners and hired supervisors and their heirs have spent the greater part of the twentieth century extolling the loyalty and virtues of their workers, saying it did not make it so.

The values of displaced white agrarians made them particularly unsuitable for the highly regimented and structured nature of factory life. Yeoman farmers who were accustomed to moving with the rhythm of the seasons and their own idiosyncratic inclinations were difficult to control. They resented all authority, claiming independence of all regulation as part of their inalienable birthright. They were quick to anger, especially in defense of their personal honor (W. J. Cash uses the term "techiness" to describe this trait). Extremely proud and easily offended, they saw interpersonal violence as the most appropriate way to solve problems. Family was the primary social and political unit to which they owed any loyalty. (Cash, 1941, 33, 43, 52, 75–76, 125; McLaurin 1971, 58–59; Carlton 1982, 10, 209; Wyatt-Brown 1986, 145–146; Hall et al. 1987, 136). Their most important demands were to be respected as equal members of the white race and to be left alone to lead their family lives as they pleased. They resented the intrusions of the mills, of unions, of "do-gooder" reformers, of uppity townspeople who looked down their noses at mill workers, of schools that tried to make their children ashamed of their parents, and of government that was controlled by the mill owners, townspeople, or social reformers (Carlton 1982, 222–25; Hodges 1986, 26–34; Hall et al. 1987, 136–40).

Mill workers were willing to follow almost any leader who would honor these wishes. That included Cole Blease (Hall et al. 1987, 120), who, as governor of South Carolina in 1911–12, vetoed an appropriation for mill safety inspections on the grounds that it would give state government too much control over workers (Carlton 1982, 234). That also included George Wallace, who in the 1960s heaped ridicule on Washington's "briefcase-totin' bureaucrats" for their unwarranted intrusions into citizens' private lives (Black and Black 1987, 217). More recently, it included Ronald Reagan, who successfully appealed to white southern workers with his promise to get government off their backs. He also tried to get the Occupational Safety and Health Administration (OSHA) off the backs of the textile industry—with some success, as we shall see. In sum, white southern mill workers have long been characterized by an exaggerated sense of individualism, and much of southern politics can be understood in terms of the manipulation of their values.[3]

Those who came to the mill villages did not come voluntarily. They came out of economic necessity. They came when they could no longer survive on the farm (Hall et al. 1987, 102). They came as failed providers for their families, and they knew it (Carlton 1982, 146). Many continued to hang on to their land and farm it part time. Others hoped to get out of debt and return to the land (McLaurin 1971, 53–54; Kirby 1987, 294; Tullos 1989, 175–76). Nearly all tried to preserve their ties to the land, even in the mill village, with tiny garden plots and small farm animals (Hall et al. 1987, 146–47). One can hear the echoes of their broken dreams in the words of southern factory workers in the 1970s who spoke of working in the factory only long enough to find a way out. They did not share the industrial goals of those who ran the factories and the town. They dreamed of escape, of fishing and hunting on the land they loved, not of building a new industrial South (Botsch 1980; Tullos 1989, 262, 267–68).

What they found when they arrived in the villages with its "shotgun" houses[4] was certainly not paternalism. Cash argued that the mill owners never did care at all for the workers' welfare, that their saying so was all a cruel hoax designed to generate worker loyalty (1941, 202–5). Beardsley's study (1987) of the neglect of mill workers' health by owners and state authorities reinforces Cash's conclusions and extends them to 1970. McLaurin (1971, 32–51) and Carlton (1982, 89–109) found that owners greatly exaggerated the building of schools and churches. Mill village schools were almost always of much lower quality than town schools; attendance rules were rarely enforced; and basic necessities of sanitation were advertised as though they were great luxuries.

Many students of southern society have observed that mill villages were modeled on the plantation system, which totally submerged its inhabitants in dependency (Beardlsey 1987, 4; Billings 1979; McLaurin 1971, 16–17). The mills provided schools, churches, stores, and even their own currency. The goal of all these institutions was to exercise social and economic control.[5] Despite these similarities, however, there were notable differences, often to the disadvantage of the workers. Carlton (1982, 106–7) points out that mill owners, unlike planters, rarely lived in their own "plantations." Usually they lived in the middle- or upper-class section of the nearby town, where they could interact with those of their own socioeconomic class. As mills were bought out by corporations, ownership became even more distant and less concerned with the daily amenities of mill village life. In short, mill workers were more isolated from their economic masters than were many slaves from their owners.

This social isolation points to the radically different visions of society held by workers and townspeople owners. Middle-class townspeople saw material wealth as the most important measure of individual worth. For many, material worth was even more important than race, although they were certainly still segregationists by any measure of the term (Carlton 1982, 157). This belief clearly placed townspeople in a superior social position to mill workers. These differences were so strong that they were characterized as establishing a second "caste" status within the white caste (Carlton 1982, 133; McLaurin 1971, 56–57). Anyone who has lived in a southern town adjacent to the remnants of mill villages knows of the class-based resentments that persist. Differences manifest themselves in school attendance zones and church and civic club memberships.

Workers adhered to the traditional world view of the equality of all whites under the banner of white superiority. They resented slights to their honor, even when the resentment was self-defeating. For example, mill workers refused to participate in a day nursery provided by middle-class women in Spartanburg, South Carolina, because of the possible negative reflections on worker competence as parents (Carlton 1982, 209).

Middle-class mill owners and their peers placed much greater value on organizational cooperation than did the workers (Carlton 1982, 238–39). The creation of the mills was a cooperative town venture that required complex social and economic interrelationships among all the middle-class participants (Carleton 1982, 29–33). As labor history demonstrates, townspeople regarded challenges to the mills as threats to their own well-being. The reaction to such challenges brought to bear the wide range of well-coordinated social control mechanisms at the disposal of those whose economic well-being was tied to the mill: evictions, loss of credit, loss of jobs, schools, and even churches (see, e.g., Pope 1942; Hall et al. 1987).

Organizational involvement and cooperation were foreign to the agrarians who had unwillingly come to the mill villages. Individual autonomy was their guiding value. They rejected external discipline from all sources. Their only social allegiance was to family. Cooperation was a matter of spontaneous neighborliness, not social contract. Occasional union support and joint actions were based more on small individual complaints than on any notion of class interest or solidarity (Carlton 1982, 251).[6] These traits remain. The sacredness of individual autonomy poses a major barrier to union organization even in the late 1900s, long after most workers have experienced formal education (Botsch 1981). A dislike of formal organizations and a highly localistic, individualistic style was a significant barrier in organizing the natives of Appalachia against the damning of the New River in the 1970s and early 1980s, and against other less obvious threats to their way of life (Foster 1988, 144, 215).

Middle-class townspeople viewed the milltown culture as simply the transplantation of the culture of poor farmers. They blamed "the mill problem" on the people who came to the villages, not on the new environment created by the mills (Carlton 1982, 173). Likewise, they blamed health problems on the poor habits of the workers, not on the mills or the mill housing (Beardsley 1987, 192). There is some measure of truth to this charge. For example, the rural habit of relieving oneself in the nearest bushes created problems when transplanted to an urban setting.

The agrarian culture's emphasis on violent reactions to personal affronts remained intact. Unfortunately, the environment of dependency confronted the workers with new reasons to feel affronted (Gaventa 1980, 72). The result was a great deal of violence within the villages, giving them a reputation that added to the insult and social stigma felt by their proud residents (Carlton 1982, 145–46, 150–51). Long work hours for all members weakened the family's status as the single strong social unit brought to the mills. Workers resented the rigidity of the hours as much as their length, and the fact that they were all spend indoors (McLaurin 1971, 26; Hall et al. 1987, 53) Long hours and factory noise reduced opportunities to socialize and interact. Yet children preferred the light work they often did with little supervision to the discipline of school, where they were constantly reminded of their class inferiority by middle-class teacher from town (Carlton, 1982, 175–79).

These unhappy conditions, combined with a propensity to solve problems through individual action, led many workers to pull up and leave whenever they were angry or had a slightly better opportunity (Hall et al. 1987, 105–9). At the beginning of the rise of the mills in the 1880s, many factories had a 50 percent turnover in labor every two years; Carlton estimates that at the turn of the century as many as 25 percent of all workers were floaters from one mill to another (1982, 151–52). This propensity to pull up roots quickly and frequently can be traced back to rural life as well as to the conditions in the mills. Kirby (1987, 277) estimates that in the early 1900s some 30 to 40 percent of the farmers in the South changed locations annually. My own work with factory operatives in the 1970s found the same pattern. Workers who were unhappy with their boss or pay would leave at the first opportunity in a futile yet proud effort to improve their condition (Botsch 1980, 92). The Occupational Safety and Health Administration used 60 percent as the annual turnover figure, with two-thirds of that being workers who simply moved from one mill to another ("Occupational Exposure" 1978, 27379). Ironically, workers who protested working conditions with their feet made more organized protests more difficult. High mobility may have posed an even greater barrier to unions than did management opposition (Carlton 1982, 142). Certainly this "nomadic tendency" undercut community ties, made the formation of any worker groups most difficult, and (especially if it involved crossing state lines) could create legal problems in claiming workers' compensation.

The holding of agrarian and individualistic values varied across the population of workers, depending on their origin. Most mill workers came from three different social groups (Carlton 1982, 146–52; McLaurin 1971, 17–18). Owners preferred the first group, the small farmers and croppers whom they saw as mainly hard working and reliable—although employers and workers both knew that most of these ex-agrarians were in the mills because they had failed at farming, even if the reasons were beyond their control. The second group was considered much less desirable. Almost every negative label one could imagine, most commonly "poor white trash," was applied to this group of wandering casual laborers who rarely achieved even sharecropper status for long. They were even less likely than the first group to submit to any form of discipline or regimentation and were very unreliable. The last group, the mountaineer "hillbillies," were pictured "as an exotic breed of barbarian . . . distrustful of the outside world, [who] regulated themselves by means of strong family loyalties, a firm code of honor, and above all, a ferocious commitment to untrammeled individualism" (Carlton, 1982, 148). They were the least desirable employees, yet their desperation for work made them useful as strikebreakers (Hall et al. 1987, 345–47).

When there was a labor surplus, the major tool for social control was to select workers from the first group. But because there were rarely enough in this group to meet employer needs, workers from all three groups influenced mill village culture. Kirby concludes that the mountaineers from southwestern Virginia, western North Carolina, and Eastern Tennessee were the "second most common migrants to the mills" (1987, 289).

The heirs of the mill village culture were left a legacy of disorganized individual powerlessness and frustration over lost social status. Each failed uprising in the history of southern labor reinforced what Gaventa (1980) calls a culture of powerlessness. We should not regard this as simple fatalism. Fatalism implies passive acceptance. Workers were not always passive and were often less than accepting (McLaurin 1971; Gaventa 1980). Carlton concludes his work by noting that "the mill workers of South Carolina remain today as they have for most of this century, acquiescent but not quite willing participants in a world not of their making" (1982, 272).

SOUTHERN POLITICS IN THE 1970s

The life of the Brown Lung Association was set in a South that was changing from total one-party dominance to a two-party system. The socioeconomic changes were perhaps even more important. The narrow traditional agricultural and manufacturing interests that had so long dominated southern politics were giving way to a more pluralistic South. Textile manufacture, which had been the major dominant interest in both Carolinas (Morehouse 1981, 108–11), was losing some of its clout. Other interests with more emphasis on economic development and education were beginning to gain political influence: banks, utilities, professional educators, real estate, and construction (Hrebenar and Thomas, 1992, 328–29). All these interests brought with them a growing middle class who would outnumber the working classes by the late 1970s (Black and Black 1987, 54–56). Textiles would still be a major player, especially in South Carolina, but leaders could no longer call all the shots.

The one-party system had really been a no-party system in most of the South. To quote V.O. Key's classic work on southern politics, "The South really has no parties" (1949, 299). This system had two related consequences. Elites could ignore class-based economic issues because there was no organized opposition, and the have-nots were the losers (Key 1949, 307). Those who later came to join the Brown Lung Association were among the losers. This was especially true in South Carolina where few stable factions existed to structure political conflict in place of parties. Local elites dominated the state through a strong legislature (Key 1949, 132, 150–51). As long as the textile industrie dominated local areas, it would be a powerful force in state government.

North Carolina, the other major textiles state in the South, had a little more structure with a relatively strong Republican party—by southern standards—in the western mountain area. In response, the Democrats had to be more organized than in southern states offering less Republican challenge. However, the conflict was more along regional lines (mountains, piedmont, and the coastal plain) than along class lines. This allowed the industrial elite to run the state in the way that best suited them. Although North Carolina was more progressive than most other southern states in the sense that it spent more on roads and education, working-class people still had no one to voice their economic interests (Key 1949, 211–28).

In sum, whether local or part of a statewide industrial elite, fairly narrow interests, including textiles, dominated both the Carolinas; interest-group politics was much more important than party politics.

The most recent comprehensive examinations of southern politics find both change and continuity. The Republicans have made tremendous inroads into southern political life, providing the potential for a two-party system on class lines. Because Democrats now need their support, the have-nots have a potentially greater voice. Yet, reality has fallen far short of the potential because of changing demographics. Working-class blacks and whites no longer constitute the largest group. Moreover, they are still split along racial lines on such volatile issues as affirmative action. As demonstrated by Jesse Helms's victory over Harvey Gantt in the 1990 U.S. Senate race in North Carolina, economic issues are usually not sufficient to attract white working-class voters when they can be so easily distracted by racial issues (Helms equated affirmative action with racial quotas) and social issues (Helms opposed federal funding of art that he had his followers considered pornographic). The conservative nature of the white working class on racial, social, and economic issues—when they are posed in terms of individual responsibility (Black and Black 1987, 61)—means that both parties must make very similar appeals. By themselves, blacks are too few in number to build any more than local majorities in carefully drawn districts. "The relevant question is not whether whites or blacks will occupy most of the vital decisionmaking arenas in state government, but *which* whites will rule (Black and Black 1987, 151).

The net result is that while two-party politics has replaced one-party factional politics, neither of the two parties has much to offer textile workers.[7] "Republicans simply offer another form of old southern factionalism—just a variation on old Democratic politics. The continuing power vacuum in southern politics is filled by interest groups. So the rise of the Republican party in the South has done little to change the environment in which these groups operate" (Hrebenar and Thomas 1992, 350). Moreover, interest groups dominate to a degree that is unmatched in any other other part of the nation (Hrebenar and Thomas 1992, 352).

The nature and number of the groups is the major change in an interest group–dominated political system. "Diversity and technology" is the new mantra. The spirit of what Black and Black (1987, 29) call "entrepreneurial individualism" is beginning to sweep across the South. Luebke (1990, 20–22) uses the term "modernizers" for members of both political parties who pursue the same agenda in North Carolina politics. That agenda stresses rapid economic development, just as did "New South" themes at the turn of the century. The advocates of this ideology want access to state government so they can pursue economic growth policies that will help them make money. Their policy agenda is a mixture of progressive and conservative positions. A better-trained work force, so long as it is not unionized, would help them achieve their ends. A more diverse economy that does not rely on just one or two industries—especially low-profit industries like textiles—would also benefit them.

This changing balance of political power presented both obstacles and opportunities for a grassroots movement aimed at textile workers. On the one hand, even if the movement succeeded in organizing both retired and active workers, its potential in terms of sheer numbers and relative size was much less than it would have been in earlier decades. At best, it could hold the balance of power between a Democratic party built on a base of black voters and a Republican party built on the higher end of the emerging middle class (the "Volvo set").[8] On the other hand, this more fluid situation offered a greater possibility of affecting state government policies and even gaining local attention. Most middle-class townspeople no longer saw the mill as the cornerstone of economic well-being. Thus, a grassroots lobbying effort had a better chance of winning middle-class sympathy than in the days when so many members of the middle class had ties to the textile industry (Pope 1942).

The late 1960s and the 1970s constituted a unique period in American political history, a period of unusual political activism with a strong theme of participatory democracy through grassroots organizing. After the most obvious sins of segregation were over, and only Vietnamese—not Americans—were dying in Vietnam, the focus turned toward finding economic justice at home. Grassroots community organization was one of the primary vehicles. Idealistic young people attempted to organize nearly all the groups that were underrepresented in the pluralistic system of interest groups that defined American democracy. The range was broad. Ralph Nader organized college students into Public Interest Research Groups (PIRGs), and activist Catholic clergy organized welfare mothers. The guiding literature and theory stressed community activism, participatory democracy, and consciousness raising. Students on college campuses read the works of grassroots organizers such as Saul Alinsky and Piven and Cloward, argued over goals and tactics and structure, and, in support of Caesar Chavez's farmworker organization, refused to eat grapes or lettuce.

The Brown Lung Association was one expression of this era of grassroots organizing. If workers would not join unions or vote for liberal candidates, perhaps they could be rallied around issues that concerned their own health. Perhaps they could be inspired by the spunk and fight of their disabled parents and grandparents. Perhaps a group like the Brown Lung Association could be the initial rallying point for the unorganized southern work force. If workers' consciousness could be raised through political education as part of their organizational activities, and if they learned some organizational skills and began to think of themselves as a collective group rather than as isolated individuals, they might begin to mobilize for larger goals of social justice. At least that was the hope.

2

COMPENSATING VICTIMS AND PROTECTING WORKERS

Those who organized the Brown Lung Association hoped to attract both disabled and active workers, to win the support of disabled workers by fighting for workers' compensation and the support of active workers by fighting for a cleaner, healthier workplace. To understand what these battles were about, we need to examine the workers' compensation system and how it neglected the needs of those disabled by "brown lung" (byssinosis). We should also examine the evolution of the Occupational Safety and Health Administration and the cotton dust standards that were supposed to make the workplace safer.

THE WORKERS' COMPENSATION SYSTEM

Clara Lewis began working at Graniteville Mills in 1925 at the age of fifteen. Her family had worked for the same company for many years. She remembers that times were very hard, in part because her father had been ill. Later, she herself began to notice breathing problems. She had the classic "Monday morning syndrome" that defines the acute stage of byssinosis: upon returning to work after the weekend, she would feel short of breath and would wheeze and cough, and the dust in the mill seemed to make it worse; however, as the week went by, she seemed to get over it. After she had worked more than forty years in the mill, her family doctor diagnosed acute bronchitis and advised early retirement. Because she did not smoke, he could not explain the cause of her problem. She finally retired in 1972, after forty-five years of service, because "I just didn't have enough breath to do my job."

She went to a local screening clinic sponsored by the Brown Lung Association in 1977 and was told she was a possible brown lung victim who could file a claim under workers' compensation. After traveling to Emory University for more extensive tests, which confirmed the diagnosis of byssinosis, she filed a workers' compensation claim in 1979. She asked for lost wages and for medical costs, which were well beyond her ability to pay. Graniteville and its insurance company, American Mutual, contested the claim. In August of 1980, after a hearing at which lawyers from both sides presented their evidence, Commissioner Harold Trask of the South Carolina Industrial Commission (now called the Workers' Compensation Commission) awarded her $37,500. At this point Lewis was surviving on social security and attempting to support a daughter who was both invalid and retarded. Things were about to get worse: she would soon suffer a heart attack (weakened lung capacity is a contributing condition to heart attacks). As was their right, Graniteville and its insurance company appealed to the full commission. In November 1980 the full commission reduced the award to $12,500 but added lifetime medical benefits. The defendants again exercised their right to appeal in the state court system. The basis for this appeal was that Clara Lewis's claim violated the statute of limitations, that she had waited too long after having contracted the disease to file her claim. The circuit court rejected that argument and, in April of 1981, upheld the full award. Some four years had now passed since the original claim was filed. By the time Graniteville and American Mutual threatened to appeal to the South Carolina Supreme Court, Clara Lewis had suffered the heart attack and was very pessimistic about her future. She settled out of court for $12,500—without any medical benefits—and of course had to pay her lawyer a significant part of the settlement (lawyers typically received a fourth to a third of the total award). And once she had settled, no further claims could be made, regardless of what medical costs she might incur.

The company announced for the record that the "Graniteville Company has always been concerned about the health and well-being of its employees and has gone to considerable financial expense to provide the cleanest, safest work environment possible. . . . Though the company could have appealed to the South Carolina Supreme Court, it was decided to settle for humanitarian reasons." Lewis's own feelings were an ambivalent mixture of loyalty, pride, and personal anger: "You know, I ain't got nothing against the company. The man who started Graniteville, he was a wonderful man. He didn't know about cotton dust. I was proud of the company when

I worked for them and I still am . . . but they're doing wrong, and they have to stop" (Roberts 1981b, 1981c).

There is probably no such thing as a typical workers' compensation case, but Clara Lewis's experience does illustrate most of the problems of the system's dealings with difficult-to-diagnose occupational diseases. She suffered high legal costs, great delay through multiple appeals, and ultimately a compromise that fell far short of meeting her basic needs—precisely the opposite of what the system is supposed to accomplish.

Prior to the enactment of the workers' compensation system in the early twentieth century, workers injured on the job had no recourse other than to sue their employers. They had to prove not only that the job caused their injury, but that the employer was negligent. In the words of the *South Carolina Workers' Compensation Commission Annual Report* (1990, 3), "this was often a very slow, costly, and uncertain legal process." Then states began adopting a kind of no-fault compensation because both workers and employers saw that a new system would be in their interests. Workers were having to endure heavy legal costs and much delay with great uncertainty in pursuing legal suits. And for industry—although it could better afford the legal expense, and delay was always in its favor—an ultimate loss could prove costly because the award might include large punitive damages (Hughes 1979, 2; Schroeder 1986, 156–57). It took a number of years for all states to adopt some kind of workers' compensation system. South Carolina, for example, did not do so until 1935.

However well the injury side of workers' compensation functions, the system has proved very weak in dealing with occupational diseases. Even though all states allow compensation for them, diseases are inherently different from accidents—yet South Carolina states that the "disability or death of an employee resulting from an occupational disease is treated as an injury by accident" (*South Carolina Workers' Compensation Commission* 1990, 5). Dealing with occupational diseases under the same kind of rules as accidents places sick workers at a severe disadvantage. Their greatest difficulty is proving that something in the workplace caused the problem. That is usually obvious in the case of accidents, but it is much more problematic in the case of occupational diseases (Schroeder 1986, 157). It is especially problematic when the symptoms are clinically indistinguishable from diseases that occur outside the workplace, such as emphysema or chronic bronchitis (Hughes 1979, 2). The claimant can present a work history, but the cause may still be subject to legal challenge, and it usually is. As of the late 1970s, employers contested only about one in ten of the accident claims that were eventually awarded, but they contested six in ten disease claims and nine in ten dust claims (U.S. Dept. of Labor 1980, 70–71).

Medical testimony is a critical part of establishing proof. Unfortunately, semantic differences in the standards of proof in medicine and in law create another barrier for those pressing a claim. Because of the medical profession's more exacting scientific standards of proof, doctors are often unwilling to attribute the precise cause of the disease. They no not always understand that compensation law requires proof to be strong enough only to lead to the conclusion that the work environment "could or might" be the cause (Hughes 1979, 32).

A related problem for textile workers is finding doctors who are knowledgeable about byssinosis and who are willing to make the appropriate diagnosis. Greenville, South Carolina, attorney Ben Bowen, who has represented many byssinosis claimants, spoke of this problem in 1980 at U.S. House of Representatives hearings. "Doctor, I said, what is the classic history of person suffering from byssinosis, and he said just what you have read on my chart [for Bowen's client]. I said, would you please tell me why you said this man had emphysema and not byssinosis? Now, I am talking about an internist, a specialist in cardiopulmonary conditions, and he said because byssinosis is not popular in Greenville, S.C." To find a doctor willing to make the diagnosis, Bowen said, he had to take his client some eighty miles from Greenville (U.S. Congress 1980, 84–85).

Restrictions in state laws pose a second kind of problem in pressing claims. Statutes of limitations have been tied to the time of exposure rather than to the time at which the worker becomes aware that the disease is related to work (Schroeder 1986, 157). Some states restricted occupational disease claims to a list of diseases, and byssinosis was not always included (U.S. Congress 1978, 163). For example, North Carolina recognized byssinosis as a compensable disease in 1963 (Hughes 1979, 12); Georgia did not do so until 1982 (Munro 1982, B1).

Workers' awareness is also a problem. They may not know about the disease or the linkage between their breathing difficulties and their work. The trouble may not occur until after they leave the workplace, and it may be misdiagnosed by physicians. No doubt many sick workers have gone to their graves without ever knowing what killed them.

Finally, employers have a greater incentive to contest occupational disease claims than injury claims because they more frequently involve permanent or total disability with higher, long-term payments (Hughes 1979, 2). From a business point of view, contesting the claim is merely a decision to minimize costs. Because time works to the advantage of a corporation that has unlimited time and to the disadvantage of the claimant who feels she or he may have a limited time and needs support right away, litigation is also a bargaining tool. Legal appeals created incentives for the claimant to settle at a lower cost.

Clara Lewis faced many of these obstacle and ultimately settled for far less than the commission had awarded. Her words also illustrate the conflict between the feelings of loyalty held by many long-term employees and feelings of betrayal. One might well ask whether the company's concern measured up to its self-congratulatory words. Did Graniteville act as an impersonal profit-maximizing corporation even while its public pronouncements portrayed a close, interpersonal, caring relationship between management and production workers? This case was not the brightest footnote in the history of one of the relatively more progressive mills in the South (Carlton 1982, 202).

The success of companies in minimizing workers' compensation costs means that someone else has to pick up the tab for medical care and living expenses. In 1979 Joseph "Chip" Hughes completed a study of disabled textile workers, funded by the U.S Department of Labor. Hughes, who was also a Brown Lung Association organizer, examined 270 disabled workers in the Carolinas, about one-fourth of all those who had at that time applied for workers' compensation. He found that the workers themselves were picking up the largest share of the costs, in the sense that their incomes fell 47 percent. More than eight of every ten dollars they did receive came from the Social Security Disability Income (SSDI) program, and whatever help they got in paying medical costs came from Medicare, not workers' compensation. Unfortunately, the waiting period for Medicare, after one is certified as totally disabled and eligible for Social Security Disability, is two years. Most workers had absolutely no health insurance during that waiting period. And even with the help of Medicare, they still spent a third of their income on medical costs (Hughes 1979, 45, 43, 16).

These findings reinforced a 1977 study by the National Institute for Occupational Safety and Health, which concluded that there were far more SSDI awards based on respiratory problems among workers in the textile industry than among the general population (Hughes 1979, 40). Unlike the workers' compensation system, SSDI does not require the disabled worker to show that the cause is work related; she or he has only to demonstrate disability. Although the national government has sometimes tried to minimize SSDI claims because of the strains they place on the Social Security system's budget, the process has been much easier for most claimants to navigate successfully (Hughes 1979, 42–43). Even if the disabled worker does win or settle a workers' compensation claim, like Clara Lewis, payment is often made in the form of a lump sum. When that money runs out, as it quickly does, the worker can make no further claim on the company and has little choice other than to turn to SSDI. The net effect is that textile companies shift a cost of doing business to all those employers and employees who pay into the SSDI system, and to the disabled worker, whose living income is severely reduced.

Workers' compensation hearings are in some ways typical administrative legal proceedings. A member of the commission (a deputy commissioner in North Carolina) presides. In both Carolinas, commissioners are appointed by the governor for six-year terms. As political appointees, they come from a variety of backgrounds that do not necessarily include law. In the early 1980s only one of three commissioners in North Carolina and four of seven in South Carolina had a legal background—and one of those had been a law clerk, not a lawyer (Covington et al. 1980b, 10). The others had a business background. The most conservative commissioner on byssinosis cases in South Carolina had spent most of his adult life in the cotton ginning business. At the first hearing, the presiding commissioner acts as a judge, interpreting points of law and ultimately rendering a written decision. Commissioners' decisions are routinely appealed to the entire commission and then to state courts. Lawyers for the claimant and the textile company, along with the insurance carrier, present their sides of the case. A clerk records the proceedings. The claimant gives testimony concerning work history and physical symptoms and undergoes cross-examination.

Byssinosis hearings, however, were unique in workers' compensation proceedings. In other workers' compensation cases, attorneys rarely have to fight for a claim (Judkins 1986, 127). But because byssinosis cases were relatively new, almost every one of them required procedural precedents, and attorneys for both sides fought hard to establish precedents that would help them in future cases. In the hearings I attended, procedural questions were raised about a wide variety of points, from the admissibility of testimony to the right of workplace access by claimants to determine the physical conditions of work. The fact that the workplace had often changed a great deal since the claimant left created additional complexity. Many of the cases involved old people who had been away from the mills for ten years or more. It was difficult for them to remember details of work histories that often dated back to the 1940s. Memory lapses or testimony inconsistent with earlier depositions could be fatal to their claims. Occasionally, lawyers for the mills employed unexpected and bizzare tactics. In one case the defense lawyer representing the mill began calling witnesses out of the audience in a seemingly random manner. He questioned them about their backgrounds and beliefs as members of the Brown Lung Association. He even interrogated a university professor who was there to do research (BLA Papers).

The workers' compensation process was very intimidating to those unfamiliar with legal proceedings and legal terminology. It was not easy to answer questions about ancient details when there was so much at stake. Having a silent cheering section of Brown Lung Association members helped calm nerves and bolster confidence, but beyond this kind of moral support, unfortunately, members could do little for one another in navigating the long and difficult process. Those who had gone through it could and did offer advice about what to say, but this created potential conflicts with the lawyers, who had their own ideas on how claimants could best answer questions.

The nature of the workers' compensation process added to the difficulties of the Brown Lung Association in recruiting members. Again, the Clara Lewis case illustrates the point. Although she was identified by an association clinic and received moral support from the group, she was never very active in the group, despite her personal anger. Physical problems, financial constraints, and a sense that individual action was the most appropriate action all stood in the way of group commitment. Her predilection for individual action was reinforced by the legal necessity of having her own individual lawyer to take her through the compensation process. Yet Lewis had more community ties and more family stability than most textile workers. If she was unable to commit herself to collective action, the probability was much lower for those who had more transient ties to their community.

Critics of the workers' compensation process argue that instead of acting as judicial bodies, commissions should perform in a more supervisory fashion, making sure claimants obtain the support to which they are entitled. As part of that supervisory function in byssinosis or other occupational disease cases, commissions should lay out standards for the diagnosis of the disease rather than relying on each side to present its own medical expert opinions (Hughes 1979,

26–27, 29). The net result of the current system is that in contested cases the claimant must obtain the assistance of an attorney and endure the same kind of long legal battle as would have existed under the tort law system that workers' compensation was designed to replace. Byssinosis cases are not unique in this respect. From the outset, court rulings have forced workers' compensation commissions to give defendants (the companies and their insurance carriers) full due process protections that invite appeals and delay (Larson 1978, 265; Schroeder 1986, 157–58).

Because of all the problems associated with occupational disease compensation, many efforts have been made to bring about reform. In 1970, as part of the same act that created the Occupational Safety and Health Administration, Congress established the National Commission on State Workmen's Compensation Laws to study the adequacy of existing state systems (*National Commission* 1972). That commission formulated a list of nineteen recommendations for all states. In 1977 another federal study group looked at problems in the state-run workers' compensation systems (*Report to the President* 1977). This task force recommended several reforms that were directly relevant to occupational diseases such as byssinosis. The most important would have shifted the legal burden from the claimant to the employer in cases where epidemiological research had shown a clear link between the disease and the workplace. It would have been presumed that anyone who had worked in that industry for a given period of time and who suffered the symptoms of that disease should be compensated, unless the employer could demonstrate that the disease was not caused in his workplace. This is called "presumption" or "presumptive diagnosis." It was a major legislative goal for which the Brown Lung Association and its supporters unsuccessfully fought on both state and federal levels.

States did little to meet the 1972 recommendations (Schroeder 1986, 159) and never came close to adding presumptive diagnosis to their own workers' compensation laws. As a result, sympathetic members of Congress proposed national laws that would have required states to meet state minimal federal standards. The Brown Lung Association provided a significant amount of testimony at hearings in 1978, 1979, and 1980 in support of federal intervention (U.S. Congress, 1978b, 1979, and 1980), and bills continued to be introduced—the last in 1983—but none passed (Schroeder 1986, 164).

Federal legislation failed for a number of reasons. In the late 1970s, with high inflation rates and growing federal deficits, the Carter administration was particularly sensitive to any legislation that would have an inflationary impact. In the waning years of the

Carter presidency, Congress never proceeded beyond studying he problem of adequate compensation for disabled byssinosis victims (U.S. Congress 1979, 130–35). The Reagan administration's philosophy of minimizing federal regulation and passing responsibilities to the states doomed any federal efforts after 1980. Federal legislation was strongly opposed by all commercial and manufacturing industries, including textiles, and by the insurance industry as well. Organized labor and its supporters simply could not match the political clout of the opposition.

The line of argument used by textile interests in opposing workers' compensation reform emphasized six main points (U.S. Congress 1979, 197–211). First, although they conceded the existence of byssinosis, they minimized the estimated number of workers who suffered anything beyond its mild reversible stages. Here they relied on scientific studies they themselves had sponsored. Second, they argued that the disease would soon cease to be a problem because they had put in place surveillance programs that would identify those susceptible to the disease and transfer them to a less dusty area. Moreover, they pointed out that dust levels were being reduced—even while they fought to have dust standards eased. Third, they argued that workers' compensation programs were best administered on the state level on grounds of both effectiveness and efficiency, pointing to the unexpectedly high costs of the federal black lung program. Fourth, they praised state programs for the progress made in meeting federal recommendations and in compensating byssinosis claims. Fifth, they acknowledged that byssinosis victims should be compensated—thus placing themselves on high moral ground—but argued that those suffering from lung disorders not caused by dust exposure should not be compensated by the textile industry. In the words of the prepared statement of the Cotton Council presented at an occupational disease hearing in 1979:

There is no hesitancy to settle workers' compensation claims which are clearly justified. But, as shown, differentiating byssinosis from non-occupationally related respiratory diseases is a difficult assignment for the best pulmonary specialists. The cotton industry cannot afford to bear the expense of disabilities caused by all respiratory diseases. No industry could, nor should Congress impose such a burden. . . . Yet the cotton industry is maligned for its efforts to make a careful investigation of claimant's eligibility for benefits. [U.S. Congress 1979, 200]

The difficulty of definitively demonstrating causality allowed the textile industry and its insurance carriers to challenge virtually all claims without abandoning the moral position of wanting to compensate legitimate claims. Finally, the industry called for research to identify the causal agent so that it could be removed from cotton before it reached the mill, thereby passing responsibility back to the farmers and the Department of Agriculture.

A number of arguments can be made for federal legislation. Ben Bowen, the Greenville lawyer who has represented may byssinosis claimants and who as a young man was a textile worker himself, argued that federal bills, even if not passed, placed a great deal of pressure on states to make compensation easier (U.S. Congress 1980, 83). Critics of the existing state system point to two, more direct benefits. First, a federal system would increase equity and uniformity across states. Why should a disabled textile worker in Aiken, South Carolina, be treated substantially differently from a worker who was employed across the Savannah River at an Augusta, Georgia, mill? Second, the federal government is in a better financial situation to support the necessary scientific studies to establish clear, uniform, standard criteria for demonstrating causality. Currently, every claimant has to bear part of this burden for her or his own particular case (Schroeder 1986, 164–45).[1]

Those who supported the Brown Lung Association differed on the optimal legislative approach. Although many association members and some U. S. representatives and senators from the Carolinas preferred a special program for brown lung victims modeled after the federal black lung program, others promoted a comprehensive approach to all occupational diseases. When Ben Bowen testified before the Senate committee on Human Resources on a comprehensive bill that would address all industrial diseases, Senator Harrison Williams, who chaired the committee and cosponsored the bill, asked him which would be preferable. Bowen strongly favored the more comprehensive approach: "I think it should be a comprehensive bill . . . because you will get bogged down in every area like asbestos and pneumoconiosis and other conditions that result from chemicals in employment. There are many chemicals now that we are not aware of. You cannot do it disease by disease" (U.S Congress 1978b, 163).

Several members of Congress from the Carolinas began to take an interest in federal legislation after the Brown Lung Association gained national attention in 1977. Although their motivations are difficult to determine precisely, one can speculate on the basis of their history and the nature and timing of the legislation they supported. Southern senators and representatives although usually stereotyped as conservative, have a populist streak that sometimes comes through. (This was especially true for South Carolina's Senator Ernest Hollings, who had discovered hunger and poverty in his home state in the 1960s and had become one of the biggest supporters of Lyndon Johnson's antipoverty programs.) Many of them had always done well with the blue-collar vote and wanted to maintain a positive image among textile workers in their states. There would be some political cost with textile interests, but that would be minimized if they could dictate the nature of a federal program so that most of the costs did not fall upon the textile companies. In supporting federally funded legislation that was limited to byssinosis claims, they could have the best of all worlds. They were playing to a significant part of their electoral base; they could argue that they were protecting textiles from more costly programs; and they could still be the champions of limited government by opposing more comprehensive occupational disease legislation.

Bills introduced by South Carolina Senators Hollings and Strom Thurmond and Congressman Butler Derrick would have created a special compensation program for byssinosis victims. Their argument for a special program rested on two grounds. First, textile workers forced into retirement by byssinosis were a large enough group to merit their own program, and they would not be covered unless a retroactive provision was included in the comprehensive bill. Unfortunately, such a retroactive provision, if covering all workers, would make the bill too expensive to pass. Senator Hollings made this point in a prepared statement for hearings on the comprehensive bill: "I believe the magnitude of the problem which exists in the Carolinas and elsewhere with regard to cotton textile workers requires more than what is promised by your proposal . . . we have forgotten those persons most deserving and most in need of our help, . . . those older disabled workers who have been selectively eliminated from state assistance . . . and who stand to suffer the same fate under the compensation standards proposed in [this bill]. . . . Targeting brown lung compensation benefits to a limited, finite population of disabled textile workers would cost only a fraction of [the cost of the black lung program], and the initial cost would decline each year" (U.S. Congress 1978b, 165–66).

The other argument focused on the question of political timing. A comprehensive law was inherently much more complex and would take longer to pass. These disabled workers did not have the time to wait. In testimony before the House Subcommittee on Labor Standards, Butler Derrick exchanged views with subcommittee member John Erlenborn of Illinois.

Erlenborn: Well, I really fear that the example we now have with the black lung is going to be the start of separate compensation programs for one dis-

ease after another—each with its own bureaucracy, its own tax to support the program. I do not think that is in the best interest of the taxpayers of this country [or] of the people who get the compensation. They will be treated unequally . . .
Derrick: You know that I have no objection to a broad compensation program, that would establish minimum Federal standards. . . . The point is, we just cannot wait 10 years. We need to move ahead with this now. [U.S. Congress 1979, 13]

Even though these men had always been supportive of the textile industry, they seemed genuinely moved by the plight of those forced into early retirement with no financial compensation. Hollings and Thurmond learned of the magnitude of the problem in hearings they held in December 1977 in Greenville, South Carolina, the center of the textile industry in the South. This was six months after Brown Lung Association members had made national headlines by their dramatic testimony at the OSHA cotton dust standard hearings. The problem clearly had publicity value.

The December hearings were dominated by members of the Brown Lung Association who told their own stories as best they could. By the time textile spokespersons came before the two senators, Hollings was ready to engage in some argument. Leaders of the South Carolina Textile Manufacturers Association argued that 1977 changes in the state's workers' compensation laws had taken care of all the problems faced by retired workers and that new programs in the mills would take care of the current work force. Hollings objected:

Have you arranged for compensation or have you dug a moat around the injured party whereby there's a sort of "Catch-22" situation that you cannot be compensated. . . . they waive their rights under the common law in order to come under the statutory provision of workman's compensation of occupational disease for awards, and instead of getting any awards whatsoever under this procedure, and it's been in with backed up cases at the time it was signed by the governor, and not a single award made by South Carolina. At least I've got you saying, wait for 2 or 3 months [for the 1977 changes in South Carolina law to have full impact], because I'm going to be here in March, and you can come back and I can meet you in March and I doubt if there'll be an award then. We'll see—I mean, I just want to see because it's a totally inadequate statute as I see it now. That's why we have to move to the federal level. [U.S. Congress 1978a, 81–82]

Employing the sarcasm for which he is famous, Hollings even attacked the surveillance programs that the Textile Manufacturers Association's Jerry Beasley praised as "excellent."

Hollings: Has there ever been anybody working for Spring Mills under that great medical and health program that you're talking of that you can name as having been diagnosed as having byssinosis?
Beasley: No, sir, I could not.
Hollings: Well, what is so wonderful or grand about the thing if they can't find at least one? Are they that good, or that clean? They don't have weave rooms? They don't have cotton dust? [U.S. Congress 1978a, 87]

Unfortunately for the members of the Brown Lung Association, they were never able to obtain the support of more than a handful of congresspersons from the Carolinas for any federal program aimed at compensation for byssinosis victims. In 1980 the *Charlotte Observer* surveyed all twenty-one members of the North and South Carolina congressional delegations. They found only seven in favor of a federal program (Thurmond was the only Republican); three were opposed (two of whom were Republicans), eight took no position, and three (including Jesse Helms) didn't reply (Ellis and Hodierne 1980, 21). Helms never took a clear position on the bill, though he did try to curry the favor of his working-class constituents at the 1977 cotton dust regulation hearings in Washington. Posing for the cameras with his arm around Brown Lung Association member Lucy Taylor, he said, "In all candor, extreme care must be exercised in connection with any brown lung legislation. I must say that it is fraught with complexity. But the bottom line is that we've got to arrive at some help for these people" (Conway 1979, 72). Helms and too many others in Congress never did arrive.

OSHA AND THE COTTON DUST STANDARD

The legal basis for the cotton dust standards that the textile industry resisted for so long came in the Occupational Safety and Health Act of 1970. Prior to the passage of this act, states had the primary responsibility for protecting workers. As has so often been the case, the federal government stepped in because the states had been doing such a poor job of meeting their responsibilities. In 1970 hearings, Bureau of Labor statistics were cited showing nearly 400,000 cases of occupational disease, and ten times the work days lost to accidents and disease as lost to strikes (Anderson, Brady, and Bullock 1978, 347).

Further explanation for this landmark legislation lies in the politics of the late 1960s (Noble 1986, 77–90). The Johnson administration began pushing the theme of quality of life as its post-civil rights and post-Great Society agenda. Workplace health and safety was the part of the agenda that was to appeal to blue-collar union workers who were alienated by programs that seemed to help the poor more than workers. The theme also reached out to middle-class environmentalists and reformers in an effort to build a coalition for Johnson's ill-fated 1968 reelection plans. When he did not run and Nixon won the White House, the efforts continued as part of Nixon's attempt to build a new Republican majority that would include blue-collar union workers.

The legislative battle pitted labor and liberal groups against business and manufacturing interests. The business group was badly divided and clearly out of touch with the times. The strategy of denial and blaming the workers was doomed to failure, especially without the help of the White House. Nixon wanted a bill that was weaker than the one eventually passed, but when presented with the bill and forced to choose between a signature and a veto, Nixon signed and took the credit (Noble 1986, 83–86, 89–94).

The result, although a victory for the labor interests, contains a few compromises designed to placate business concerns. While the secretary of labor, through OSHA, which is in the Labor Department, sets the standards and enforces them, there is a presidentially appointed review commission to which standards can be appealed. The research arm to help establish standards, the National Institute for Occupational Safety and Health (NIOSH), is administratively housed in a separate department. A provision allows states to establish their own OSHA inspection programs, as did both Carolinas (Anderson, Brady, and Bullock 1978, 348). How well the states enforced regulations on industries vital to their economic well-being became a major point of concern of the Brown Lung Association and its supporters.

The act specifically set a temporary standard for cotton dust of no more than 1 milligram per cubic meter of respirable cotton dust. ("Respirable cotton dust" means the nearly invisible dust particles that are small enough to be inhaled.) This was the limit that the American Conference of Governmental Industrial Hygienists had recommended in 1966, and in 1968 the secretary of labor had applied the same limit to mills with federal contracts under the Walsh-Healey Act. Neither this nor later temporary standards were ever rigorously enforced.

The original 1970 act directed the secretary of labor, using the advice of NIOSH, to set a permanent cotton dust standard. After a great deal of delay, part of which was caused by the Nixon administration's promise to move slowly, NIOSH submitted its recommendations to the secretary of labor in September 1974. Following more administrative delay and petitions from the Textile Workers Union of America and a Nader research group for a 0.1 milligram standard, OSHA finally published a proposal of 0.2 milligrams three days after Christmas in 1976. This set the stage for extensive hearings that began on 5 April 1977, in Washington, D.C., moved to Greenville, Mississippi, and ended in Lubbock, Texas, on May 12. Additional documents were received until the process was closed on 2 September 1977 ("Occupational Exposure" 1978, 27350–51). By then, some 5,000 pages of material had been gathered for consideration. (Hodierne 1978).

While this long administrative process was taking place, the national political climate had changed dramatically. Nixon, who was philosophically hostile to any regulation of this kind, had resigned from the presidency; Gerald Ford's brief tenure had ended; and Democrat Jimmy Carter, who was more receptive to the plight of workers, had been in the White House since January. Because of severe inflation and declining employment in the textile industry, however, Carter had critical economic concerns to take into account.

In the months before the final standards were published in June 1978, a political battle took place in the Carter White House between economic advisers and the Department of Labor. The administration was under pressure from a federal district court to issue the final standards, as a result of a suit by the Amalgamated Clothing and Textile Workers Union and the North Carolina branch of Ralph Nader's Public Interest Research Group. In late May the Labor Department had been about to issue the order but was blocked when Charles Schultz, Carter's chair of the Council of Economic Advisers, ordered the standards to be examined on the grounds that they would be inflationary. Ray Marshall, Carter's secretary of labor, challenged the order, setting up a confrontation that only the president could resolve ("Marshall Fighting" 1978). After two weeks of news stories about the internal dispute, Carter reversed the order he had previously given that the regulations be revised to reduce costs ("Carter Cutting Costs" 1978). Unfortunately for the president, the public airing of this kind of infighting was typical of his tenure. It contributed to an image of weak leadership, which was partially responsible for his electoral defeat in 1980. That defeat was to have grave implications for the Brown Lung Association.

The critical issue in this fight concerned the means whereby dust would be reduced. Administration economists preferred cheaper personal protection devices such as disposable masks, coupled with medical surveillance. Labor preferred mechanical dust controls that would be engineered into the equipment, thereby requiring no worker cooperation. In addition to pressure from within the executive branch, organized labor and members of the House of Representatives reminded Carter of his promise to safeguard workers from occupational illness ("Carter OKs" 1978).

As is typically the case in regulatory policymaking, this was not the end of the fight. Both sides went to the courts. The Amalgamated Clothing and Textile Workers filed suit in federal appeals court charging that the standards were set too high and that the four-year period allowed for compliance was too long ("Tighter Cotton Dust Standards" 1978). The American Textile Manufacturers Institute challenged the legality of the standards in the courts and pressured Congress to fund additional studies focusing on the question of costs. The Circuit Court of Appeals issued a stay pending its ruling. In October 1979 the stay was lifted when the appeal was rejected, and the clock began running on the four-year timetable on 27 March 1980.

The legal basis for this dispute can be found in the original wording of the 1970 law that created OSHA. The law states that the secretary of labor "shall set the standard which most adequately assures, to the extent feasible, on the basis of the best available evidence, that no employee will suffer material impairment of health or functional capacity." The standard would be based on "research, demonstrations, experiments," and "other considerations shall be the latest available scientific data in the field, the feasibility of the standards, and experience gained in the field" (sec. 6 (b) (5) of the 1970 Occupational Safety and Health Act).

The disputed word here was "feasibility": did it mean both technological and economic feasibility? Could cost-benefit analysis be used to determine feasibility? Textile interests wanted to limit the meaning to those technologies that were already available and would not place any significant economic strain on the industry. That would translate into much higher allowable dust limits and different means of control (such as the use of personal respirators—disposable masks—rather than engineering controls) from those envisioned in the final standards.

OSHA anticipated these objections in publishing of the final standards in June 1978. Citing court opinions, the agency argued that "conditions of technological feasibility are not limited to devices already developed [but] may require improvements in existing technology or require the development of new technology" ("Occupational Exposure" 1978, 27352). On the question of economic feasibility, OSHA tried to have it both ways. On the one hand it argued that a higher dust level was acceptable in weaving and slashing operations because otherwise "massive reorientation of the mill would be required [and] the capital costs to comply with the 200 microgram [0.2 milligram] per cubic meter standard [would be] $1.3 billion." In the very next paragraph the agency declared that it was "primarily concerned with the health of weavers." Yet OSHA admitted that the best research of the time showed that there would be no byssinosis with a standard of a 0.2 milligram but a 10 percent rate with the higher limit of 0.75 milligram that it was mandating ("Occupational Exposure" 1978, 27360). OSHA attempted to resolve the difference by arguing that the 0.75 standard would afford about the same protection for those in weaving as the 0.2 standard would for those in carding operations.

The decision-making rule for OSHA was to achieve a rough balancing of several considerations. The agency would set the standard for dust as low as was technologically possible, so long as the "costs of compliance [were] not overly burdensome to industry" and "the benefits to worker health [were] likely to be appreciable." Although the agency talked about many estimated costs and projected benefits and admitted that such exercises should "be encouraged within the limits of the estimation techniques," it refused to acknowledge an obligation to engage in precise cost-benefit calculations. It concluded that benefits were difficult to quantify and that previous efforts to do so had not been helpful. Ultimately, OSHA's decision as to what was technologically and economically feasible rested on the claim that Congress had given the agency "discretion which is essentially legislative in nature" (Occupational Exposure" 1978, 27378–79).

This claim of legislative discretion practically invited textile interest groups to lobby Congress to reduce that legislative discretion, as well as to continue to challenge the figures and studies used by OSHA in making its decision. OSHA had anticipated that conflicts among the many scientific studies would be the basis for appeals to move more slowly. In discussing its legal authority to issue a standard, the agency argued that even though Congress understood that "conclusive medical or scientific evidence . . . may not exist," the legislative intent was clear: Congress wanted the secretary of labor to set a standard anyhow, using "the best available evidence" ("Occupational Exposure" 1978, 27351).

At the direction of Congress, which was under pressure from the textile industry, Department of Labor economists performed a more precise cost-benefit analysis whose purpose was to "develop viable alternatives which are less costly and more technologically feasible." The 122-page study completed in May 1979, (excluding appendixes), concluded that OSHA's final standard was "in fact the most cost-effective of the available alternatives." The study estimated that the cost of each avoided case would be about $8,000, while "a conservative estimate of benefits was more than $100,000 for each case avoided. . . . [Costs] are more than offset by the benefits of regulation" (U.S. Department of Labor 1979, iv–v, 10–11, 14).

Ultimately, though the textile interests were able to delay the standards with court challenges that went all the way to the Supreme Court, they lost. On 16 June 1981 the Court ruled in favor of the standard as set by OSHA in 1978. The case had taken so long, however, that a new administration was in office. Ronald Reagan's OSHA was much less enthusiastic about safety regulations than Jimmy Carter's OSHA had been. The solicitor general's office, representing OSHA before the Court, had argued in favor of the standards in 1980.[2] Under pressure from the new president in 1981, the solicitor general made the highly unusual request that the Court refrain from rendering an opinion until the new administration had reexamined the standards (Greenhouse 1981b). The Court ignored the request and decided the case. The lesson was that the president is obligated to enforce the policies set by Congress (Greenhouse, 1981a).

Unfortunately for the Brown Lung Association, the lesson may have sounded clear, but it was muddied by the fact that one of the most important steps in the policymaking process is implementation. Enforcement of the standards was in the hands of an administration that was hostile to the regulations, the union, and the Brown Lung Association. Implementation afforded Reagan's OSHA more opportunities for review. That part of the story comes later.

3

WORKPLACE RISK AND SCIENTIFIC RESEARCH

The likelihood that a worker will contract byssinosis depends on the precise work setting in a cotton textile plant. The more dust associated with a stage of production, the more likely it is to produce the symptoms. Therefore, a complete understanding of byssinosis and the grassroots movement that arose out of this occupational disease requires an understanding of the textile industry and the production of cotton cloth.

PRODUCTION AND RISK

Most generally, the cotton textile industry has three major components.[1] First, yarn production involves taking the baled cotton through several stages to produce cotton yarn or some blend of cotton and synthetic yarn. "Opening" involves breaking open the cotton bale, cleaning it, and mixing the fibers. "Carding" rakes these fibers into a single direction and removes more impurities and trash, along with unusable short fibers. The result is a loose, ropelike blend of cotton fibers called "sliver." Next, the slivers are drawn together to produce a thin strand called "roving." "Spinning" involves twisting the roving to form yarn. Yarn may be twisted together to form stronger yarn, depending on the need. The twisted yarn is then wound onto spools, or bobbins, and is ready for the next stage.

Weaving is the second major stage in textile production. In this complex process the yarn is taken from the bobbins, loaded onto the loom, and then fashioned into cloth. Most basically this is accomplished by raising and lowering alternate parallel strands while a shuttle carries another strand back and forth in a perpendicular direction. The finished product, called "gray goods," consists of two sets of yarns that cross over and under each other.

Finally, the gray goods need to be "finished" before they are commercially useful. Finishing varies greatly, depending on the intended use of the material. If the yarn was dyed before weaving (in which case, it was not really "gray"), then the cloth may only be washed and treated with conditioners. If it is to be dyed or printed, then it may first be cleaned and bleached.

The amount of cotton dust and the risk of contracting byssinosis decreases at each stage of production. It is highest in the opening and carding rooms, lower as the cotton moves through roving and spinning, and lower yet in weaving. Most experts do not consider byssinosis a significant problem in finishing. Chemicals and dyes are potential threats to health but threats more difficult to identify. The Brown Lung Association never became concerned with them except it attempted to form coalitions with other groups of workers suffering occupational health problems.

As a result of this difference in risk, workers in the less dusty parts of textile plants simply did not feel the threat as much as those in opening and carding rooms. The political implication was that these workers had much less personal incentive to join in any action to changing working conditions with respect to dust or to join the fight for easier workers' compensation laws. In effect, this variation in risk divided the workers so that most saw little personal danger and were therefore poor candidates for recruitment into the Brown Lung Association.

In addition, attitudes toward those who were sick influenced individuals' motivation to become involved. In his comparative study of occupational health movements, Bennett Judkins (1986, 16–17) argues that the social meaning of illness in America places a negative label on the person who becomes dependent. A person who is no longer physically independent is viewed as abnormal. To release a person from the norm of independence, society demands proof that the illness is both severe and that it was not self-inflicted. Society frowns upon those who ask for help but do not suffer a serious disease. We do not feel responsible to help those who caused their own problems. Judkins cites these as American values. If they hold for America, they are even more powerful in the context of the American South, where independence and rugged individualism are elevated to the level of religious commandments among those in the working class (Botsch 1980, 64–65). Violation of these commandments raises suspicions of weakness and sin.

Denial provides the psychological means to avoid these uncomfortable possibilities. It is easier to deny that others are really made sick by their work and to deny that you can become sick than it is to challenge your employers or find new work when you have little education and few marketable skills.

Many mill people were reluctant to get involved with the Brown Lung Association and their organizers for two reasons that are both related to how illness is seen. First, as argued by Judkins (1986, 18), they saw that mills treated past claimants of byssinosis as lazy people looking for an easy handout. They did not want to suffer that degrading charge themselves. Because they had few employment alternatives, they were inclined to deny any illness of their own and keep on working.

Second, many of them, as true believers in the southern commandment to make do for yourself, viewed the Brown Lung Organization with some degree of suspicion. Those who canvassed door to door to identify disabled workers for potential workers' compensation claims sometimes ran into these negative feelings (Interviews). Even workers who expressed sympathy did not want to associate too closely with the group. To do so would be to admit their own vulnerability and potential weakness, to risk raising their own self-doubt and others' suspicions about their intent to live up to the commandment. Once again, denial was the easier option.

DISCOVERY, NEGLECT, AND CONTROVERSY

Workers and researchers have used a number of terms to describe the breathing afflictions of textile workers. A British physician, Adrien Proust, began using the name "byssinosis" in 1877 to describe an industrial disease that had long been associated with exposure to cotton dust. The term is based on the Latin word *byssus*, which originally referred to flax or linen but commonly included cotton fibers as well (Harris et al. 1972, 200). In 1705 Bernarino Ramazzini, considered the father of occupational medicine (Jacobs 1987, 1), recorded the earliest description of the disease. He characterized it as having both short-term acute effects and long-term chronic effects (much as researchers do nearly 300 years later) originating with a foul mischievous powder, that entering the lungs by the mouth and throat, causes continual coughs and gradually makes way for an asthma . . . at the long run if [those who contract the disease] find their affliction grows upon them they must look out for another trade." In this treatise on tradesmen's diseases, Ramazzini concluded by pronouncing a moral judgment: "'Tis a sordid profit that's accompanied with the destruction of health" (quoted in Harris et al. 1972, 199).

In 1831 an early British researcher called the disease "spinner's phthisis" (Kay 1831). In the late 1800s and early 1900s the terms "mill fever" (Arlidge 1892) and "weaver's cough" (Collis 1915) were used to denote breathing problems associated with mill work. In the early 1940s, doctors coined the term "mattress-maker's fever" to describe a similar reaction to cotton dust in a related industry (Neal, Schneiter, and Cominita 1942). A number of common popular names have also been used down through the years: cardroom fever, cotton fever, cotton cold, dust fever, dust chills, and heckling fever (Harris et al. 1972, 201). Most of these terms apply to syndromes that, unlike byssinosis, have a sudden onset, have associated fever, and do not follow the classical pattern of progressive byssinosis stages (Harris et al. 1972, 200–201). The link with byssinosis is that those who experience these symptoms—"reactors"—have a higher risk of contracting byssinosis (Bouhuys et al. 1967, 170).

Two generic medical terms that cover a whole range of lung diseases are often used by physicians dealing with those suspected of having byssinosis: chronic obstructive pulmonary disease (COPD) and chronic obstructive lung disease (COLD). The latter term is most unfortunate in that its acronym suggests a mild and temporary malady. But though byssinosis in its early stages, acute byssinosis, may be mild and reversible, in its later chronic stages it causes permanent lung damage.

The most widely used popular term, "brown lung," is fraught with controversy. Ralph Nader is frequently given credit (and sometimes blame) for coining the term in a 1971 article that brought national attention to the problem (Williams et al. 1980). In the first sentence of that article, Nader (1971, 335) notes that brown lung was already the popular name for the disease. A *New England Journal of Medicine* editorial ("Respirator Disorders" 1967, 209–10) listing popular names for byssinosis, however, does not include brown lung. Given that Nader had helped launch the battle over black lung in 1968, the label seemed a natural one for him to choose. When asked about the origin of the term, Nader (1991) confirmed that he did coin the term and that his choice was influenced by the black lung experience.

The descriptive accuracy of "brown lung" is a much more important and controversial question. Spokespersons for the textile industry and some medical researchers often protested that the term evokes inaccurate images. They pointed out that autopsy studies show no discoloration of lung tissue with cotton dust (see, e.g., Williams et al. 1980; Heyden and Pratt, 1980, 1798). Nevertheless, the term stuck because of its powerful image and because of the accepted use of the term "black lung" in the coal mining industry. In addition, the black lung organizing experience served as a kind of model for the organizers of the Brown Lung Association, several of whom had experience in and close contacts with the black lung movement.

In an important and highly readable work on the health care history of mill workers and blacks in the South, Edward Beardsley (1987, 229–42) likens the discovery of byssinosis in southern textile mills to the erupting of "Old Faithful." The final realization that it does exist was preceded by a number of promising false starts separated by long periods of silence. Beardsley traces this story of false starts and neglect up to the early 1970s, which is the beginning of the period in which we are primarily interested. The British, who had known something about the dangers of work in textiles for a long time, failed to take any significant action until the 1900s. The government studied extremely high rates of respiratory disease among textiles workers in the late 1920s. Baffled at first by autopsy studies that revealed physical lung damage with no obvious cause, researchers later found that the affliction was associated with work in the dustiest parts of the mill and with the length of exposure to the dust. The conclusion the British drew in 1932 still stands today: the major distinction between this industrial disease and similar diseases found outside the mill were in the cause rather than the clinical results (Beardsley 1987, 230). Doctors can't diagnose byssinosis from medical examinations alone; they must combine medical examinations with the patient's work history. This ambiguity in medical research created a huge problem for workers trying to collect workers' compensation in a system based on proof of cause for any disability.

Reacting to the British findings, in 1932, the U.S. Public Health Service performed a study on one cotton mill in South Carolina. The researcher found a higher rate of respiratory complaints among cardroom workers than other textile mill workers but discounted those complaints for several reasons: no problems showed up in chest x-rays; breathing capacities were no different from those of other workers in the mill; and absences that workers attributed to breathing problems were explained away with the argument that they were staying home merely in order to give other workers a chance to make some money. No follow-up was performed on those who had complained about breathing problems. Beardsley (1987, 230–31) concludes that this biased and incomplete examination allowed health authorities to ignore the problem for another decade.

In 1941, reacting to a number of studies performed in the 1930s, the British Parliament made compensation available to textile workers who suffered complete disability following at least twenty years of exposure. One of the most important findings of those studies was the 1936 identification of what are now considered the classical symptoms and stages of byssinosis. It was the ability to identify the disease from unique symptoms proceeding in stages that enabled the British to set up a compensation system (Beardsley 1987, 232). Initially, the worker feels only chest tightness and mild dyspnea (difficulty in breathing) on Monday morning after a weekend off or on other days following holidays. This acute condition may last years until it advances into more chronic stages. Then the condition begins to persist beyond Monday morning and to increase in severity until the worker becomes totally disabled. One can find this description in many industrial health books and medical journal articles (e.g., Milby 1964, 56–57; Kilburn, Kilburn, and Merchant 1973, 1952). We now know, however, that not all those afflicted with the disease experience these classic symptoms (Wegman, Levenstein, and Greaves 1983, 189). Unfortunately, that has made it more difficult for some to prove their claims of byssinosis in workers' compensation proceedings.

The British action caused Americans to reexamine the problem, and a number of studies with different methodologies and conflicting findings appeared in the 1940s. In 1947 a U.S. Public Health Service team attempted to resolve the conflicts in a review of all the research. They were unsuccessful. Their conclusions provided ammunition for both sides: textile spokespersons could cite the conclusion that "the problem . . . is hardly known to exist in the United States"; industry critics could cite the warning that it did exist but was unrecognized because those who were afflicted left work before they were disabled. The study called for more definitive research (Beardsley 1987, 233), but the problem fell into a state of neglect until the 1960s.

Once again the catalyst came from the work of British research. During the 1950s Dr. Richard Schilling performed the most thorough study that had ever been done. He found high rates of byssinosis among British textile workers, few of whom were winning workers' compensation. This work led to thorough changes in the British compensation system. In 1959 the *Journal of Occupational Medicine* published one of Schilling's studies that identified the source of byssinosis as not the cotton itself but rather something in the boil that becomes ground up in the early processing stages. Schilling argued that if byssinosis was not a problem in American mills, it would be important to know why. In 1960 he was allowed to examine workers in two mills in Alabama. He found that although there was less dust in these mills than in most British mills, all those who worked in the cardrooms—one of the dustiest places in the mill—had byssinosis symptoms (Beardsley 1987, 236).

Schilling's research created a system of grading the peculiar symptoms, which is generally accepted by most doctors. This system analyzes the progression of the disease in more detail than the simple acute/chronic dichotomy. At Grade 1/2 the worker only occasionally feels temporary chest tightness or coughing upon returning to work after time off. At Grade 1 these first-day-back symptoms occur consistently each time the worker returns to work. Grade 2 describes a progression to the point where the symptoms continue for longer periods during the work week. Finally, Grade 3 adds permanent lung damage to these symptoms (Kilburn, Kilburn, and Merchant 1973, 1952–53).

Schilling's work stimulated a barrage of studies by researchers in the United States; he collaborated in a number of them himself. The 1964 work of the late Dr. Arend Bouhuys in examining inmates working at the mill located in the federal penitentiary in Atlanta was significant for both medical and political reasons (Bouhuys et al. 1969). He found that nearly a third of those workers had byssinosis, a striking medical finding that flew in the face of industry claims. Politically, the study was significant in that it had to be performed in a federal facility; the textile industry had openly opposed the study and would not allow Bouhuys access to privately owned mills (BLA Papers, letter from T.M. Forbes, executive vice-president of the Georgia Textile Manufacturers Association, 4 June 1964). Industry leaders were taking an aggressively defensive posture on the issue to keep medical evidence from turning against them.

This research, along with findings of many abnormal chest x-rays among mill workers, led the North Carolina Board of Health to conclude in 1966 that more research was needed. With the support of the state government, the board was successful in obtaining the cooperation of a few mills in the state. Meanwhile, as Bouhuys and others were continued their research, their findings were generally consistent with those of Bouhuys's earlier work in Atlanta: in the dustiest part of the mills, the cardrooms, one-fourth to one-third of the workers had symptoms of byssinosis (Beardsley 1987, 237–38).

The outburst of research that began in the 1960s continued into the early 1980s. The results were complex enough that all sides in the controversy could cite some evidence to support their political positions. A number of medical questions have never been fully answered (Wegman, Levenstein, and Greaves 1983, 189–90).

First, the etiology, or cause, of the disease is not precisely known. Researchers are relatively certain that the causal agent of the acute symptoms of byssinosis is an endotoxin from the cell walls of certain bacteria that often colonize in cotton plants (Castellan et al. 1987, 608). When the cotton is harvested and ginned (the process in which seeds are removed), these bacteria are mixed with the cotton brought into the mill to be processed. This theory is supported by studies of experimental exposure to the endotoxin (Castellan et al. 1987) and by the fact that byssinosis levels of incidence are progressively lower as the cotton is cleaned. The industry experimented a great deal in the early 1980s with washing the cotton and using additives to remove or trap these materials. In 1985 OSHA made the last modifications of the dust standard, including provisions that reduced requirements for washed cotton ("Occupational Exposure," 1985). Unfortunately, washing tended to make cotton more difficult to process into yarn, and despite the time and money spent in experiments and pilot studies, these processing problems were never overcome. Consequently, very few mills employ washing as a means of dust control (Interviews). This aside, it is not known exactly how these microscopic particles adversely affect the lungs, although it appears that the damage is in the narrowing of the airways as opposed to the destruction of the tissue called "parenchyma" (Wegman, Levenstein, and Greaves 1983, 190).

Second, the pathogenesis, or progression of the disease from the temporary acute stages (Schilling's Grade 1/2 through Grade 2) to the chronic stage (Schilling's Grade 3) when irreversible damage has been done, is also unclear. Though some researchers still question the relationship between dust and the chronic stages of the disease (Heyden and Pratt 1980, 1798; Diem 1983, 403), most conclude that the relationship is certain, even if the biological logic of the causal sequence is not completely understood (Merchant 1983, 138; Beck and Schachter 1983, 411).

Third, the relationship between byssinosis and cigarette smoking has been a hot topic of debate among researchers. Some researchers have argued that smoking is really the cause of lost lung function (Heyden and Pratt 1980, 1798). Most research, however, has concluded that smoking has an additive or multiplier effect in the likelihood of contracting the disease (Wegman, Levenstein, and Greaves 1983, 189). In issuing regulations governing dust levels in the cotton industry, OSHA specifically rejecting the argument that tobacco was the real culprit after reviewing the medical research record ("Occupational Exposure" 1978, 27353). A 1986 study of those diagnosed with byssinosis in Great Britain was composed of a sample of more than 500 cases in which about one in five were lifelong nonsmokers (Rook et al. 1987, 5–6). Nevertheless, smokers have had a most difficult time in winning workers' compensation claims.

CONTINUING UNCERTAINTIES

In 1982 the National Research Council of the National Academy of Sciences, under a grant from the U.S. Department of Agriculture, attempted to resolve much of this controversy by reviewing all the research that had been done up to that time and issuing a report to clarify the scientific findings and issues (Committee on Byssinosis 1982). That effort was no more successful than the ill-fated 1947 Public Health Service review. Members of the committee were so divided that they issued a minority report attached to the majority report. The majority took the traditional conservative scientific position that without conclusive evidence, cotton dust could not be judged to be the sole causal agent of chronic byssinosis. The chair of the committee conceded, however, that this conclusion should "in no way be interpreted to say there is no chronic effect" ("WHO Disputes" 1982). A week after the academy report appeared, the World Health Organization (WHO) issued its own report based on the same studies. It concluded that cotton dust caused both acute and chronic byssinosis ("WHO Disputes" 1982).

Much of the difference in these conclusions rests on the notion of causality, or what medical researchers call "etiology." The research methodology for most byssinosis studies has been epidemiological: that is, populations of workers were studied and compared to other populations in terms of a number of variables, including exposure to cotton dust. These studies established a strong statistical correlation between cotton dust exposure and byssinosis. However, according to the old statistical saw; correlation does not necessarily mean causation. In addition, researchers faced problems in establishing even this statistical relationship. The data used depend on individuals' memory of work history as well as on company records, which are often not available. Memory and records do not tell exactly how much dust exposure actually occurred.

The results of the disease can be more precisely measured. Medical researchers measure lung function loss in terms of the volume of air the lungs can hold and the rate at which the air can be exhaled, which are then compared to known values for generally healthy populations. Ideally, to reflect change with dust exposure, these measurements should be longitudinal. This was not possible until after the late 1960s, when mills began to employ medical surveillance.

An exchange in *The American Statistician* in 1983 illustrates the nature of the technical differences between those who claim statistical causality and those who claim that the evidence falls short. Diem (1983, 403) argues that all past studies used imperfect methodologies. He insists that sample populations must be completely randomly selected and that the variation in dust exposure must be measured more precisely to satisfy the demands of statistical causality. In their article in the same journal, Beck and Schachter (1983, 405, 408–411) counter in three ways. They find the demands made by Diem unreasonable in field research: records of precise individual dust exposure do not exist but can only be approximated by years in the mills, because workers often change jobs. They defend their own sample selection methods as the best that can be done in field research, showing that appropriate statistical controls and checks were made. Finally, they argue that all existing evidence points in the same direction, "that cotton dust can cause chronic lung disease in cotton textile workers."

While less than statistically perfect, the case for causality is convincing. Indeed, given what is known about the nature of the disease, the perfect case linking dust exposure to the chronic irreversible stages of the disease could be made only in a laboratory setting in an experiment that would be ethically unacceptable. Hence, though we may be relatively certain about the cause of initial acute symptoms, we will probably never have scientific certainty about all aspects of byssinosis.

In sum, science has been incapable of providing policymakers the kind of exact definitive answers they would like. Industry often used this lack of precision to argue against action, but the Occupational Safety and Health Administration and most researchers argued that enough was known to require action. Current workers needed protection, and retired disabled workers needed compensation before it was too late (Wegman, Levenstein, and Greaves 1983; Merchant 1983, 138).

In recent years the textile industry has played a greater leadership role in byssinosis research. Since 1977 industry groups have helped sponsor an annual Cotton Dust Conference and publish its proceedings. Industry provides some funding, and the National Institute for Occupational Safety and Health has its own annual budget to support research. The bulk of research money, however, comes from the U.S. Department of Agriculture, which has broadened its interest from simply the endotoxins found in cotton to other organic dust that may be harmful. Indeed, Dr. Robert Castellan of the Division of Respiratory Disease Studies of NIOSH believes that byssinosis may be but one of many organic dust diseases, each of which may have acute symptoms occurring in patterns peculiar to the work schedules and exposure levels of a particular industry (1991).

Research continues, but at a less urgent pace. Nevertheless, even if byssinosis is no longer a major problem in the United States, it is still a danger in Third World nations where there are few regulatory controls. The issue has become a global one as the industry has shifted to other nations with lower labor costs.

Mills in the United States tend to see the problem in terms of a few continued claims from workers who were exposed before the late 1970s. They are not worried about future claims because current industrial medical practices screen out those who are most likely to develop problems, identify those who have problems in early stages, and remove both from the workplace, thereby protecting workers from medical risk and the industry from financial risk.[2] According to a mill safety official who did not wish to be quoted by name, the removal is in the form of transfer to a less dusty area and retraining if possible, although retraining is difficult for many workers with little education, and there is no guarantee that a new job assignment will pay as much as the original one. Being able to work in a mill without developing breathing problems is seen simply as an additional job qualification: if one does not meet that qualification, one should not work for the mill.

Ironically, cleaner mills may have created a new problem that will not be recognized for some time to come. Because it is still unclear whether the acute stage must precede the chronic stage, some researchers are concerned that a cleaner mill environment may mask the acute early warning symptoms in those who are susceptible until they contract the chronic form of the disease. The classic Monday morning pattern may have been the result of high exposure to endotoxins in a specific work schedule. Had the schedule or exposure been different, the early symptoms might have followed a different pattern. Lower levels of endotoxin exposure over time—which can still happen even with the current standards in place—may still result in chronic byssinosis. This will not be known until a generation of mill workers lives their work lives under the new standards (Castellan 1991).[3]

The most recently published research underscores the continuing research controversy and debate over policy implications.

Tulane University School of Medicine researchers examined 1,800 workers in nine Burlington plants in North Carolina between 1982 and 1987. They concluded that nonsmokers would lose about 14 percent of their lung capacity over a twenty-year period of work. For smokers, the loss would almost double with a 25 percent loss. The researchers made two recommendations: first, that smokers be kept out of cotton textiles work (this is already done in many personnel offices in preemployment screening; Lord 1991b, 1B); second, that current dust limits be reexamined. Industry officials responded that current limits are adequate ("Smokers Shouldn't Work" 1991). Without an active Brown Lung Association in the South, few people will effectively challenge that claim, and the controversy will be relegated to the status of a nonissue.

A review of medical research with its cold clinical descriptions couched in antiseptic euphemisms reveals little about the precise impact of byssinosis on the daily lives of real human beings. Among sympathetic works employing an oral history approach (see Terrill and Hirsch 1978, 155; Conway 1979, 10–29, 58–87; Tullos 1989, 255–84), McCarl (1982 16–18) provides the best description for those of us in the comfortable and usually healthy middle class: "One man told me to hold my breath until I felt that panicky tingle when you can't get any air, then imagine having that all day every day for the rest of your life." What led some of these suffering people to fight back?

4

THE BIRTH OF THE
BROWN LUNG
ASSOCIATION

Having examined the political and cultural settings, government policies with respect to workers' compensation and dust exposure, and the scientific and medical controversies surrounding the nature of byssinosis, we now turn to the grassroots movement itself. We begin by considering the obstacles that stood in the way of such a movement and the challenges its members and organizers faced. The obstacles were many, and they were formidable. Then we shall turn to the people who brought about the formation of the Brown Lung Association and examine the group's embryonic stage and early growth. Finally, we shall assess the role of organized labor in the formation and life of the association.

OBSTACLES

History is filled with the sufferings of many peoples, yet often their only response to that suffering is human endurance. Social scientists have developed a number of models that help explain when hardship will be translated into social protest and when it will not (Gamson 1968; Piven and Cloward 1977; Gaventa 1980). At a minimum, we might argue that a number of conditions must be met before any significant protest takes place and before that protest is mobilized and directed into an organization.

First, a significant number of people must be undergoing the same hardship and must feel that the cause of their trouble is some identifiable outside agent rather than mere personal misfortune (Piven and Cloward 1977, 12). This outside agent provides a target for protest. Next, the potential protesters must feel that they can actually do something about their grievance; otherwise, they will cope somehow or acquiesce, feeling some mixture of fatalism and anger (Gaventa 1880, 255–57). Finally, they must have leadership to direct and organize their disparate energies. Whether this leadership should aim at mobilizing and creating pressure though protest (Piven and Cloward 1977) or at creating a formal, ongoing organization (Gaventa 1980, 257–58; McAdam 1982, 54; Pope 1989, 94–95) is a matter of controversy among social movement theorists. But in either case, leadership, whether it comes from within or without or from some combination, is essential. Each of these requirements might be seen as one in a series of barriers that must be overcome before the movement can enter the competition among interest groups that is so central to our political system.[1]

Were there a significant number of people undergoing the hardships associated with byssinosis? We have already seen that a minority of those who work in cotton textiles were at risk, depending on the amount of dust associated with their particular jobs. Was this minority enough? One can find a variety of suggestive figures in several studies. The figures used by the U.S. Department of Labor in its 1979 *Report to Congress* (36–39) estimated that in 1977 there were "83,610 expected cases of byssinosis among the nearly 560,000 workers exposed to cotton dust at current levels." This estimate, based on prevalence rates established from the research work of Merchant and others in the early 1970s, included those experiencing the first mild and infrequent symptoms as well as those who were suffering permanent damage. It represented about 15 percent of the 1977 cotton textile work force. The Department of Labor considered it to be a conservative estimate, however, in that many of those with respiratory problems had already left the work force (1979, 39). Bouhuys estimated that 35,000 employed and retired workers had permanent damage and should have been considered disabled in 1973 (Bouhuys et al. 1977, 183).

Based on Bouhuys's rates, the number of disabled workers in North and South Carolina was estimated to be about 18,000, a figure frequently cited in press accounts in the Carolinas.[2] Although industry was very critical of Bouhuys's conclusions (U.S. Congress 1980, 528), the Department of Labor accepted his work and cited it in the 1978 cotton dust standards. Bouhuys estimated that about 800 workers were becoming disabled each year (U.S. Department of Labor 1980, 17). In calculating the number of cases that various dust standards would prevent, OSHA used an incidence rate of 25 percent for the estimated 200,000 workers in the cotton yarn industry, a higher-risk area than other segments of the industry ("Occupational Exposure" 1978, 27379). Other estimates were consistent with this figure. If 15 percent of those in all textile operations were suffering some kind of symptoms, and if 25 percent of the workers in the yarn industry would eventually become disabled, we might conclude that the scale of frustration among textile workers should be great enough to meet the necessary critical mass requirements for active protest. Even though they represented a minority of the entire work force, potential recruits numbered about 50,000 yarn workers and more than 30,000 in other parts of the industry. Until changes took place, there would be a significant number of additional potential recruits each year as workers began to suffer initial symptoms.

Did these people know enough about the nature of byssinosis to blame it on something other than their own bad luck? Workers lacked knowledge of the subject because there was so little publicity about the disease. Suffering was seen as a matter of personal misfortune. Even if a few knew about byssinosis, there was no social framework within which they could communicate with others. Their work lives reinforced social isolation. Mill work involved tending a large number of noisy machines with little opportunity for social intercourse. With a few notable exceptions, textile communities were typically transient in nature. Most workers lived in rental housing and moved frequently. Transiency then became another barrier to political involvement and, perhaps even more important, to any sense of collective solidarity. Therefore, even if there were 18,000 workers in the Carolinas disabled by byssinosis, isolation decreased the probability that they would be aware of their collective problem.[3]

Did those afflicted with byssinosis have a great enough sense of personal effectiveness—what political scientists call "efficacy"—to feel that they could actually do something about their problems? In his classic work on protest, William Gamson (1968, 48) argues that protest is most likely when the discontented hold attitudes of low trust toward authorities, coupled with a high sense of efficacy. Shingles (1981) found that even the disadvantages of low levels of education and income could be overcome by those who had this combination. Most of the demographic characteristics of disabled textile workers would predict political attitudes of moderate to low trust but low, not high, efficacy. The environment in which they lived did little to give any workers a sense that either their personal or cooperative actions would be effective in yielding positive results. They resided in a region where political participation had been depressed by one-party politics for over a century. Active political participation, especially if it challenged the local elites in a milltown, could cause them to be labeled as a troublemakers, and that could cost them their jobs. Low levels of education and a dearth of the organizational memberships that might have compensated for a lack of formal political socialization made politics a forbidden mystery zone in their world.

Mill workers' only significant political involvement was a highly personalized "friends and neighbors" kind of politics. They would take pride when someone they knew in the community won a legislative seat. They might ask a local legislator or congressperson for some kind of help on a highly personal problem. But they paid no attention to votes or issue positions. Brown Lung Association staff who were not from the South found this both surprising and frustrating in their work with local chapters. They were surprised that a number of these uneducated people did not seem reluctant to talk to legislators about their personal problems and frustrated that workers paid so little attention to legislative action on group concerns. Staff sometimes found it hard to persuade these members to be more critical of legislators whom they considered their friends and neighbors (Interviews).

Did disabled workers have the leadership and organizational skills to play the game of interest-group politics effectively? Active workers had little time, money, or skill to devote to group associations. Retired disabled workers had time but were even more lacking in money, skills, and energy.

The one organization to which most older and disabled workers belonged, the church, had traditionally promoted a set of values that opposed political involvement, especially in liberal causes. Traditional fundamentalist religious values led members to a posture of fatalistic deference in this life and hope for better conditions in the next. The political activism of some fundamentalist churches on conservative social issues was at best irrelevant to the concerns of the Brown Lung Association; at worst, it was counterproductive. It created cross-pressures for those in the textile community. The politicians who stood with them on social issues were the very same ones who were least likely to support regulation of the textile industry and reform of workers' compensation laws.

With little organizational experience, few textile workers had any leadership experience or skill. One of the greatest resources of the black lung movement in West Virginia was the union experience of those who built the movement. Very few textile workers had had any union experience.

Early organizers were aware of these cultural and attitudinal obstacles. In a report to a union funding source on how early grant monies had been spent in 1975, Mike Szpak, one of the founders, described the members as "a people who move cautiously, believe in God's profound power and are so basically individualistic in nature that collective action is a new and sometimes jolting experience" (BLA Papers). Frank Blechman, another founding organizer, wrote to a United Mine Workers official that because "the industry is not unionized . . . there is no tradition of militancy to draw upon" (BLA Papers, Blechman letter to Steve Early, 2 May 1975).

Given all that was lacking in essential requirements, it is little wonder that so many suffered so long with so little effective group action. And there were additional obstacles, many of which have also been barriers to the organization of labor unions. Southern mill workers are characterized by low pay, low skill, and declining job opportunities. Between 1972 and 1985 there was a loss of 43,000 jobs in textiles employment in South Carolina (Martin 1988, 10). In early 1991 the number of textile jobs in South Carolina fell below 100,000 for the first time since before World War II. By the end of 1991 the number had fallen to 94,000, and only a little more than twice that (209,500) in North Carolina ("Smokers Shouldn't Work" 1991). Nationally, textiles employment (including both cotton and synthetics) dropped nearly 6 percent in 1990, from 724,000 to 683,000 (Associated Press 1990). As a result discontented workers could be replaced rather easily should they leave or threaten to leave the mill. With few skills, many had no alternative to the mill. Even if active workers joined the fight, protest had very little potential to create any real pressure on the mills.

The obstacles for retired workers were especially great. My own conversations with them revealed a fear of even expressing their discontent, based on perceived threats to jobs held by relatives and friends. Organizers and staff cited fear as their greatest barrier to greater member involvement. Whether these fears were real or imagined did not matter. They served to reinforce a culture of powerlessness that made any attempt to redress grievances almost unthinkable. They are evidence of what Gaventa (1980, 15–30), building on the work of Bachrach and Baratz (1962) and Lukes (1974), called the "third face" of power. That third face is the power of control through culture. Elites had created a culture down through history which gave workers a sense of defeat and powerlessness (Gaventa 1980, 255). Open challenge was almost beyond conception for most.

Health problems too posed almost insurmountable barriers for retired workers. The poor health of disabled brown lung members made physical disruption of any institutions impossible and mandated a complex and costly physical support system for any significant group activity. For example, in May of 1981 the AFL-CIO sponsored a demonstration for disabled brown lung workers in Washington, D.C. More than a hundred members were bused from the Carolinas. They were to march from the AFL-CIO headquarters to the Department of Labor Building for the purpose of protesting Reagan administration efforts to revise a proposed standard for cotton dust in the mills set by OSHA under the Carter administration ("Brown Lung Protesters" 1981; Roberts 1981a). Several of the nine members of the Aiken chapter who attended explained to me that the help of nurses, first aid stations, and wheelchairs provided by the union made the march possible. The few members who were able to gain access to the building were quickly and easily ejected after officials refused to see them. Even holding chapter meetings was difficult. Organizers might have to spend several hours before and after ferrying members who could not drive to and from the meeting. In addition, health problems forced sudden changes in leadership and caused leaders to miss meetings.

Even if all of these barriers could be overcome, changing public policy on byssinosis posed a most difficult challenge for several reasons. First, the name of the system that was failing to protect workers disabled with byssinosis is something of a misnomer. It is a workers' compensation "system" only in the sense that all states have such laws. Beyond the basic similarity of requiring industries to provide compensation, states vary widely with respect to legal requirements for claims based on occupational diseases. Therefore, the Brown Lung Association had to lobby for different reforms in different states (Larson 1979). We will review these differences when we examine the tactics employed in attempting to create pressure on the compensation system.

Second, because there had also been some movement to impose minimal federal standards on state workers' compensation laws since the early 1970s, the group had to lobby actively on the national level in order to bring pressure for state legislative action.[4] This requirement placed considerable strain on already thin resources.

Third, the issues surrounding the disease raised the many complex medical and scientific questions discussed in the preceding chapter, such as the cause of the disease and how to prevent it. The mills, not the Brown Lung Association, were in the best position to generate studies. They had easier access to those who were exposed. Fortunately for the association, the mills pursued a "head in the sand" strategy for many years and did little research until independent studies had produced ample data upon which to build a policy argument.

To be effective, the association had to place pressure on both medical scientists and medical practitioners. The scientific studies that the mills and their insurance companies did sponsor had to be challenged if federal and state regulations were to be changed. This challenge required a great deal of technical knowledge and the financial means to hire experts. The knowledge and attitudes of medical practitioners also had a great impact on individual workers' compensation claims. The testimony of doctors was a critical factor in determining the outcome of claims. One North Carolina lawyer told me that medical testimony made up 80 percent of each case. Unfortunately for would-be claimants, only a few doctors were willing or able to distinguish byssinosis from nonspecific lung disorders (Hughes 1979, 18–38). State laws sometimes limited the choice of doctors to special medical panels chosen by those administering the compensation laws. Almost from the outset, organizers and staff complained that their greatest problem in winning cases was finding cooperative doctors (BLA Papers; Interviews). Even into the 1990s, lawyers claimed they were having a hard time in finding doctors who willing to diagnose byssinosis (Bowen 1991).

Fourth, the group had to engage in bureaucratic lobbying at both the state and national levels. OSHA had been considering standards for allowable dust in the mills since its creation in 1970. After hearings were finally held in 1977 and standards were issued in 1978, the Brown Lung Association faced the task of making sure that the standards withstood review and were properly implemented. Just because federal regulations set standards did not necessarily mean that the states would hire inspectors, make the inspections, levy fines, and force compliance.

Finally, because both dust standards and workers' compensation awards to brown lung victims were commonly appealed in the courts by industry, judicial lobbying was necessary. This added one more strain on the resources of an organization that already had so much going against it. Judicial lobbying may be the most expensive kind of interest-group activity, because it requires highly trained and consequently quite expensive lawyers to fight the battle. Members could personally contact legislators, give testimony in bureaucratic hearings, and even utilize the findings of independent scientific research to question industry-sponsored research, but they needed a lawyer to fight legal appeals. Paying the lawyer in personal compensation cases was the lesser problem, for fees would be generated from successful claims—usually 20 to 33 percent of the award or settlement. Fighting appeals of the cotton dust standards was another matter: there was no built-in subsidy for legal expenses and winning would not generate money. Consequently, the Brown Lung Association had no choice but to play a minor role in these legal fights. It did file a "friend of the court" brief in the 1981 challenge to the standards before the Supreme Court, but the Carter administration and the textile unions carried the brunt of most of that legal battle.

Given this set of initial conditions and lobbying challenges covering nearly the entire spectrum of interest-group activities—legislative lobbying on the state and national level, lobbying in the scientific and medical communities, bureaucratic lobbying on the state and national levels, and judicial lobbying on the state and national levels—we might wonder how byssinosis escaped the realm of nonissues and arrived on the issue agenda.

BEGINNINGS

There are three reasons why the Brown Lung Organization came into being and why byssinosis forced its way onto the political agenda: the political environment of the 1970s; the organizers who were created by that environment, along with the circumstances that brought them together; and the actions of Ralph Nader, a key opinion leader in the period.

The birth of the Brown Lung Association took place in an activist political environment that stressed grassroots participation. There was increasing popular awareness of occupational health problems and a growing concern among social activists that workers were being denied any say regarding health and safety in their places of work.[5] In Ralph Nader's article in *The Nation* titled "Brown Lung: The Cotton Mill Killer" (1971, 335–37), the theme was one of industry interference, intransigence, and inhumanity coupled with political insensitivity. Nader detailed the problems researchers were having in even studying the problem, including Arendt Bouhuys's difficulty in gaining access to Georgia mills.[6] He charged that the industry itself spent nothing for research on the problem, despite the fact that the British had recognized the disease as work related and had made it compensable under law since 1941. When the industry did contract with the Industrial Hygiene Foundation of Pittsburgh for a study to establish the existence and prevalence of byssinosis, Nader sarcastically noted, this was "the same foundation that defended the coal mine industry during the recent struggle to make black lung disease compensable." Further, this study was used to reduce the scope of a legislative investigation in

South Carolina. In a letter to all members of the legislature, the South Carolina Textile Manufacturers Association had argued that another study would just "result in a variety of research findings which would conceivably confuse the situation rather than finding answers to whatever problems may exist" (quoted in Nader 1971, 336). Finally, Nader reported that his 1969 request to the Nixon administration for federal funding to support research, alert workers, and set standards for dust control in the mills had been answered with symbolic support and substantive inaction.

In closing this short, but important article, Nader suggested a strategy for organization: "The textile industry will probably continue to do nothing until it is threatened with large expenditures to compensate its workers for loss of their health—expenditures considerably larger even than the present costs of early retirements, sick leaves, and loss of efficiency among its injured employees" (1971, 337).

Si Kahn, a young community organizer and protest song composer and performer, first heard about byssinosis in 1970 (Kahn 1992). He and his wife at the time, Kathy, had created Cut Cane Associates, a community development and organizing team that operated out of the small town of Mineral Bluff in the hills of northern Georgia. The name "Cut Cane" came from the creek that ran in front of their house. The year after the Nader article appeared, the Textile Workers Union of America (TWUA)—which merged with clothing workers in 1976 to form the Amalgamated Clothing and Textile Workers Union (ACTWU)—considered sponsoring a project of Kahn's Cut Cane Associates. According to an internal memo dated 4 February 1972, the TWUA had already given the Kahns $500 in 1971 to interview cotton textile workers. Kahn had gone to four different mill towns and interviewed many people who he thought had byssinosis. Some of them later became members of the organization (Kahn 1992). In 1972, the idea was to take the next step along lines suggested by Nader: begin in places that had a union base, interview and test workers for breathing problems, educate them, build interest, publicize the problem, and press for government action (BLA Papers). This larger project was not funded at that time, however.

What Si Kahn learned from his early exploration was applied later when he brought together the young people who would be the founding organizers of the Brown Lung Association.[7] Although he himself played no official role, Kahn was the single most important intellectual force behind the organization. Minutes of the group's meetings for the first several years indicate that he attended many staff planning meetings. He played a major role in initial grant writing because of his contacts with foundations and his previous experience in writing proposals. In addition, the other founding organizers regarded his speed-typing skill with awe.

Kahn's books on grassroots organization, *How People Get Power* (1970) and *Organizing: A Guide for Grassroots Leaders* (1982), outline the philosophy behind the association. It was to be a self-governing, self-sufficient, member-run, nonhierarchical, highly egalitarian, democratic, grassroots group that would develop links to other groups and widen its scope in order to promote a populist political agenda to offset corporate power. Kahn strongly believed that movements should develop their own music and culture as they grow (1982, 334–36). To this end, Mountain Musicians Cooperative produced a benefit long-playing record, *Cotton Mill Blues*, which was released in early 1976 and featured Kahn performing a variety of protest and folk songs that he and others had written (BLA Papers).

In the early 1970s Kahn went to the mountains of Appalachia to become involved in community development among the coal miners who lived there. Organizing mill workers around byssinosis was put "on the back burner," but Kahn's experiences with disabled coal miners created a model that he would later apply to the mills (Kahn 1992). He became involved with the Black Lung Association, a group of disaffected members of the United Mine Workers (UMW) who fought not only for occupational health but also for reform of their corrupt union. Kahn was related to Bernie Aronson, a close associate of Arnold Miller, a leader of the Black Lung Association who eventually won control of the UMW when he was elected union president in late 1972 (Bethell 1976, 115).

In the mining towns of Appalachia, Kahn met a number of the young people who would found the Brown Lung Association: Charlotte Brody (whom he later married), Michael Szpak, Frank Blechman, Thad Moore, and Eleanor "Len" Stanley. He also linked up with Bob Hall, Joseph "Chip" Hughes (who later married Len Stanley), and Bill Finger of the Institute for Southern Studies, which publishes the populist pro-labor quarterly *Southern Exposure* out of the Chapel Hill, North Carolina, area. They would later play important supporting roles for the Brown Lung Association.

This group first worked together on the UMW strike at the Brookside mine in Harlan County, Kentucky, from 1973 until late summer of 1974. Blechman was there as a part-time volunteer, as he was still employed in East Tennessee. Szpak was doing the organizing work in North and South Carolina to bring consumer and stockholder pressure on Duke Power, owner of the Brookside mine.

Moore was with the North Carolina Public Interest Research Group, a Nader-inspired organization funded by college student contributions, which was also working in support of the miners striking for a contract. The three members of the Institute for Southern Studies were supporting efforts in the Carolinas with the help of people like Len Stanley. Brody was working with Kahn at Brookside.

These individuals came from varied backgrounds and had varied reasons for becoming involved in the movement. Beyond his general commitment to the ideals of community organization, Mike Szpak found motivation in his own family history. His grandfather had been a cotton mill worker who reportedly died from byssinosis. His father and mother were both mill workers who had left their native Massachusetts for mill work in Greenville, South Carolina when Mike was four. After his father was killed in a mill accident, his mother took him back to Massachusetts, where she worked as a loom fixer. Szpak attended Boston College at the height of the social and political turmoil of the 1960s, obtaining a B.A. in history in 1968. He went on to earn master's degrees in educational administration and social work, specializing in community organizing. Between 1971 and 1973 he worked in a factory and was a member of the United Rubber Workers, serving on the union's Health and Safety Committee (BLA Papers).

When Szpak went to work on the Brookside effort, he was a field staffer for the Movement for Economic Justice, on loan to Carolina Action, another activist group working in the Carolinas (Szpak 1991). Other organizers remember that he initially went to Brookside to help, but Kahn decided that his "bullhorn Boston" style would not work with the local people there. His credentials in collective action and grassroots organizing also included the Amalgamated Clothing Workers strike against Farah and work with the Massachusetts Welfare Rights Organization (BLA Papers).

Szpak, incidentally, was not the only organizer who had connections to the Welfare Rights Organization. In the fall of 1975 Dee Steele joined the Brown Lung Association as an organizer, working with the Greensboro chapter. The next summer she became the administrator for the association, responsible for keeping the books. A letter of recommendation for Steele from a United Auto Workers official described her as an experienced Welfare Rights organizer who had "creatively adopted the urban oriented model of welfare rights to rural Virginia" (BLA Papers, letter dated 8 July 1975).

Although he joined the effort after Szpak, Frank Blechman had a greater influence on what the Brown Lung Association was eventually to become. A native of Virginia whose father was a prominent corporate lawyer, Blechman earned a B.A. in international relations at the University of Virginia in 1969, worked as a newspaper photographer for a year, and then went to Navy Officer Candidate School (OCS) for a year after his father used political connections to obtain the assignment. Blechman was opposed to the Vietnam War but regarded himself as a "person of conscience" who might find it useful to know how to fight. As he learned more and more about military weapons, however, he came to the conclusion that these terrible tools of destruction should never be used. Consequently, he refused his assignment following his completion of OCS and clerical error enabled him to receive an honorable discharge without ever having to complete his required time of service.

That would have been the end of the matter, but he prolonged the ordeal by applying for conscientious objector status with his draft board. It decided that he should do alternative service to fulfill his obligation. He became a Community Program Developer under the VISTA program, working primarily in the Johnson City area of East Tennessee, where he helped organize tenant unions and food co-ops. Si and Kathy Kahn were the VISTA trainers there at the time. They persuaded him that his photography and press skills would be of use in the black lung movement. He did volunteer work for the Brookside strike under the guidance of Kahn after he left VISTA in March 1973, supporting himself by working as a welder in an East Tennessee factory. He first met Szpak in the Carolinas when they were both lining up people to testify in public hearings against Duke Power's requested rate increase in the spring of 1974.

Charlotte Brody was significant not only because of her relationship to Kahn but because of her long tenure with the Brown Lung Association. A Detroit native who was trained as a nurse, Brody had spent most of her working life as an organizer, working with Kentucky coal miners, with antiwar groups, and with the Student Nonviolent Coordinating Committee (SNCC) on civil rights issues (Drogin 1980a, 17). She was the only founder still active with the remnants of the Brown Lung Association after its rapid decline in the early 1980s.

Thad Moore, who put together the Greensboro chapter, did not stay with the association very long. According to other organizers, he left after Szpak convinced him that he was not a very good organizer. Nevertheless, he deserves credit for "discovering" Lacy Wright, perhaps the strongest and most highly publicized member leader of the association.

Len Stanley came into the movement out of her combined interests in community organizing and public health. She was a product of the antipoverty programs of the 1960s, helping to organize minority women. She attended the School of Public Health at the University of North Carolina, Chapel Hill, where she learned of byssinosis and became involved in groups that were trying to organize workers around health and safety issues. Later, she and Chip Hughes went to Erwin to organize a Brown Lung chapter.

The group was preparing a long-term campaign against Duke Power when a striking miner, Lawrence Jones, was shot and killed by a foreman at the mine (Bethell 1976, 116). Mike Szpak, still working in Charlotte, North Carolina, to bring pressure on Duke Power's corporate headquarters, remembers that Si Kahn called him at three in the morning to tell him of the shooting. Szpak then called all members of Duke Power's board of directors. The next day, Szpak was distributing leaflets outside the church of Duke's president, Carl Horn. Horn avoided him publicly but then doubled back in his car and spoke to Szpak, telling him that they were going to end the strike and sign a contract.

With the strike abruptly over, the group faced the question of what to do next. Kahn's romantic involvement with Charlotte Brody, who held a strong commitment to occupational health, had increased his own interest in byssinosis as an occupational health issue around which to build a grassroots movement. Blechman remembers Kahn's rhetorical question: "What is to the rest of the South like coal mining is to Appalachia?" The answer, of course, was textiles. The Black Lung Association had helped in the Brookside strike and assisted in returning control of the UMW to the rank-and-file miners. Perhaps byssinosis could provide the wedge for organizing the southern textile work force and taking power for the workers.

Len Stanley (1992) remembers that this initial brainstorming actually took place before the end of the Brookside strike, when most of the initial organizers were attending an alternative energy conference related to the pressure they were trying to bring to bear on Duke Power. In the basement of the building where the conference was held, they began talking right after lunch, and the excited discussion about the possibility of an occupational health movement lasted until after midnight.

In addition to the sudden ending of the Brookside strike, the August 1974 pro-union vote by textile workers at the J. P. Stevens mill in Roanoke Rapids, North Carolina, played a role in turning the attention of organizers toward the Carolinas (Hughes 1992). After a bitter struggle (captured in the docudrama film *Norma Rae*) Stevens employees had voted to be represented by the Textile Workers Union of America, and this seemed to represent a historic opportunity:

southern workers were finally ready to be organized, if only they had the right kind of help. Little did these would-be organizers know at the time that it would take another six years just to get a contract signed with Stevens and that there would be no domino effect following that hard-won victory (Luebke 1990, 97–98).

Even before the end of the Brookside strike and the Stevens vote, the group had participated in discussions about the possibility of building a movement around byssinosis. Highlander, a school for political and social activists, founded by Myles Horton in the mountains of Tennessee near Knoxville, held a conference on occupational health in July 1974.[8] In addition to Kahn, Szpak, Blechman, Moore, Hughes, and Brody (who attended only the second day, after most of the discussion was over), members of the Tennessee Legal Aid, the Tennessee Health Care Organization, the Black Lung Association, and the Knoxville Brown Lung Project were also present.

The Knoxville Brown Lung Project was one of a few early false starts in organizing byssinosis victims. The two organizers, Fran Ansley and Brenda Bell, had hoped to identify enough victims to create an organization, but they found too few victims in the area. They attributed this to two factors. Knoxville had a diversified economy in which anyone who had an adverse reaction to cotton dust could rather easily find industrial employment outside the textile mills. In addition, the mills there had been blending cotton with synthetics for a long time, thereby reducing cotton dust exposure. Ansley and Bell concluded that the organization required an area that was dominated by the textile industry (BLA Papers, Report by Ansley and Bell). The Knoxville Brown Lung Project was funded by Youth Project, which also helped fund the earlier Brookside efforts and later brown lung organizing in the Carolinas. Youth Project was a Washington-based funding group that pooled money from many small donors into large grants. It then entered into "contracts with organizers whose job it is to build organizations [that] involve the 'victimized constituency' into a democratic organization which works to assume power to change the status quo" (BLA Papers).

Also present at the Highlander meeting was an observer from the TWUA, who saw some possibility "to harness the efforts of many of these people to our problems in the South in the future. . . . We certainly need any help we can get from sympathetic Southerners, if we are to organize the South" (BLA Papers, Memo from Bruce Raynor to Sol Stetin, 23 July 1974). His report and exploratory work done in the next several months led Sol Stetin, president of the TWUA, to support the funding of initial organizing efforts in 1975.

The first person to act was Mike Szpak, who visited Si Kahn at his home in northern Georgia right after the end of the Brookside strike and remembers Kahn's asking him to go to South Carolina to try organizing around brown lung. A limited amount of money was available in Youth Project grant funds left over from the Brookside effort. Szpak also received critical help from the TWUA in making initial contacts.

From September through November of 1974, Szpak explored the possibilities of building an organization in the area of Greenville, South Carolina. Greenville is located in the heart of textile country, and the Textile Workers Union of America had an organizing drive going on at the J. P. Stevens plants there. After considerable effort, however, Szpak concluded that the industry's ability to pressure workers and their families was too strong in Greenville and that state and regional media coverage would be too limited in this small city. Moreover, he was also followed around on his house-to-house calls by someone who reported his activities to the South Carolina Chamber of Commerce. The November 29, 1974, issue of the chamber's newsletter described in ominous terms the flyers he was giving out, though it concluded that because this group was so new, "we are not able to evaluate at this time." He did receive help in making contacts in the mill neighborhoods from an Office of Economic Opportunity worker who knew the area; nevertheless, the going was very slow. He found very low worker awareness of any problem and remembers that the people he visited were very suspicious and rarely invited him inside their homes. No doubt his Boston accent did not help very much.

By December 1974 Szpak had decided that Columbia, South Carolina, would be a much better place to start an initial chapter. It had the advantage of being the state capital, where there was access to the legislature and to media with a wider impact. In addition, the mills there were unionized: 80 to 90 percent of the workers at M. Lowenstein's Pacific Mills and the Mt. Vernon Mills belonged to the TWUA. The union provided lists of retirees and Szpak also found names and addresses of retired workers from studies performed in those mills by Bouhuys and a morbidity study done by Mt. Sinai Hospital. These lists allowed Szpak to perform three highly efficient and well-targeted mailings to potential members. Those who returned the attached postcards got another letter, a phone call, and finally a personal visit. In addition, because the mills were not a major part of Columbia's economy, "industry monitoring of our activities was slight" (BLA Papers). The relative economic unimportance of textiles had been a barrier in the earlier Knoxville effort but was a slight advantage here because organizers saw Columbia as just a place to get started before moving to locales where the industry was dominant.

BUILDING CHAPTERS

The actual organizing work began in early 1975, with grants from several sources supporting a number of efforts. Szpak had obtained additional money from the Youth Project and $10,000 each from the United Church of Christ and the AFL-CIO's Industrial Union Department. Youth Project also funded Thad Moore's efforts to organize a chapter in Greensboro. The group applied to the Catholic Church's Campaign for Human Development in January 1975, but those monies did not begin until November. Blechman, who had arrived in South Carolina in December 1974, worked with Szpak to build the initial chapter in Columbia.

Szpak remembers that in early 1975 there was a kind of race to see who would build the first chapter because Youth Project would not fund two separate projects. After he and Blechman held the first successful mass meeting of 125 retired and disabled workers on April 25 and elected temporary officers on May 22 (BLA Papers), Szpak felt he had become the "kingpin" of the group. Others remember that even though Szpak was officially designated head organizer by Youth Project and other funding groups, there was an informal agreement that staff would act collectively to make decisions. These differing perceptions about the division of power among organizers pointed to trouble down the road.

From the initial organizing efforts in 1975 until mid-1976, there was very little formal structure, if any, tying the different chapters together. As Charlotte Brody remembers it, organizing came first and structure came later. In March 1975 Szpak and Blechman attempted to provide a more formal structure by forming a new organization called the Southern Institute for Occupational Health (SIOH). The SIOH was to serve as a sponsoring agency for the Brown Lung Association chapters, contracting with them to give help in planning, implementation, and evaluation (BLA Papers). The SIOH board of directors included Wib Gully of the North Carolina PIRG, Bill Finger of the Institute for Southern Studies, and Charlotte Brody, who in a 21 May 1975 letter (BLA Papers) was described as "related in some close way to Si Kahn." (In 1975 Kahn and Brody moved to Roanoke Rapids, where Kahn worked as a union consultant helping the TWUA in its strike against J. P. Stevens (Kahn 1992).

Brody had a small grant to organize a new brown lung chapter. They hoped that a group of older retired workers could provide inspiration for younger workers to organize.) Len Stanley, a Chapel Hill epidemiologist, was another SIOH board member. In 1975 she and Chip Hughes began organizing another chapter in Erwin, North Carolina, with a small grant obtained through the Institute of Southern Studies. The other seven members of the board were two college professors, a minister, an attorney, the head of the black legislative caucus in the South Carolina General Assembly, the director of the South Carolina Human Rights Council, and Daisy Pittman, a Brown Lung Association member who would be the last president of the Columbia chapter when it finally folded in February 1990.

There were two reasons for the creation of the Southern Institute for Occupational Health. First, it would allow Szpak and his associates latitude to organize workers in other industries, such as asbestos workers, on the basis of occupational disease. The Brown Lung Project (the original name) was to be just one of several efforts. In 1975 SIOH made a number of contacts with workers outside textiles in the hope of creating a much broader movement (BLA Papers)—but work with the brown lung groups soon occupied all available time and energy.

Second, organizers hoped the more neutral name of the new organization would make it easier to work with government agencies (BLA Papers, letter from Frank Blechman to Carl Dykes, 28 July 1975). That point turned out to be moot, as organizers who survived the conflicts of early 1976 turned their full attention to the Brown Lung Association and began applying for direct funding. SIOH remained alive for a year or two after 1976, but only as a legal entity. After 1977 the Brown Lung Association obtained tax exempt status and raised its own funds.

With the benefit of more than a decade of hindsight, Blechman now feels that perhaps organizers should have remained outside the Brown Lung Association in a consulting agency like SIOH. This might have forced members to assume more responsibility for their own fund raising and made them less dependent on the external funding of grants obtained by staff.

In 1975 the organizers identified and brought together enough victims to build chapters in three cities. Columbia held its first mass meeting in April, and by mid-1976 the chapter claimed 103 members. Meanwhile, Thad Moore was organizing the Greensboro, North Carolina, chapter. Having chapters in both states would enable them to give the organization a regional basis. In August the Greensboro group held its first meeting, and by mid-1976 it claimed

52 members. Late in 1975 a chapter was begun in Spartanburg, South Carolina, mainly because it was a less hostile place than neighboring Greenville but shared media with Greenville, thereby giving the group a foothold in the Greenville area. Spartanburg did not exactly welcome the organization with open arms. Organizers had to move the first meeting from a church to a union hall when mill managers among the church leadership forced the minister to refuse the group the use of the building (BLA Papers). Nevertheless, the first meeting attracted 50 people, and the new chapter had 89 members by March 1976. Organizers planned a drive in Greenville in early 1976, beginning with a mailing of 2,500 letters with return postcards. From a commercial list broker they bought mailing labels for all retired persons in selected zip code areas corresponding to mill villages.

By early 1976 the efforts of four more of the original organizers had born fruit in North Carolina. Brody, with informal help from Kahn, created a chapter in Roanoke Rapids; Stanley and Hughes organized one in Erwin. Szpak (1991) regarded these newer North Carolina chapters as having been organized differently from the Columbia chapter. He describes them as "fast track" models, with lower membership and no mass meeting required: "They would get five people together in a living room and call it a chapter." How to merge these disparate groups into a larger organization with a formal structure was a question that would bring to a head the differences between Szpak and the other organizers.

In locating and recruiting their first members, the organizers began a process that became the principal method of building the organization. Along with the help of mailings to whatever lists they could obtain, they knocked on doors in the neighborhoods of former milltown areas, attempting to locate disabled workers. In Greensboro, Thad Moore found the rather remarkable Lacy Wright (Drogin 1980a), a former textile worker who in 1966, at the age of sixty-one, had retired from Cone Mills with severe breathing problems. Like so many other workers, Wright had been diagnosed as having emphysema or bronchitis, not byssinosis. Unlike most textile workers, he had worked in a union plant. As a former president of his TWUA local, he had organizational experience and skills and put them to use in a very personal cause that involved him for the rest of his life (Finger 1976, 64). Unfortunately for the group, there were not very many Lacy Wrights to be found. But they did find enough people like him to get the association started: among them, Hub Spires, Gertrude Brown, Essie Briggs, Shorty Gamble, and Daisy Pittman in Columbia, Alvin Wood in Greenville, Florence Sandlin in Greensboro, Lucy Taylor in Roanoke Rapids, Elsie Morrison in Erwin.

In early 1976 the internal crisis that had been brewing for some time nearly split the association into two warring factions. The conflict revolved around two of the founding organizers, Mike Szpak and Frank Blechman, and involved questions of power, style, and organizational philosophy. Blechman and Szpak, both very strong-willed and committed young men, found working together impossible. Each had a different vision of what the group was to become; each had a different style of leadership. Szpak, recognized by funding agencies as the person in charge, used a hierarchical command style with other organizers, inviting little collective discussion or decision-making. At the same time as he embraced hierarchy in his relationship with other organizers, he insisted that members assume responsibilities. In the words of a Youth Project officer who visited the chapters to ascertain the problem, he "made members work and does not baby them" (BLA Papers, letter from Heleny Cooke, 10 May 1976). Many members in fact found Szpak too demanding and too abrasive. Blechman, on the other hand, was more open to the feelings of other staffers and not so demanding on members or staff (BLA Papers). His style and philosophy were nonhierarchical, egalitarian, and collective. He was clearly influenced by the thought of Si Kahn, who had trained him as a VISTA worker in Tennessee. Szpak was influenced by Herb White, an organizer for the United Church of Christ who stressed a stronger role for lead organizers. Szpak disparagingly labeled the leadership philosophy of Blechman a "1970s Chapel Hill" genre of "collectivity and congeniality" with too little regard for necessary discipline.

Beyond questions of philosophy and power, the struggle centered on how to bring together chapters that had been organized in a variety of ways by a variety of people under a variety of grants. When the conflict came to a head in the spring of 1976, there were six chapters. The original Columbia chapter, the largest and strongest in the association, was closest to Blechman, who had stayed with it when Szpak left to organize chapters in Spartanburg and Greenville. These three and the Greensboro chapter were included under the SIOH framework. The two new newest chapters, Erwin and Roanoke Rapids, had no official relationship to the others. Blechman and his old colleagues from the Brookside strike wanted to bring all the chapters together as equals as quickly as possible. Szpak did not consider the new chapters strong or large enough to be equal partners in an association.

The conflict was not resolved until after Blechman gained enough support from the other chapters to force Szpak out. That support came rather naturally as the other organizers embraced Kahn's model of grassroots organization and resented Szpak's unilateral assertion of sole authority. In July 1976 a joint meeting of all the chapters was held, ostensibly to attempt to resolve the differences. The member who was chairing the meeting asked Blechman to outline a possible agenda for the discussion. Blechman also took the minutes. It was clear that he and the other organizers already had the necessary votes to carry the day; the meeting was only to ratify what had already taken place. Prior to this meeting Blechman had gained support of the board of directors of SIOH. Szpak had resigned as director of SIOH's Brown Lung Project and was under threat of suit from the board to return resources over which he had control. Szpak announced that he was thinking about leaving the area and terminating his association with the group. By the end of the summer he was gone (BLA Papers). SIOH dropped the suits against him in September, explaining to the Youth Project people that the money under Szpak's control had been returned and that the atmosphere was now better and "more democratic" (BLA Papers). With one antagonist gone, the group regained its funding support from Youth Project and continued its expansion.

In an interview fifteen years later, Charlotte Brody patiently answered questions about the Szpak/Blechman struggle but insisted that the dispute was not really germane to what the Brown Lung Association eventually became. From her perspective, the association was not Michael Szpak; it was other organizers—Betty Bailey, Dave Austin, Mary Lou Seymour, Karen Hart, Len Stanley, Chip Hughes, David Dotson, Jerry Wingate, Mike and Kathy Russell—who worked closely with their chapters, each of which was unique.[9]

The dispute was important, however, in determining the organizer philosophy and leadership style that would dominate the association for the rest of its life. Never again would any organizer dominate the association as Szpak did during the first year. From this point on, organizers and the more active members collectively made decisions—with all the strengths and weaknesses that characterize collective decision-making. Once made, decisions would carry a greater sense of legitimacy. All too often, however, no decision would be made because consensus was lacking. Necessary planning rarely went beyond the discussion stage because no one had the legitimate power to make and enforce needed decisions on funding, staffing, policy positions, or negotiating postures. Negotiation with other groups was especially difficult in that no one other than the amorphous collective was in a position to negotiate.

Of course, this is one of the classic problems for any democratic organization: to what extent can it concentrate power for the sake of efficiency and tactical agility without sacrificing legitimacy and risking autocracy? The Brown Lung Association, employing the vision of Si Kahn (1970), clearly came down on the side of dividing and spreading power as much as possible. It shifted a great deal of power to the chapters, and the influence of organizers over their individual chapters was considerable. This practice may have fit best with the political culture of members, who embraced southern values of localism and volunteerism, and who rejected almost all forms of concentrated power that could impose on their individual discretion.

Still, the fight left some long-lasting scars on the organization. The rumors and accusations had created an atmosphere of distrust among several of the original chapters. Even years later they were reluctant to send money to the central fund out of fear that it was being mismanaged or misused by organizers or other chapters. The experience reinforced the parochial, territorial, localistic orientation that was already such an important part of members' culture. It reinforced their distrust of authority based on generations of experience in the mills. The addition of new chapters reduced the legacy of distrust somewhat, but given that the chapters involved in the fight were generally the strongest and largest, the legacy remained. The fight also cost the association some resources. Both the AFL-CIO's Industrial Union Department (IUD) and the United Church of Christ pulled their funding when Szpak left. Others hold him responsible for these losses, but Szpak maintains that he was not. He claims that he even sent a memo to the IUD asking that funding for the Brown Lung Association be continued.

After 1976, the group branched out to other towns across the South. In late 1976 the organizers had bought an offset printing press to publish flyers and announcements. In early 1977 they adopted formal bylaws governing the bi-state board they had set up the previous summer (BLA Papers). In October they began publishing an association newsletter, the *Brown Lung Blues.* By late 1977 organizers were in the process of creating six new chapters in North Carolina (Rockingham, Lincolnton, Eden, and Stanly County in the Kannapolis-Concord area all became chapters eventually; Albemarle and Reidsville never fully developed) in addition to the three chapters already in existence (Greensboro, Roanoke Rapids, and Erwin). They had three chapters in South Carolina (Columbia, Spartanburg, and Greenville), and another was being organized in the Horse Creek Valley—"the Valley"—area of South Carolina between Aiken and Augusta, Georgia.

Federal programs such as the Comprehensive Training and Employment Act (CETA) and Volunteers in Service to America (VISTA) provided many of the organizers over the next several years. They were assisted by volunteers and interns from university programs, some of whom later stayed on as paid staff. Their methods were those pioneered by Szpak with the help of Blechman in 1974 and 1975: going door to door, advertising with posters, and holding screening clinics. Members helped by talking to potential recruits.

John Kassell, Dave Austin, and David Dotson were typical of many of the new staff who came to help organize. Kassell, who was an organizer and staff coordinator in South Carolina during the peak years of the association, signed on initially as a VISTA volunteer in early 1979 and later became regular staff. Just after finishing college, he had learned of the Brown Lung Association through his involvement with the J. P. Stevens boycott movement. He rode a bus from his home in Washington, D.C., to Greenville to help (Kassell 1992).

Dave Austin learned of the association through his work at the School of Public Health at the University of North Carolina at Chapel Hill, which was the source of a number of staff, including Fran Lynn and Len Stanley. After graduating in 1976, he joined the regular staff as a coordinator. He helped recruit health care workers to run screening clinics, placed CETA and VISTA volunteers in new chapters, investigated the criteria used by physicians in diagnosing byssinosis, and established a medical bank of information on the disease (Austin 1992).

David Dotson was working on his M.A. in social work at the University of Georgia when he read Kahn's 1970 book on grassroots organizing. As the practicum part of his graduate program, he went to help organize the Valley. His first day's efforts were less than a total success. An organizer dropped him off on an extremely hot mid-summer day in 1977 and told him to knock on doors for the next several hours. After he had tried about twenty houses without getting an answer, one resident did come to the door and explained that everyone was out of town because it was the Fourth of July week, when mills traditionally close for their annual vacation. Dotson returned later to begin the slow process of locating the Valley chapter's first potential members (Dotson 1991).

The Highlander school in Tennessee continued to be involved. Members of Brown Lung and Black Lung associations met there in January 1977 to compare experiences and learn from each other. In October 1977 members of the bi-state board that governed the association and some of the organizers attended a Highlander workshop to review progress, set new goals, learn organizational skills, and improve their knowledge about federal laws and the compensation process (*Brown Lung Blues* 15 November 1977). They met once again in May 1979 to discuss future directions.

In 1979, deciding to expand into Virginia and Georgia, the association stopped calling itself the Carolina Brown Lung Association and became simply the Brown Lung Association (the name used throughout this book for the sake of simplicity). Leaders received a $37,000 grant from the Catholic Church's Campaign for Human Development to begin this expansion effort (BLA Papers). By early 1980 there were fifteen chapters in the four states (Drogin 1980a, 18) and some chapters were publishing their own newsletters. Up to this point, it seemed that the original organizers' plans were working quite well.

The overall strategy for change centered on building and maintaining a people's organization that may be described in terms of the general model and philosophy of Highlander founder Myles Horton, social activist and theorist Saul Alinsky, and, of course, Si Kahn. Bring the discontented together around a common problem. Build a sense of collectivity and attract new membership in confronting this problem. Build confidence by staying within the people's experiences and concentrating on winnable issues. In doing so, teach self-reliance and organizational skills. Move on to tackle more difficult issues as the organization grows (Alinsky 1971; Adams with Horton 1975; Kahn 1970, 1982; Glen 1988).

The staff viewed the organization as one small part of a long-term struggle to raise class consciousness and build organizational ties and political skills among the lower classes. Some early organizers may have held a quite radical vision for the future, but most were clearly well within the American populist tradition. John Kassell (1992) described the goal as building a self-sustaining grass-roots organization. Mike Russell (1992) differed from many others in that his vision was somewhat more limited. He thought the group itself would probably never move beyond a rather narrow focus, but he saw the effort as one that could change the atmosphere so that others could organize. He described his actions as "applied high school civics."

As a conscious policy, organizers tried to restrain their rhetoric. A few of the doctors who volunteered their help at screening clinics were not so careful. One of them castigated those who attended a clinic for not being Communists, saying that he was speaking for the association. The organizers responded as quickly as they could: "We pulled him aside quietly and told him if he ever did that again we'd . . . break his knees" (Drogin 1980a, 18; Blechman 1991). Some of these doctors were members of a radical leftist group called the Communist Worker's Party (CWP). Two of them were killed and a third was wounded in the well-publicized confrontation between the CWP and the Klan in Greensboro, North Carolina, in November of 1979. These kinds of connections, even though they were few in number, did create some image problems for the group. A well-known South Carolina lawyer condemned the association in terms that expressed the traditional values and prejudices of the South: "Hell, they're nothing but a bunch of damn Catholics and labor unions agitating" (Drogin 1980s, 18). However, a prominent mainstream South Carolina legislator who was friendly to the group said that anyone who talked about workers' rights was likely to be labeled a socialist in the state (Lourie 1991).

A related image problem arose from the nonsouthern origins of so many of the staff. Any time they communicated with state political leaders, their speech betrayed them. One state senator told me it was obvious to him that the association was organized by outsiders instead of being a legitimate local group whose members decided things for themselves. Although he had no problems with most of the members, whom he had known all his life, he resented seeing an outsider "calling all the shots" (Interviews). The South has a long tradition of blaming "outside agitators" for its problems.

The best defense against both these images was the involvement of retired workers in media events—including the use of their own words. In an early learning experience, members at a disastrous press conference read a staff-written statement that included such sophisticated terms as "promulgate" (Stanley 1992). By contrast, in the words of one organizer, "when you see old retired textile workers coming and talking to you, you can't really think of them as being radical, you can't believe it" (Interviews). Because organizers and staff understood this quite well, it became imperative to have members be as visible and vocal as possible.

Some of the members as well understood the need for staff to stay in the background. John Kassell (1992) remembers that active members such as the Hardin family of Greenville, South Carolina, played the role of protective grandparents to Yankee staff, though they were not above kidding about cultural differences. Mr. Hardin once slipped one young woman a few hot peppers to eat. When she later invited the Hardins over for a vegetarian dinner, he jokingly asked her if she shopped at the same stores as they and if she was from the same planet.

Organizers sometimes had to adjust their life-styles in order to fit in with the Bible Belt communities in which they worked. Len Stanley and Chip Hughes, for example, decided it would be easier to work as a couple in organizing Eden, North Carolina, if they were formally married rather than just living together. Len laughingly describes the ceremony as an outdoor organizer wedding and remembers that Si Kahn sang a song he composed for the occasion (Stanley 1992).

Most of the organizers are best understood as interest-group liberals, not Communist radicals, as opponents sometimes charged (M. Russell 1992). They came to volunteer their time and energy with a very American vision: to organize the unorganized so that there would be a better balance in the struggle between interest groups that characterizes American democracy. They labored to make pluralism a reality in the South. Working for the association was often a stopping-off place between college and graduate school or law school. It was somewhat like a tour in the Peace Corps for these idealistic and highly motivated young people with a strong sense of social justice. They wanted to make what they saw as a backward part of the nation live up to the ideals they thought America should stand for. A young woman who worked as organizer for the Aiken chapter in 1979–80, after graduating from Radcliffe, explained her activism in these terms: "I felt like a lot of organizing needed to be done in the South . . . that southern workers didn't have a sense that they needed to organize the same way that most workers in northern industrial cities seem to" (Interviews).

THE ROLE OF ORGANIZED LABOR

One of the controversies surrounding the Brown Lung Association was whether it was anything more than a stalking-horse for organized labor. Textile officials often regarded the group as a back-door effort on the part of the union to get into the mills. An article in the *New York Times* in 1977 assumed a strong union connection (King 1977; Hall 1978, 33). Union officials feel that the role of unions in the birth and life of the organization has been grossly undervalued and underappreciated by some of the organizers and observers of the group (Frumin 1991). Organizers themselves hold a range of views on the role of unions. Those who helped at the outset tend to credit unions for laying the groundwork in many of the places where they initially organized; at the same time, they hold some contempt for unions, feeling that they lacked energy, skill, and true commitment to the workers. Those who came later and worked in places where there was no union base see the union role as minimal.

The connections that did exist between unions and the Brown Lung Association fell far short of union domination. A memo from a TWUA observer at the 1974 Highlander meeting made it clear that the union had its hopes: "It would probably be possible to harness the efforts of many of these people to our problems in the South in the future . . . probably [they would be] valuable allies. We certainly need any help we can get from sympathetic Southerners, if we are to organize the South" (BLA Papers, memo from Bruce Raynor to Sol Stetin, 23 July 1974).

In a grant proposal to the Textile Workers Union of America in late 1975, Mike Szpak did all he could to encourage those hopes. After recalling that the safety concerns of miners had been a valuable organizing issue in the coal industry, he made the obvious comparison: "Because 15 to 25% of active cotton mill workers are partially disabled by Brown Lung [it] offers a legitimate means of approaching both active and retired mill workers. . . . dust control [and] compensation [are] something concrete [that organizers can give] to mill workers. . . . Successes, by giving workers a taste of the usefulness of organizing, can help open workers to later drives by the union" (BLA Papers, Carolina Brown Lung Project Proposal to IUD).

Although Szpak's argument persuaded the union to fund his proposal, the logic of the argument was flawed. The Brown Lung Association could not give workers anything they considered to be concrete. Safety and health were not highly salient issues for most mill workers. They certainly did not carry the weight that safety did among mine workers, where everyone worked in fear of all too frequent accidents and all were exposed to coal dust. Because these issues were not important to most mill workers, even after efforts to educate them, they saw no concrete benefits. If you needed workers' compensation, you hired a lawyer. You didn't get it through the Brown Lung Association.

A year later, reporting his progress under the union grant, Szpak listed a wide range of activities in recruiting disabled workers in Columbia, Greensboro, and Spartanburg and in getting them started on filing for compensation. But on the key question of how much all of this effort was helping the union cause among active workers, he admitted having "no ready answer." He could offer only hope: "One thing [is] certain: Brown Lung is an issue which organizes people . . . disabled people. As the publicity and consciousness of the dangers of cotton dust to the health of workers increases, effects of active worker attitudes toward the organization may change. . . . It's hard to imagine that these people and their activities aren't going to have some impact on the area and its attitudes toward organizing" (BLA Papers, letter from Michael Szpak to IUD, 11 December 1975).

In reality, Szpak was probably far more interested in obtaining financial support than in the validity of his arguments, even though he had and continues to have strong personal union ties and sympathies (BLA Papers; Szpak 1991). Frank Blechman, the other major figure in the initial organizational effort, also had obvious union ties and sympathies. Having come from the United Mine Workers struggle, like many of the initial organizers, he saw obvious parallels with the miners' black lung movement. At the least, he hoped to replicate part of what had taken place in Kentucky. He wrote a former co-worker in the Brookside effort to ask for a list of contributors. He thought the efforts were similar enough to warrant trying to interest them in supporting the brown lung movement: "In many ways, it's a lot like the black lung fight seven or eight years ago, with all the same possibilities for union reform, union building, and shaking the industry" (BLA Papers, letter to Carl Dykes, 19 February 1975). In a later letter, however, he noted the huge caveat: there was no history of unionization or militancy upon which to build (BLA Papers, letter to Steve Early, 2 May 1975).

According to the early correspondence of the Brown Lung Association, the textile union provided the association considerable help and cooperation (BLA Papers). Strong union membership in the Columbia mills made initial organizing efforts possible there. Unions provided lists of retirees. A union official introduced Szpak to Dr. Arendt Bouhuys, who provided him with a list of over a hundred people in the Columbia area whom he identified as having symptoms of byssinosis. The first mass meeting in April 1975 took place in a union hall in Columbia (Szpak 1991).

A weaker union base slowed the Greensboro organizing efforts. A minority of mill workers in Greensboro were union members, compared with a clear majority in Columbia (Szpak 1991). But even in Greensboro, much of the leadership—most notably Lacy Wright—had gained skills and confidence from former union activities. Organizing efforts in Spartanburg too began with membership and retirement lists from textile unions (BLA Papers, letter to Steve Early from Frank Blechman, 2 May 1975). Unions were active and provided a significant base of support also for North Carolina chapters that were created in Erwin, near a Burlington Mills plant (Stanley 1992), and in Roanoke Rapids, where the J. P. Stevens struggle was taking place (Szpak 1991; Frumin 1991). In Erwin, initial meetings were held in a union hall until the new group rented a small cinderblock building where a restaurant had been located (the Coca-Cola company replaced the restaurant name with the Brown Lung Association chapter name between two round Coke emblems above the door; Stanley 1992).

Union contacts were used even in unsuccessful exploratory efforts at such mill locations as Newberry, South Carolina (BLA Papers, letter to Steve Early from Frank Blechman, 2 May 1975). Frank

Blechman (1991) remembers that those who slammed the door in the organizers' faces tended to be workers who had opposed union movements in earlier decades—whereas many who welcomed their initiative were workers who had memories of management "beating the tar out of them" in efforts to unionize in the 1930s and later. Now they were retired and felt they should give it one more shot. Without this small base of support created by decades of repressed anger and frustration, Blechman believes, the organization would never have started.

Staff who organized later chapters found that any previous successful union activities in the area made a difference. Kathy Russell (1992), who went door to door to organize the Anderson, South Carolina, chapter in the summer of 1978, remembers that Anderson's workers had a greater sense of community and empowerment than workers in Greenville. She attributed this difference to an active union organizing drive at a nearby fiberglass plant. Residents felt less dominated by the mill.

Throughout the life of the Brown Lung Association, the union cooperated in publicity efforts and continued to offer limited financial help. After the first couple of years, however, the interests of the two groups went in different directions. The organizers of the Brown Lung Association and many of its other sponsors envisioned a broad movement of community empowerment going beyond the workplace. The union did not place a high priority on retired workers, especially given that many of them had opposed union organization when they were working in the mills. Nor did union officials object when some mills that couldn't afford to modernize to meet the standards were forced to close. From the union's perspective, job losses because of forced modernization were quite acceptable, "so long as most of the people in the new jobs are unionized at relatively high wages" (Berman 1978, 156).

The union became disenchanted with the Brown Lung Association as it became clear that the association would not be able to help in organizing active workers. On an October 1977 trip to explore funding possibilities, Brown Lung members and staffers were given the cold shoulder by Sol Stetin, executive vice-president of the Amalgamated Clothing and Textile Workers Union. They described their meeting with him as the "least successful of the trip." Rather than listen, the union official lectured them on what they had not done for the union and then left for another meeting without even giving them a chance to respond (BLA Papers).

Resentments arose between the young, idealistic Brown Lung Association staffers, who were new to the southern organizing battle arena, and the war-weary veterans of the union. Association organizers believed that they had been able to gain national media attention for a problem that the union had failed to deal with for decades. They thought the union lacked commitment to organize on a wide scale (Hughes 1992). They felt a little arrogant and were convinced that their tangible results merited those feelings (Brody 1991; Kahn 1992). Len Stanley (1992) remembers their winning the Department of Labor "New Directions" grant—to educate active workers about the dangers of cotton dust exposure—as a major victory over the union. She felt that unlike union officials, Brown Lung staff really cared about the workers. One staff member described a union official as fitting the negative stereotype that textile management used to arouse distrust between workers and union organizers: "a fat, cigar-smoking New York Jew driving a big Cadillac" (Interviews).

Union officials regarded Brown Lung Association staff as neophytes who had not yet paid their dues. At a joint planning meeting in 1977, when they happened to see part of a grant application in which the association claimed to be "the only one working for workers health," union officials boiled at the insult, even though it was explained as just part of the rhetoric of grant writing. When organizers thoughtlessly added that the union could prove the claim to be untrue by giving the association financial support, the officials were outraged. Attempted blackmail had been added to insult (Blechman 1991).

Part of the problem was a mutual basic distrust between the union officials and these young activists. Many association staff came from the black lung movement, which had been much more than a crusade against an occupational disease. It was a reform movement in which a faction of the United Mine Workers organized around black lung to overthrow the existing UMW leadership. That history was enough to make textile union officials nervous (Stanley 1992).

The Brown Lung Association staff's rhetoric and style of decision-making added to the distrust. When union and association representatives were to meet to plan for the 1977 OSHA hearings on proposed cotton dust regulations, the union wanted only two or three members to serve as association representatives; instead, the association insisted on sending twelve to fifteen, some from each chapter. The union did not want to foot the bill for so many people. Moreover, they didn't care for the collective decision-making style that was so characteristic of the Brown Lung Association. They were more comfortable with the greater concentration of power at the top of a hierarchical structure (Blechman 1991).

Other differences had to do with where the association would organize. From the union's perspective, the group would ideally concentrate on areas where there was little union base, acting as a third force in building a climate that would better support later union organizational efforts. Union officials did not want the Brown Lung Association to focus its efforts on mills that were already unionized. Most of these were small independent mills, and if were forced to clean up, the extra expense might place them at a competitive disadvantage with larger non-union mills (Kahn 1992).

Union officials made association organizers feel somewhat unwelcome in union areas, especially when Brown Lung organizers asked to help in strike negotiations concerning health and safety issues, or to play a greater role in determining the provisions of proposed federal legislation dealing with occupational diseases (Blechman 1991). From the union's point of view, those who wanted be involved should join the union, not the Brown Lung Association. From the association leaders' point of view, they had to remain separate, especially if they were to recruit members who had anti-union feelings. Even though most organizers hoped that the group would lead to a better atmosphere for union organizing, for short-term tactical reasons they wanted to avoid the charge of being a front for the union (Kahn 1992). Trying to have it both ways proved difficult.

The evidence supports a conclusion that the union was a necessary and vital factor in getting the Brown Lung Association off the ground. It provided initial contacts and some funding, and gave the group legitimacy in contacting retirees who had been union supporters in their earlier years. Former union members also provided an important experienced and assertive segment of the member leadership. The union base in the mill villages of the South was so small and narrow, however, that the group could not go very far using that base alone. The association did expand into areas with no union support and did enlist members who were hostile toward organized labor. Unions were disappointed that the group was unable to penetrate further and obtain the support of active workers. Combined with a significant distrust of organizer goals and styles, this disappointment weakened the relationship between the Brown Lung Association and the Amalgamated Clothing and Textile Workers Union. Rather than an enduring symbiotic relationship as originally hoped, it became a relatively brief affair of convenience.

5

ORGANIZATIONAL
STRUCTURE
AND LIFE

This chapter examines the Brown Lung Association from an organizational perspective. How were members recruited and retained? What were the membership incentives? How was the group governed? How did these far-flung, tiny chapters, spread out over five southern states, communicate with one another? Finally, what was the relationship between organizers and members (a critical question for a group that had a goal of becoming a grassroots, member-run organization)?

RECRUITMENT AND MEMBERSHIP INCENTIVES

Helping disabled workers through the workers' compensation process was the primary tactic for recruiting new members, just as earlier welfare rights organizations had approached potential members by helping them secure welfare benefits. The activities of the Brown Lung Association chapter in the Valley just outside Aiken, South Carolina, are illustrative. In 1977 two organizers came to the Valley area and identified potentially compensable cases by knocking on doors and asking questions. They invited these people to a screening clinic to have a breathing test and find out if they had a compensable problem. Following the clinic, they invited participants to an organizational meeting to learn more about the compensation process. Enough came and were enlisted to form a chapter, and they were assigned a staff member to help them get started. Later they would have a say in choosing their staff help (Interviews).

Congressman Butler Derrick helped the group obtain a spirometer, the machine used to test breathing capacity. It was kept in the chapter's storefront office in Bath, South Carolina, one of the small milltowns in the Valley. From that time on, nearly all of the chapter's public communications contained an invitation to mill workers to come to the office and have their breathing tested if they thought they had any problems. Chapter leaders also offered to help workers interpret the results of the tests that the mills were required to give under federal law. They could not persuade many active workers to take them up on this offer, but they did find several retired workers to test each month in their never-ending door-to-door canvassing.

Periodically, the chapter held well-publicized clinics, repeating the initial organizational tactic. A Saturday clinic held in late August 1981 was typical. Staff placed announcements in local newspapers, had them broadcast as public service messages on area radio and TV stations, enlisted members to spread word about the clinic, and passed out about 2,000 leaflets in mill parking lots and in the usual door-to-door visits. The staff organizer and a local college student intern performed this thankless labor. Only one member helped. For most members, walking for more than a few minutes placed too much demand on their limited physical capabilities.

The routine in the door-to-door canvassing followed a well-established pattern. The organizer or intern or member would introduce him- or herself as a Brown Lung Association volunteer and ask if anyone living there worked in the mills. If so, the caller would ask about any breathing problems and whether a doctor had been consulted, tell about the breathing clinic that was planned, and explain the possibility of filing for workers' compensation. If an active worker lived there, the organizer would invite the worker to bring the results of the OSHA-required breathing tests to the clinic for interpretation.

As might be expected, the turnout for these clinics diminished with each effort. The first clinic held in an area might attract 75 to 100 people, as was the case in Augusta, Georgia. Approximately 25 people came to the Aiken chapter's 1981 clinic, and three were identified by breathing tests and case histories as good prospects for claiming workers' compensation. Staff gave them information about the cotton dust standards and how to file claims, and invited them to a follow-up meeting the next week. Nine of those who attended the clinic came to the follow-up, and three came to the next regular chapter meeting. They came because of their personal interest in compensation. Two of the three had possibly winnable cases, and the organizer made appointments for them with lawyers. The third was not eligible for compensation under South Carolina law. After working most of his life in South Carolina mills, he had worked for several months in a Georgia mill before coming disabled, and claims had to be filed against the last place of employment. Georgia compensation laws were even more difficult than South Carolina laws. Thus, he was victimized by the nature of the federal system as well as by byssinosis.

Those attending the clinics were told little about the Brown Lung Association at the time. Rather, the association tried subtly to involve them as they provided information about and helped them through the compensation process. Information and help with workers' compensation were the major membership incentives. Without them, there would have been no Brown Lung Association.

In mid-1981 the organization reached its peak (BLA Papers). Door-to-door canvassing and screening clinics had built an organization with seventeen chapters: seven in North Carolina (Greensboro, Roanoke Rapids, Erwin, Richmond-Scotland, Lincoln-Gaston, Eden, and Ephraim Lowder Memorial, formerly Stanly County), six in South Carolina (Columbia, Spartanburg, Greenville, Aiken, Anderson, and Greenwood, which was added in 1981 but lasted only about a year), two in Georgia (Augusta and Columbus), and two in Virginia (Danville and Martinsville, which lasted only a short while). Efforts to build new chapters and to expand into Alabama continued for the next couple of years, despite the association's decline, because remaining staffers concentrated their efforts on building new chapters. A chapter in Opelika, Alabama, was added, but the Martinsville, Virginia, chapter was closed. In early 1982 organizers attempted to build chapters in Ware Shoals and Gaffney, South Carolina, but these never got off the ground because no full-time organizers could be assigned to help them. The chapter in Griffin, Georgia, also organized in 1982, was more successful. It lasted several years and was instrumental in helping many of its recruits file for compensation before the July 1984 deadline set by Georgia. Many achieved settlements (Seymour 1991). After the deadline, however, the Georgia chapters folded within the next year. Without individual material incentives, people dropped out.

Because the group did not place a great emphasis on records of paying membership, (defined by the payment of $3.00 in annual dues) the total membership was uncertain. In 1981 the Aiken organizer estimated that chapters averaged 50 to 60 members each. If this was true, then total paying membership was around 1,000, much lower than the figure of 5,000 that was given in many newspaper accounts (Drogin 1980a, 17). More than likely, the figure quoted to newspapers was derived from the circulation of the association newsletter, which was mailed to about 7,000 in the fall of

1981. In a December 1981 fund-raising letter, the association claimed seventeen chapters and 7,000 members in five states, counting all people on its mailing list. The association mailing list combined all chapter mailing lists. If the Aiken chapter list was typical, the 7,000 included a wide variety of people only marginally concerned with the organization. The Aiken chapter had about 400 names on its mailing list, including local ministers, media persons, and all workers and ex-workers who had expressed any interest in the group.

Piven and Cloward (1977, 287) argue that there is a fatal flaw in any poor people's organization that is formed around a specific grievance. Once the problem is settled or reduced in scope, then fewer people will join. Moreover, if the grievances are settled on an individual basis through payment of claims or grants, then what incentive does the individual have for remaining active in the organization? Piven and Cloward maintain that the exhaustion of individual material incentives contributed to the failure of the Welfare Rights Organization. Poor people joined to obtain special grants, and "once people received a special grant, many saw no further purpose in affiliating with the organization."

The logic of this argument applies rather easily to the Brown Lung Association. Screening clinics may have been enough to attract people who had breathing problems; they joined in order to learn about possible legal recourse. However, much greater incentives were needed to retain members whose individual cases had come to a final legal resolution. Organizers reported that many did drop out after their cases were settled. As previously noted, none of the three chapters in Georgia lasted very long after the July 1984 deadline for filing old claims. Once the claims were settled—every member of the Augusta chapter did receive some compensation (Seymour 1991)—activities stopped within a year or so. The only economic self-interest remaining for those who lost their worker's compensation claims was the hope that organized lobbying and protest would bring changes in the law so that they could refile.

My interviews uncovered little evidence that this faint hope played any significant role. Any motivation for continued activity on the part of those who won some monetary settlement, and those who had no hope of ever winning a claim, derived primarily from altruism, anger, and some need for solidarity and fellowship. They continued to come, bake cakes, sell plaques, and hold barbecues out of a combined sense of rage at the mills and hope that their own efforts would lead to healthier lives for the next generation of mill workers (Kassell, 1992; M. Russell 1992). I asked the Aiken chapter president why he was involved, especially since his own legal case appeared so bleak. Melvin Turner haltingly explained, literally gasping for air between phrases as he spoke, that it was for his family and friends, so that they would have better lives and a safer place to work. Less than a year later Turner died as a result of complications of his lung problems. Mike Russell, an organizer who worked in the Greenville area, remembers the anger of another member who had initially been reluctant to get involved. She had worked in the mill all her life. When her disability began, the mill allowed her to work part time. When it became too severe even for that, the mill allowed her to work a few odd hours. At the time she thought the mill was doing her a favor. But after learning that her problem was byssinosis, she concluded that the mill hadn't been doing her a favor; it had been working her down to her last breath. She felt betrayed and exploited (M. Russell 1992).

The problem of limited membership incentives was compounded by the fact that the association had no monopoly in providing expert help. Once an individual was identified as having a compensable breathing problem at a group-sponsored clinic, the help of the group was not really necessary. All the individual needed was help from a lawyer and doctors to provide medical evidence. Some organizers felt that lawyers tended to break members off from the group, pushing them down a path that stressed only individual goals (M. Russell 1992).

Potential members' first contact with the group was as "free riders," who received absolutely free of charge the most important thing the group could provide: awareness that they had a compensable problem. They received this benefit regardless of whether they attended any meetings after the initial ones. Many potential members never went beyond the free benefits the association provided (Michael Russell 1992).

Potentially, the mills themselves could have undercut the association's efforts had they provided their own screening clinics for retirees. Mills did claim that the association was unnecessary because they tested their own workers and informed them about possible compensation. Given the history of well-publicized cases in which mills had ignored breathing problems and failed to tell workers that they were work related, however, this claim had little credibility. In April of 1979 Cannon Mills, which has most of its operations near Charlotte, did attempt to reduce the association's appeal by offering brown lung screening to 4,000 of its retirees. Just over 300 came to the clinic, and six of those were diagnosed as having byssinosis (Covington 1980, 12). Even though there were obvious economic disincentives for mills to seek out potential claimants among their retirees, more of this kind of activity could have severely undercut the clinics provided by the Brown Lung Association.

Any organization that faces a free-rider problem as severe as that of the Brown Lung Association must offer some side benefits that are contingent on participation. Although it could not supply the individual legal or medical help that was needed, the group did provide another kind of help. For those whose cases were pending, the group served a psychological support function. A great deal of time at each meeting was devoted to small talk, comparing notes about how cases were going, complaining about lawyers, discussing hearings and the commission members who heard the cases. Many of the same stories and incidents were retold each month by the same people. Verbalizing served as an outlet for frustration and a source of hope. Underlying their stories was the reassuring feeling that "if I can make these others understand the reasonableness of my claim, then surely those who administer workers' compensation will also understand." Attendance at compensation hearings by staff, organizers, or fellow members provided further psychological support for those with active legal cases. Having supportive friends present as a silent cheering section made it easier for claimants to answer the complicated and sometimes hostile questions posed by lawyers representing the insurance companies and the mills.

Although the association itself was not directly involved in any of the workers' compensation claims and each individual making a claim had to secure his or her own attorney, the group did provide some helpful information on lawyers. This information served as another inducement for involvement. Lawyers varied a great deal in experience and success in byssinosis cases, attention they gave the client, and fee structure. The group compiled a list of lawyers who handled brown lung cases and offered this list, without recommendations, to those who needed it. Like the screening clinics, this sort of help was not contingent upon membership. Members provided much more useful information on an informal basis, however, frequently speaking at meetings about the relative merits of their lawyers. One could quickly learn which lawyers to use and which to avoid by just listening—but one could do so only by attending meetings. Unfortunately, this inducement for continued participation evaporated once a lawyer was chosen.

The net result of these membership incentives and recruiting techniques in Aiken County was a chapter of about 45 paid members at its peak in the early 1980s. Including the eight most active, some fifteen could be considered regular members who frequently attended meetings, occasionally took part in protest activities, and offered some help in fund raising. All fifteen had some brown lung claim. The cases of nine were settled one way or the other and six had active cases while the organization was at its peak.

Aiken was one of the larger and stronger of the seventeen chapters. If we make the generous assumption that the number of regular participants in other chapters matched the number in Aiken, then the entire organization never had more than about 255 regular participants at one time. Probably not more than half that number were really active members who played some leadership role. These estimates are smaller than those of Frank Blechman. He thought that each chapter probably averaged about 25 active members, and that over the entire life of the organization some 1,200 people played significant roles (Blechman 1991). Either estimate falls far short of what is required for a grassroots popular movement. Spread over a wide geographical area, the group had too few votes to concern many public officials and too few members to mount any mass protests. Such numbers are enough, however, to create an effective interest group if other resources—information, expertise, public sympathy—can be brought to bear upon policymakers.

During the eighteen-month period during which I observed meetings of the Aiken chapter, no active workers—those still employed in the mills—ever attended meetings. There were a number of active workers on the mailing list, but none played any significant role in the chapter or paid membership dues. Organizers said this was typical of most chapters (Interviews; Brody 1991; Kassell 1992; M. Russell 1992). The failure to induce active mill workers to join and participate was a major stumbling block to building an effective organization. Active workers had access to the institution that was the major focal point of discontent—the mill. There was little that retired disabled workers could do to bring pressure upon the mills directly beyond pressing their own legal claims. They were relegated to passing out leaflets at the gates and generating negative publicity. Nor could they threaten owners by providing a beachhead for the anathema of all mill owners—unions.

Though the Amalgamated Clothing and Textile Workers Union of the AFL-CIO was generally sympathetic and supportive—for example, funding association members' attendance at the Department of Labor protest in May 1981—it naturally cared more about the dissatisfactions of employed workers than about those of retired workers. Dissatisfied employed workers could provide the basis for an organizing drive. Retired workers, many of whom had rejected unions in the past and many of whom were still anti-union, could at best provide only access to the active workers. But the Brown Lung Association was failing to provide that link. One ACTWU organizer bluntly declared, "Hell, anybody can organize retired textile workers. They got nothing to lose. It's active workers who are at risk, and Brown Lung don't do nothing for them" (Drogin 1980a). Another professional union organizer told me at a conference that the inability to attract active workers was the association's fatal flaw as far as the union was concerned (Interviews).

The futile efforts of the Aiken chapter to attract active workers underscores this criticism. Though staff were assigned to work specifically on recruiting active workers, none were successful. Organizers understood the importance of this failure. Following the defeat of their legislative program in the South Carolina legislature in 1976, an internal memo noted that the association must have active workers as members in order to place sufficient pressure on legislators (BLA Papers).

The failure to do so is best explained in terms of a lack of incentives for active worker membership. Organizers attempted to use worker education to recruit active workers. Until the Reagan administration cut off OSHA grants in late 1981, those grants funded efforts to tell workers about the dangers of cotton dust, their rights to a clean work environment, their ability to complain and request inspections by OSHA without employer reprisals, their rights to employer-provided health examinations, and the obligation of the company to give workers the results of these examinations whether requested or not. From the perspective of organizers, most of whom were college educated, the value of knowledge about potential dangers to long-term health was of the highest priority. Mill workers saw it differently. To those for whom daily life posed a continuing and physically exhausting challenge to obtain and maintain a few of the material symbols of the middle-class dream, education about a possible health risk years down the road was much less important. In fact, expressing concern might endanger their livelihood. Most workers knew they could be easily replaced. Moreover, personal danger was easily rationalized away or denied: the problem might not develop, or if it did, one could change jobs before permanent damage was done (the current practice of screening workers to identify what the mills call "reactors," those who react adversely to cotton dust, serves to reinforce these feelings). In addition, many young workers didn't plan to spend their lives in the mills. They saw work as temporary, a way to make a living until they could start their own small businesses or move on to better-paying jobs.

When I asked one organizer what her greatest disappointment had been, her answer touched on many of these problems: "That more active workers are not involved. I concentrated for a lot of the time on active factory workers, trying to get them involved in some way or another in changing the mill, and that's been much slower than I thought it would be. [There's] a combination of fear—they stand to lose their own jobs; it's a more direct fear—plus a certain lack of strong enough interest to take whatever risk there is. Some of them have serious breathing problems, but most . . . are not in bad shape right now. They may get in bad shape, but they're not right now. It's not the central issue in their lives, to try and make the mill a healthier place to work. The younger people even hope not to stay there, so it's even a less important issue for them" (Interviews). Looking back retrospectively, Charlotte Brody, the organizer with the longest tenure of any, concluded, "We never came up with an organizing model that could attract them" (1991).

These problems were never solved. The records show that despite its best efforts, very few active workers ever became interested in the association. A screening of the documentary film *Song of the Canary*, a highly sympathetic portrayal of the association, attracted seventeen active workers. In February 1979 chapter meetings drew a total of about 300 members but only 35 active workers. The association was successful in talking to active workers at union organized mills—for example, an organizer addressed forty-two at a union meeting in Erwin, North Carolina (BLA Papers)—but as far as the union was concerned, this was preaching to the choir.

One can make an instructive comparison between the Brown Lung Association experience and the community organizing efforts of the 1960s and 1970s. Both needed to attract members with some leadership skills from the general population. Individuals with the most personal confidence and ambition generally make the best leaders, at least until others can be empowered. As long as they had grant monies, the Community Action Programs of the 1960s used paid jobs to recruit persons who had these desirable traits. These jobs offered a stepping-stone out of poverty to those who were ambitious for upward mobility, but the hard-core poor were often ignored. (Matusow 1984, 251; Lemann 1991, 232, 250–52). The Brown Lung Association was never able to offer either paid work or a career path out of low-paying work in a declining industry to potential members with leadership skills. Workers with ambition and energy had to decide where to spend their efforts. They had two choices. They could join the Brown Lung Association and make a long-term commitment to the improvement of work life in an industry that offered them little future under the best of circumstances, or they could expend their energies on education and individual small business opportunities. The latter choice offered a potentially higher payoff and a higher probability of success. It was no contest, especially in an individualist culture.

In addition to its problems in attracting active workers, the association had difficulties in locating and recruiting black members. For most of their history, the mills themselves had employed whites only (Carlton 1982, 158), excluding blacks from all but the most menial and low-paying jobs. Mills did not begin to employ blacks in larger numbers until the 1960s, as a result of the civil rights movement. Consequently, in the 1970s relatively few blacks had a long work history of cotton dust exposure. For that reason alone, initial organizing efforts found few blacks as potential members.

The norm of segregation that had been a part of the lives of the older retired workers posed an additional barrier. Whites and blacks of this older generation had few interactions of any kind and were not comfortable with each other. Because so much member recruitment came through networking with family and friends of existing members, few blacks were recruited through the membership (Blechman 1991; Kassell 1992).

When staff did locate potential black members, they found it difficult to convince them that they would be welcome. As one staffer put it, "If you're having a meeting at a white person's house, a black person's just not going to come. At a black person's house, a white person's not going to come" (Interviews). Having a Brown Lung chapter office made biracial meetings much easier, but even so, though not hostile to blacks who attended, members did occasionally and openly use racist terminology. Terms like "nigger" were part of the etiquette system they had lived with all their lives. This sometimes shocked northern staffers, who had been used to more refined forms of racism: "Even at the height of racial tension in [the North], people are embarrassed to say 'nigger,' embarrassed to say 'I hate blacks.' It was like you were supposed to find other kinds of justification for being against busing. You weren't supposed to say you didn't want your kids to be with blacks. Where here, if you're completely in a white group, there are plenty of people who aren't the least bit embarrassed to make racist comments" (Interviews). One of the founding organizers described this barrier in more sanitized terms, explaining that cultural and stylistic differences separated the two races of this generation (Blechman 1991).

There were some small victories. One of Charlotte Brody's fondest memories of the chapter she organized in Roanoke Rapids in volved race relations. The group was scheduled to drive to Raleigh for a group action. Word spread that some of the white husbands did not want their wives to go if they were to ride in the same cars as black males. Lucy Taylor, who was a leader in both the chapter and the association, confronted the problem head on. She told the whites that if that was how they felt, then the group didn't need them to go. They went—in integrated cars. Black males rode in the front seat and white females in the back seat (an interesting historical reversal) because of differences in required leg room, not race (Brody 1991).

Finding blacks willing to play leadership roles proved even more difficult. Older blacks, with even less education than whites and with a lifetime of third-class citizenship behind them, found it nearly impossible to assert themselves. According to one staffer, "There's still a lot of sense among older blacks—I haven't known many younger blacks, mostly older blacks—still a lot of deference to whites, politeness, not wanting to upset whites, and a lot of fear that they've had to live through in the past is still with them. . . . You keep quiet and keep your place and curse at 'em when you go home" (Interviews). A photograph of those attending a retreat for staff and members at the Highlander School in October 1977 shows twelve white staff, eighteen white members, and one black member (*Brown Lung Blues*, 15 November 1977). There were a few exceptions. Judkins (1992) remembers that at one point the Gaston County chapter in North Carolina had a black president, and a few blacks did play leadership roles in the Roanoke Rapids chapter, where blacks and whites had a history of working together in union activities (Brody 1991), and in Alabama, where blacks composed a larger part of the work force than in the Carolinas (Blechman 1991).

A staff attempt to link the struggle of older textile workers with the much more well-known struggle of blacks for civil rights illustrates the problems of crossing racial lines. A joint program appearance by Essie Briggs, an active Columbia chapter member and leader in the association, and Mojeska Simpkins, a nearly legendary figure in the early South Carolina civil rights movement, turned into a disaster. The appearance seemed like a good idea to organizers because both were female leaders of oppressed groups, and both had been born in the very same year. speaking first, Simpkins told of all the troubles they had with the Klan when she was young. Briggs interpreted this as an accusation and a personal insult. She walked out before she was scheduled to speak, complaining that she was not part of the Klan (Blechman 1991).

One of the Highlander School's principal purposes was to promote interracial cooperation among black and white workers and to

"confront the issue of race relations in the South" (Glen 1988, 30).
At another Highlander conference in the spring of 1979, both staff
and members pledged to take positive steps to recruit and include
more black members. A year later, at an association board meeting on
9 June 1980, members and organizers discussed this earlier pledge
and the need to do things to make it a reality. Finally, members passed
a motion to accept all the blacks they could as members and to
"treat them right" when they did join (BLA Papers, meeting minutes).

A governing board committee memo, dated June 10, 1980, out-
lined the reasons why blacks should be recruited. Blacks also suffered from brown lung. Blacks were a large part of the active work
force that the association was committed to work for. They had civil
rights skills and experiences. Achieving adequate numbers to make
a political impact required the association to involve both races. According to the memo, the focus was to be on outreach into black
communities and encouraging black members to run for offices
in the association. In its yearly report, each chapter was to include
a description of its efforts to recruit blacks (BLA Papers). Such
reports may have been made, but none appear in the association's
papers. Only in a few monthly reports was there any reference to
black recruitment. On some of the reporting forms sent to the central association by chapter organizers in 1981 (including such items
as number of new members, number of outreach contacts made to
retired and active workers, and so on), someone had added a hand-
written category breaking down new members by race. Blacks constituted a mere handful.

The defining question of southern politics—what role blacks
will play in society—was also a question in the life of the Brown
Lung Association. Racial barriers separated members from a significant number of potential recruits, especially from blacks in the active work force, where their numbers were much larger. Even
though the organizers forced the member leaders to confront the
problem of race relations in principle, for the most part the promises and pledges made by the association leadership never made it
down to the chapter level.

Although blacks did not play a large role in the organization, the
other traditionally subservient group in the South was a major
player: women were involved and in leadership positions from the
beginning. In fact, women composed a clear majority of the leaders
throughout the life of the association. In the early years, women
outnumbered men at governing board meetings by as much as a two
to one ratio (BLA Papers). Judkins (1992) remembers that during his
years with the association women not only outnumbered men

among the member leaders but were generally better leaders. My own observations tend to reinforce this generalization.

Necessity explains much of the important role that females played. In a number of instances, women who were the spouses of byssinosis victims had little choice. The men were simply too sick to take an active part. In addition, a woman who became involved as a victim's spouse usually lived longer than her husband and had more time to develop her leadership skills. It was rare for the relationship to work the other way, with the husband of a female victim playing a leadership role. Traditional gender roles probably made the difference. A woman was more likely to stand by her man than a man was to stand by his woman.

The other part of the explanation lies with the organizers. Many, perhaps most, of the staff were young college-educated females who had modern views about the role of women. Even though female members, as traditional southern working-class women, might have preferred for men to lead (Judkins 1992), staff encouraged them to play leadership roles themselves.

GOVERNANCE AND DECISION-MAKING

Each chapter was essentially self-governing, electing its own officers, keeping its own books, and raising about half of its operating funds.[1] Three delegates were selected from each chapter to represent it on a state board (because so many members had health problems, the bylaws allowed chapters to elect alternate delegates with full voting powers). The association as a whole was governed by a board consisting of all the delegates on the state boards, and all voting majorities had to include at least one delegate from each state. The association governing board set broad policy, planned protest events focused on Washington, spoke for the association to other groups such as unions, oversaw association grants, and hired staff. Because most of the available money came from grants to the association, the board held quite a bit of power. Moreover, the association board was the employer of the staff, because virtually all staffers were paid from grant monies. Association board meetings were to take place at least three times each year ("By-laws" 1979). During years of peak activity, such as 1977, it met four times (BLA Papers).

To keep any one state from dominating the association, the bylaws limited each state to no more than seven chapters. In practice, North Carolina exceeded this limit with nine chapters, but the two extras were given the status of "satellite" chapters associated with nearby regular chapters. Many chapters were in fact a coalition of what could have been several chapters in different towns ("By-laws" 1979). This did create occasional problems and disputes over the location of chapter offices, given the highly localistic orientation of members and the fact that many members found it difficult to travel even short distances (BLA Papers). Organizers had hoped that as the other states caught up, this restriction on chapter numbers could be eased. That hope was never realized.

An executive committee made decisions as necessary between board meetings. It was composed of officers, standing committee chairs, and the state board presidents. They had the power to hire and fire staff with the approval of the subunits to which the staff were assigned ("By-laws" 1979).

The committee structure was designed to maximize opportunities for member involvement. There were only three standing committees in 1980 (Finance/Fundraising, OSHA/Active Worker/Education/Training/Communication, and Legal/Legislative), but the by-laws required that each chapter have a delegate on each of these committees. In theory, this meant that each of a chapter's three delegates would have a committee in which to work. Including the three association-level officers (president, vice-president, and secretary) and the three officers for each standing committee (chair, vice-chair, and secretary), there were twelve association-level leadership positions to fill. State-level officers and committees further expanded leadership opportunities.

Attendance was quite high at governing board meetings, despite the health problems of members. During the peak years of late 1976 through 1981, all chapters usually sent representatives. There are few records of board meetings after 1981, probably because of the loss in staff, who generally kept the records and made logistical arrangements.

High turnover was a problem in building and maintaining a strong leadership. Health problems—or death—forced most of those who had a few years of experience out of active participation. According to the minutes of governing board meetings where attendance was recorded by name, forty-five different members attended between late 1976 and late 1978, but only one of those names reappeared in a list for a spring 1982 board meeting (BLA Papers). This overstates the rate of turnover, because according to other records and interviews, several persons named on the earlier lists remained active well into the 1980s. Nevertheless, turnover was extremely high. Without the involvement of active workers whose prospects for longevity were higher, the only way the group could survive was through continual replacement. That required a tremendous amount of energy dedicated on an ongoing basis to recruitment and leadership training. Organizers provided most of that energy until late 1981.

The association adopted a complex grievance procedure in December 1979. Two years earlier it had rejected the suggestion of Frank Blechman that such a procedure be adopted when Lacy Wright, one of the strongest members until his death, argued that there could be no grievance procedure without a signed contract. Wright was incorrect, but board members went along with him, and Blechman did not pursue the issue (BLA Papers, minutes of board meetings, November 1977, December 1979). Once adopted, the procedure was used several times in such matters as the location of a chapter office serving two areas and occasional disputes over expenses filed by staff (BLA Papers).

The association did give theoretical autonomy to local chapters and state boards in "accepting the right of each chapter and each state to conduct its own business" ("By-laws" 1979). That autonomy was meaningful only to the extent that each chapter could raise all the money needed to survive. Most could raise only part of what they needed to rent office space and pay telephone and utility bills. Aiken, one of the more prosperous chapters, raised about half of its operating costs, but very few activities beyond mere survival could be funded by most of the chapters. A few of the more prosperous ones did help keep the central organization going for several years after government funding was cut in 1981, but most were unable to pay even their own office bills, let alone salaries for the staff needed to recruit new members.

The terms "staff" and "organizers" can be used interchangeably. In a behavioral sense, "organizer" is more descriptive of reality, although many staff at the association level expended more time in writing grant proposals than in organizing. When those grants disappeared, virtually all the grant-writing specialists disappeared as well.

In 1986, after all paid staffers were gone and the organization was surviving on the basis of a few volunteers, the association rewrote its bylaws to create a simpler structure. Fewer active members would be required to fill positions. Terms of office were increased from one to two years. State governing boards were dropped. The number of delegates from each chapter was reduced from three to two and required meetings each year from three to one. Each chapter was made responsible for hiring its own staff at its own expense (in fact, that had been a reality for several years). The standing committees were dropped entirely. Because so few chapters remained, all protections against single-state dominance were also dropped. Moreover, these bylaws included provisions for disbursement of remaining assets should the association dissolve ("Bylaws" 1986).

STAFF-MEMBER RELATIONS: SYMBIOSIS OR DEPENDENCE?

Organizers placed major emphasis on teaching members organizational skills and self-reliance, and encouraging them to accept responsibility. The building of a self-governing, self-reliant grassroots organization was to serve two important purposes. First, the organization was an end in itself. Those who began and staffed it believed in participatory democracy. Helping powerless people to discover collective power through organization and to assume the responsibility of defining the goals and directions of that organization is what grassroots organization and participatory democracy are all about (Kahn 1970; 1982). The second purpose was to legitimize the organization in the eyes of the community. It is much more difficult to publicly discredit a group that is run by people who have spent their lives working in the community than it is to discredit outside troublemakers, especially in the South with its long history of paranoia toward outsiders.

Organizers never really achieved their primary organizational goal, except on paper. The last two assigned to the Aiken chapter both felt that one of their greatest disappointments was the failure of members to assume greater responsibility and control. This was evident in chapter decision-making. In an ongoing struggle, members sought to defer to staff opinions, advice, judgments, and initiatives, while staff pushed, prodded, and cajoled members to make their own decisions, even on the most routine matters. Inevitably, "suggestions" made by staff were ratified by members.

Furthermore, because few members assumed responsibility beyond attending meetings and participating in events that were organized by staff, those plans made by members took place only when the staff decided to act. For example, in 1980 the Aiken chapter decided to raise funds by compiling, publishing, and selling a cookbook. At the meeting at which this decision was made, every key motion that led to the ultimate decision was formulated by the organizer as a question. Should we publish a cookbook? Who should compile the book? This question was related by the organizer until someone finally volunteered. How many should we publish? This was asked after the organizer had discussed the economics of publication and suggested some reasonable numbers. The organizer later explained that she was very conscious of this problem and terribly frustrated by her inability to induce members to do more (Interviews). The reality was that despite her best efforts, virtually nothing would have happened without her leadership.

The lack of participation by members was apparent in virtually all activities. An intern noted in his work diary that "ninety-nine percent of the active members are seen only at the monthly meetings and sometimes at *important* events (then only after persistent begging by the organizer)" (Parks 1981). On a day-to-day basis, it was the staff that ran the office, answered the phone, passed out the leaflets, wrote newsletter articles, ordered materials, and organized protest and fund-raising events.

Newsletters performed an important communication and educational function for the organization. Their formats varied, but the general content was similar. All contained news about state and federal governmental actions (such as the 1981 Supreme Court decision to uphold the OSHA cotton dust standards against the industry's legal challenge), news about the legal problems of local members, upcoming events such as clinics or leafleting, and inevitably, pleas for help in and news of fund-raising efforts. In most cases they were little more than one or two legal-length sheets folded twice and stapled, but they were an effective way of letting members know that the group was functioning. As noted above, most of the writing and production tasks were performed by staff; members usually helped with folding, stapling, and addressing, but even here staff often did the brunt of the work. Once staff was lost, the newsletters stopped. The last issues published carried pleas for members to come and help with story writing, typing, and layouts. Not enough help came.

Organizers certainly tried to teach self-reliance, hoping to avoid an atmosphere of deferential dependence. In the short period of training that new staff received, training leaders placed great emphasis on the idea that the Brown Lung Association was to be a member-controlled organization. They told new staff to be careful not to make decisions for members, even if such restraint slowed the decision-making process. One staffer discussed this at some length:

The commitment is not just to the cause of eliminating brown lung, but also to the type of organization it is, to having democratic organization run by members. . . . In other grassroots organizations you find staff who say they believe in that, but think it will work a lot better if they just run it themselves, and you can't build a real strong grassroots organization unless you have a strong and real commitment to having it run by members, and letting them run it. . . . If I'm doing something all by myself, that's a bad sign. A lot of times it's easier to do something yourself than to help someone else do it. . . . The more you see them invest, be concerned, and want to see what's going on, the better. . . . You should make them have more responsibility to see that something succeeds.

Despite this general failure to induce self-reliance and responsibility, there was a small corps of members who were quite active in the organization. In the Aiken chapter these member-activists, numbering about eight, developed their own special areas of expertise. Most participated in fund-raising events, but five or six always seemed to be central in assuming responsibilities. When physically able, they all participated in protest events, but three or four seemed to specialize in communications: writing letters, appearing on news programs, testifying at hearings, and holding news conferences. The organizers were quite careful to have no one except members speak at media events. One state legislator was impressed; he reported that several members, though obviously uneducated, seemed to have become relatively knowledgeable about byssinosis and rendered effective testimony before the legislature (Interviews). Philip Smith, a member of the Aiken chapter who exhibited an unusual amount of interest in organizational matters, was elected president of the entire Brown Lung Association. Unfortunately for the hopes of staff, he was the exception rather than the rule.

Even those who did develop some expertise needed significant help in maintaining their efforts. In September 1981 a mill official wrote a letter to the Aiken newspaper blaming byssinosis on cotton farmers and praising the mills for all the money they had spent on dust removal. The president of the Aiken chapter read the letter and took the initiative to ask the chapter's staff organizer to help her write a letter in response. He delegated the task to the college intern working in the office. The intern, who was very impressed with the woman's innate intelligence and common sense, assisted her in two ways. First, he did the physical writing, because she lacked confidence in her own handwriting. Second, he helped her put her thoughts into clear sentences, although he found that she needed only a little help in that task (Parks 1981). Had staff not been available to support her initiative, however, there would have been no response.

Most other members required much more assistance. When the intern helped another member write a letter in response to the same letter from the mill official, the process was much more difficult: "We got the letter in this fashion. She would start airing her complaints and expressing her views in random fashion. When she came across something applicable to the letter that she felt strongly about, I would ask if she would like me to write it down. She would say yes or no and we would proceed" (Parks 1981).

At the extreme end of helplessness was an elderly gentleman who had virtually no formal education and lacked even the skill to dial a telephone by himself. After a great deal of effort, the organizer persuaded him to talk to state senators on the phone about the association's opposition to the reconfirmation of the head of the state's Department of Labor. What followed was painful for the intern to witness:

He wanted [the staff member] or me to make the phone call and say that we were [him] because we would know what to say. [The staff member] finally dialed the home of Senator Russell and handed him the phone. He asked to speak to the senator, but she was not home. Next, [the staff member] dialed Senator Shealy and handed him the phone. He asked for Senator Russell. [The staff member] whispered that this was Senator Shealy's house. He then asked for Senator Shealy Russell. This eventually being straightened out, Senator Shealy waited to hear what [the member] had to say. He froze, could not open his mouth, until Senator Shealy hung up." [Parks 1981].

Next, the intern made a nearly unsuccessful effort to help the same member write a letter. This time the major barrier was fear. They did get the letter written, but before it could be mailed, the member "became terrified. What if Senator Moore called the mills and had his children and grandchildren fired" (Parks 1981). Only the letter was toned down by removing all references to his family was it finally sent. The intern noted that this member was an extreme case, yet he knew that others also feared retaliation.

Ironically, despite his fears and almost total lack of self-confidence, this old gentleman was the "most active member" of the Aiken chapter during the six months the intern kept his diary. He was the only one who could be counted on to help pass out leaflets and regularly come to the office to do routine tasks. In the last years of his life this man did conquer some of his fears, though not without a great deal of help and patience from staff and volunteers. In a sense, the staff acted as midwives to deliver the bravery that lay within him.

Several organizers with whom I have spoken feel that this description underestimates member independence and self-reliance.

They argue that the Aiken chapter was atypical. They remember that other chapters did develop relatively greater self-sufficiency, even though they acknowledge that building independence was a continuing problem. One of the last organizers said that the only sure test was what would happen to the organization after there were no advisers left (Interviews). If that was the acid test, Aiken was not atypical: with a couple of notable exceptions, members were unable to keep chapters open and functioning after the organizers left. A few individual members remained as contacts in some places, but offices closed and, more important, meetings and protest activities virtually stopped.

Len Stanley (1992) takes a middle position. She argues that members needed staff and should not have been expected to make it on their own. She saw the process as symbiotic: staff and members educated each other. The disease and the legal questions were all complicated, but if staff explained, listened to what the disabled workers were saying about their own experiences, and then said it back, eventually both would understand the problem and be able to express it in words that all could understand. The process built confidence and trust.

At the associational level, dependency was less of a problem. Association officers were the most skilled and self-confident members; they at least partly self-selected themselves from all over the region. In the minutes of meetings one can find numerous instances where members did initiate proposals or disagree with staff— though staff usually carried the day when there were disagreements (BLA Papers).

In the summer of 1978 staff made a number of proposals to reorganize the association. The major questions concerned redefining the responsibilities of committees, allowing staff to serve as committee members, and dividing staff into two categories. In addition to staff assigned to chapters, a new category called resource staff was proposed. The idea was to give persons in this new category central responsibilities so that they could make better use of their specialized skills. In the August 1978 meeting the association president, Woody Clark, asked organizer Frank Blechman to present and explain the proposals. A number of members opposed giving up any chapter staff to create this new group and asserted themselves quite clearly in attempting to protect the parochial interests of their chapters. The initial vote was split. President Clark said he wanted time to study the matter before he cast the deciding vote. The next day he voted in favor of the recommended changes. Between August and the next board meeting in November, several members complained that improper procedures had been employed and that staff had improperly interfered. At the November meeting, trying to placate dissident members, Clark said "there should not be any interference by the staff." Then the member board voted to reapprove the reorganization plan that staff had proposed (BLA Papers).

Early in the life of the organization Heleny Cooke, an official from Youth Project, the principal funding agency at the time, observed this problem while investigating the conflict between founding organizers Mike Szpak and Frank Blechman. After visiting the three chapters of the association that existed in March 1976, Cooke wrote a report that was quite critical of Blechman's style. She saw him as "clearly manipulating these people" and orchestrating the member movement against Szpak. In contrast, she saw Szpak as "one of the better organizers Youth Project has seen in awhile. He works to build leaders who are responsible by transferring skills to them such as (a) how to run a meeting, (b) how to write by-laws, (c) how to contact the press, and (d) how to hold a hearing" (BLA Papers, letter from Cooke, 10 May 1976). Basically, she thought, he forced members to do the things they needed to do if they were to survive. Blechman, while seeming more kind, ran the risk of making the members dependent on him and his friendly suggestions.

Staff had frequent meetings to plan the agenda for board meetings and discuss association matters and policy. Although a number of strong-willed members would sometimes put up a fight, staff suggestions routinely became de facto association decisions for most of the Brown Lung Association's existence. The May 1977 board meeting illustrates this point well. Of thirteen motions presented and passed at the meeting, ten came from staff. Of the three from members, only one was clearly contrary to staff wishes, and that was to reject some extra staff pay (BLA Papers).

It is clear that a number of members did gain enough skill and confidence to speak up and did play important leadership roles. Several overcame significant personal obstacles and achieved great personal victories. There is also no question that staff did try to teach all members greater self-reliance and organizational skills. They frequently held member workshops and wrote manuals on how to do such things as plan and hold press conferences (BLA Papers). Given the fact that old age and poor health required ongoing leadership replacement, however, there were too few member leaders with the necessary skills to sustain the association at its peak level without considerable staff help. Blechman's style established quite early a pattern that may have been somewhat harmful. It proved to be a major weakness when the funding used to pay organizer salaries dried up.

In looking back at the failure of the association to build self-sustaining chapters, a long-lasting organizers who later served as an adviser to the remnants of the group argued that the original organizers had done everything backward. In her view, they built a central organization before chapters were strong enough to sustain it. Then organizers made the association too dependent on outside monies with too many strings attached. She thought they should have kept the group decentralized and stressed building independent, self-reliant chapters (Interviews). Given the localistic orientations of members, many of whom gave up when they lost their local chapter offices, she was probably correct. The central association was somewhat like a tree that grew too fast, with shallow roots that could not sustain it without massive doses of outside nourishment.

6

NOISE AND
INSTITUTIONAL
DISRUPTION

The Brown Lung Association utilized a number of traditional interest-group tactics in their overall strategy, a strategy that required pressure on many targets. They attempted to generate information and favorable publicity, held protest rallies, testified at hearings, rewarded and punished political candidates, and formed coalitions with other groups, worked at building legitimacy, placed pressure on the workers' compensation system, and encouraged strict enforcement of the cotton dust standards.

Throughout its life, the organization provided extensive human evidence of the failures of the existing system of worker protection and care.[1] The retired workers themselves were the most effective publicity the group could bring to bear. During U.S. Senate and House hearings on workers' compensation reform in 1978 and 1980, the Brown Lung Organization and its members directly produced eighty-six pages of testimony and reports. This compares to only twenty-eight pages produced by textile interests.

In the late spring of 1979 there was a third hearing in which the textile industry chose not to participate. The Subcommittee on Labor Standards of the House Committee on Education and Labor was investigating the extent and severity of occupational disease. The investigation only indirectly involved workers' compensation issues while the other two hearings focused on legislation to impose minimal federal standards on workers' compensation. The industry told Chairman Edward Beard (D-R.I.) that textile companies were not participating because they were currently party to litigation in occupational disease cases. This hearing was dominated by testimony of the Brown Lung Association and its supporters (U.S. Congress 1978b, 1979, 1980).

The activities of the Aiken chapter during the year and a half it was most active fell within the range of traditional interest-group tactics. Between March 1980 and September 1981, members of the Aiken chapter contacted public officials on at least twelve different occasions, including meetings with the governor of South Carolina, Senators Thurmond and Hollings, members of the state legislature, Congressman Butler Derrick, and the chairman of the state Industrial Commission (later called the Workers' Compensation Commission) to request data on compensation cases. Twice they sponsored campaign-related activities: a debate between candidates for the state senate at a chapter meeting, and a survey of legislative candidates for their views on proposed reforms in the state workers' compensation system. Grassroots lobbying activities included participation in nine different protests and rallies, three screening clinics, four interviews or editorial statements on television or radio, dozens of leafletings, and dozens of news releases and letters to the editor in the local papers.

These efforts generated 179 column inches of favorable news stories in Aiken's afternoon newspaper during this period, not including wire service stories on important events such as the U.S. Supreme Court decision. By comparison, mill officials generated only 50 column inches during the same period, defending and praising their own efforts to provide a clean work environment.

Eight members of the Aiken chapter attended a South Carolina senate committee hearing to support the testimony of two association members in an unsuccessful effort to block the reappointment of Commissioner of Labor Edgar McGowan. They thought McGowan had not adequately enforced regulations through mill inspections. In March 1980 one member accompanied an association delegation to Washington to testify in favor of a U.S. House bill to set federally mandated minimum workers' compensation standards. The chapter was also party to written testimony opposing a U.S. Senate bill that would have resulted in fewer OSHA inspections. In the area of judicial lobbying, the Aiken chapter as such took no direct action, but members did attend a judicial hearing in which a mill had challenged the legality of cotton dust standards, and they contributed fifty dollars toward sending a member of another chapter to attend the U.S. Supreme Court oral arguments on the challenge to the OSHA cotton dust standard. Along with the rest of the association, they were party to an *amicus curiae* brief the organization filed with the Supreme Court in the same case. Finally, chapter members met at least three times with outside groups in an attempt to form coalitions. Two of these meetings were with unions, and the last was with other grassroots organizations that focused on industrial disease: the Black Lung Association, the White

Lung Association (asbestos), and Legal Services, which provided the association with legal interns during the summer.

Although most chapters in the association mainly engaged in the same kinds of traditional, nonconfrontational interest-group activities, members occasionally participated in confrontational protest actions. These actions were designed to generate publicity about the plight of the workers, so that they would be harder to ignore and to bring the pressure of public opinion to bear on officials. In 1979, for example, members of the Greenville chapter made an uninvited visit to the classroom of Clemson University economics professor Hugh MacCaulay to challenge an editorial he had written for the *Greenville News.* The editorial argued against compensating byssinosis victims on the grounds that they knew of the risk when they entered the mill, had other employment options, and did receive higher wages to offset these risks. When association members occupied his class, MacCaulay threatened to call the campus police. Members stayed long enough to tell their side of the story and pass out leaflets to students and the media, whom they had notified in advance (BLA Papers).

Some attempts at confrontational protest were defused when the other side did not appear, but they generated press coverage nevertheless. When Dr. Philip Pratt of the Duke Medical School published a study that blamed byssinosis health problems on smoking, association members staged a press conference in front of Duke University Hospital to challenge his findings. They had sent a telegram to Pratt inviting him to come and discuss their own little "study," which consisted of the personal testimony of several nonsmoking members who had byssinosis. Without benefit of the doctor's presence, the members told their stories to the press (BLA Papers).

Confrontation had its risks. After several months of negotiation over the conditions of a proposed meeting, William Stephenson, chair of the North Carolina Industrial Commission, agreed to meet with members at his office in August 1978 (BLA Papers). The members used the meeting to accuse the commission of dragging its feet and attempted to generate maximum press coverage. Stephenson clearly felt burned; he accused the association of exploiting the meeting for publicity in an atmosphere that was "accusatory," rather than using the opportunity for "calm talk about common problems" (BLA Papers,) letter from Stephenson, (26 October 1978). Following this confrontational meeting, the association lost most of its access to Stephenson. This may not have been a great loss, given the publicity value of the confrontation and the fact that they were able to place pressure on him later through the governor's office.

Some actions were intended to create extreme psychological discomfort among officials who were not used to being confronted by poor sick citizens. Frank Blechman described what he called a new technique in their early efforts, the "no-demand confrontation": "We take a group, visit a guy, and just smile and say hello. We cough some, and wheeze a little. When the guy is braced to fend off demands, it scares 'm shitless. They know what we want, but we just wait until they make an offer, and then we laugh and keep on waiting making them sweat until we get something acceptable. It's slow, but it works" (BLA Papers, letter from Blechman, 7 May 1975).

COMMUNITY LEGITIMACY

The success of publicity efforts depended on how the group was perceived by those in positions to help. To get government grants, it needed to be seen as a legitimate service organization. To obtain favorable local news coverage and raise any significant money in the community, it needed to be seen as a legitimate locally operated and run organization that really represented at least the retired workers. To gain the ear of legislators, governors, representatives, and senators, it needed to be seen as representing a significant number of voters. Although community legitimacy was a goal in itself, it was also a tactic—or at least an intermediate goal—to enable the association to achieve its larger strategic goals of public policy and building an ongoing grassroots organization.

Although there was not enough community participation of the necessary quality to create a self-reliant, permanent grassroots organization, the limited number of local residents who did participate helped the group achieve community legitimacy. Members of the community who served in formal leadership positions and acted as the most visible spokespersons for the association made community legitimacy possible. Organizers regarded this as one of the strengths of the group and felt that it blunted the typical southern establishment charge that all the problems were created by outside instigators (Interviews).

The achievement of legitimacy was supported by the fact that chapter announcements of meetings, clinics, and events regularly appeared in newspapers and on local radio and television stations along with announcements for other noncontroversial community groups. A state senator said that even though he had the impression that someone from the outside was "calling all the shots," the association should be regarded as credible because he had known many of the members all his life (Interviews). A 1981 public opinion poll run in the Aiken area indicated that the Brown Lung Association had both a higher recognition rating than the Moral Majority (88 and 55 percent respectively) and a higher approval rating (69 and 29 percent respectively) (USCA Survey Research Services 1989, 56–57).

Building community credibility and visibility took years of effort. The association had great difficulty in gaining any news coverage in its first two years. A turningpoint came in April of 1977 when fifty-five members traveled to Washington to talk about their difficulties at the OSHA hearings on the proposed cotton dust standard. National media, including the *Washington Post*, NBC News, and ABC News, covered the compelling and tragic stories these people told with dramatic and credible simplicity. This attention legitimized coverage of the association for regional and local media (Hall 1978, 27–28; Conway 1979, 58–59). Although coverage was uneven and dropped off quite a bit after the hearings ended, most newspapers did give the group enough favorable coverage to make industry spokespersons complain about bias in the media (Hall 1978, 28).

From the Brown Lung Association's point of view, the high point in media attention came in a week-long Pulitzer Prize–winning series titled "Brown Lung: A Case of Deadly Neglect," which ran in the *Charlotte Observer* in early February 1980. Fifteen staff reporters worked on the series for four months. The series included enough stories and pictures to fill twenty-four full pages. In the introductory piece, the hard-hitting themes were highlighted with bullets by editor Rich Oppel: the workers' compensation system was a "bureaucratic nightmare" characterized by "limp-wristed inspections" of mills, "deception" on the part of state-employed doctors, "injustice" and "foot-dragging" in paying compensation, and "state secrecy" in commission records (1980, 2). Only two items in the series gave the textile industry any comfort at all: a short piece that praised one small mill for trying to clean up (Ellis 1980, 8), and the article "Does Group Help or Hurt the Cause?" (Drogin 1980a, 17–18), which discussed some of the controversial aspects and confrontational tactics of the Brown Lung Association.

The editors of the paper included an editorial with each day's installment. That the editorial positions were clearly on the side of the disabled workers can be seen in the titles: "A Test of Society's Morality," "Non-enforcement Is No Joke," "Benefits System Isn't Working," "Doctors: They Can Provide Proper Medical Care without Ever Diagnosing a Case of Brown Lung," "Inertia: Business as Usual Means Illness as Usual for Many Mill Workers," "Charity: Brown Lung Isn't a Socially Acceptable Disease," and "It's Time to Do the Obvious." In that last editorial, the paper pronounced its judgment of the two contending interests.

Leaders of the textile industry complain bitterly about the Carolina Brown Lung Association. It is, among other things, a political pressure group, and it sometimes exaggerates and makes questionable charges. The charges are particularly irritating to companies that have worked hard to make the mills safe. But the harm done by the association's irresponsibility is minuscule compared to the harm done by mill owners who wail about federal intervention instead of providing basic safeguards for their workers. ["It's Time to Do the Obvious"]

In late 1980 public television aired a one-hour documentary on occupational diseases that devoted half its length to the Brown Lung Association. *Song of the Canary* had been made three years earlier, just after members had presented their dramatic personal testimony at OSHA hearings in Washington and at the hearings on workers' compensation problems held by Senators Hollings and Thurmond in Greenville in December 1977. Public television had been hesitant to broadcast the film because of its clear commitment to the association's side of the controversy (O'Conner 1980). Its premise was that workers were being used to test the safety of the workplace just as miners had once used canaries to test the mines for gas. The most powerful aspect of the film was the contrast between the obviously ill retired workers who were unable to gain compensation from the mills and the comfortable mill executives who proclaimed that they cared about their workers. Switching shots from suffering ex-workers, some tethered to oxygen tanks, to a well-dressed executive standing in front of a large mill left a greater impression than any dialogue possibly could have.

Most of these tactics could be classified as "noise" (Lipsky 1968). Piven and Cloward regard such activities as largely ineffective because they only invite "weak and tokenistic" symbolic responses. In their view, effective protest involves the disruption of important institutions in order to gain some substantive response (1977, 23–24). Options in the area of disruptive protest, however, were quite limited. Members had little physical energy and no physical access to the mills, and the group was unable to recruit active workers who had both energy and access.

OVERLOADING THE WORKERS' COMPENSATION SYSTEM

The Brown Lung Association did make some attempts at institutional disruption. The same tactic that was used to recruit members was also aimed at disrupting the workers' compensation system by overloading it with cases. Identifying those with possibly compensable problems and encouraging and supporting them to collect compensation placed an administrative burden on workers' compensation agencies. Quite obviously, the more cases, the greater the burden. The greater the burden, the more likely the commissions would be to seek ways to speed the process and reduce the burden. Reforms would afford an opportunity to make it easier for ex-workers to collect compensation. The more workers collected, the greater the financial strain on the mills and the insurance brokers. The long-term strategy here was similar to what has always been an argument for workers' compensation: high costs "would encourage employers to maintain safe conditions in order to reduce their payment for casualty insurance" (Shaffer 1978, 191). It is the same strategy Ralph Nader (1971, 337) had laid out. At some point, the group hoped to make it cheaper for companies to improve conditions than to pay compensation. Members were quite aware of this goal and frequently said that their claims would force the mills to clean up the workplace. To that end, every chapter placed major emphasis on identifying possible cases through their well-publicized screening clinics and in encouraging and helping victims to press their claims.

A significant obstacle in pursuing the strategy of pressure through workers' compensation was that each state had been allowed wide latitude in designing its own workers' compensation system. Despite periodic federal pressures to bring some uniformity, varying state laws and judicial interpretations of those laws meant that the legal obstacles facing byssinosis claimants would be different in each state and that reform had to be pursued separately in each state.

The least reform took place in Virginia and Alabama. In Virginia the state courts ruled that the claimant must prove cotton dust the sole cause of disability before any award could be given (Brown Lung Reporter, 3, no. 5, 1981, N.C. ed.). The result was that no one has ever won an award in Virginia. In Alabama the association never became strong enough to mount significant pressure on state government, although claimants have won a few awards there in recent years (Interviews). Most of the action and reform took place in the Carolinas and, to a lesser extent, in Georgia.

The association created two legal offices—one in West Columbia, South Carolina, and the other in Durham, North Carolina—which tried to help lawyers deal with the obstacles and legal complexities in compensation claims. At their peak, they employed two full-time lawyers who provided resource material to lawyers litigating cases, kept track of all legal changes, and published information about those changes in a bimonthly newsletter, the *Brown Lung Reporter.* The newsletter also kept lawyers informed of efforts to change state laws. Organizers knew that lawyers were among the more important interest groups lobbying the legislature and that their support could be of significant help in securing legislative change.

North Carolina passed its first workers' compensation law in 1929. In 1935 the state added an occupational disease section, but byssinosis was not one of diseases listed. In 1971, with the growing awareness of byssinosis as a significant disease and following the creation of OSHA, the state amended the law so that byssinosis could be considered compensable (Stephenson 1982). The law covered "any disease . . . which is proven to be due to causes and conditions which are characteristic of and peculiar to a particular trade, occupation or employment, but excluding all ordinary diseases of life to which the general public is equally exposed outside employment" (G.S. 97–53 [13], cited in Stephenson 1982, 5). Unfortunately for byssinosis claimants, this language also provided ample grounds for appeal by mills and their insurers. Because byssinosis is clinically indistinguishable from other lung diseases, mills could always claim that this was an ordinary disease of life and not caused by the mill. If the claimant smoked, the problem was blamed on smoking.

The commission administering the law created a medical panel of physicians certified in lung disease to examine claimants. Lawyers consider the diagnosis of panel physicians to be the single most important determining factor in the outcome of a case (Interviews). At first, the mill's insurance company, if it agreed to pay the costs, was allowed to select the member of the panel to perform the examination. This proved highly controversial: doctors who were least likely to diagnose byssinosis were the most likely to be chosen, with the result that many claims were assigned to only a few doctors, and cases backlogged. The commission then began assigning cases.

The state courts had to sort out many complex legal questions involving jurisdiction, procedure, and interpretation. One question was the date when the new law applied. Before the North Carolina Supreme Court decision in 1979 *(Wood v. J.P. Stevens)*, the commission had ruled that anyone contracting the disease prior to 1971 had to be considered for compensation under the more restrictive laws that had existed at the time they contracted the disease. The court decided that a better rule was to apply the law in effect at the time the claimant became disabled and unable to earn wages. This decision also allowed plaintiffs to present their own medical expert witnesses in addition to the state's medical panel witness (Singletary and Hammer 1980, 2, 4).

The statute of limitations was another major impediment for older retired workers who had been disabled for a long time but had had no idea that their problems were work related. Prior to 1980 the North Carolina Industrial Commission had ruled that claims had to be made within one year of the last exposure to cotton dust, regardless of whether the person knew that he or she had byssinosis or not. In *Taylor v. J.P. Stevens*, the North Carolina Supreme Court ruled that the statute of limitations would run from "the date that the employee has been advised by competent medical authority that she has the occupational disease."

The result of these rulings in North Carolina was a significant increase in the number of byssinosis cases successfully settled. By January 1980, claimants in 286 cases had won $3.76 million in awards or settlements. By February 1981 the number had nearly doubled, with 543 claimants winning a total of $8.01 million. In August 1981, just when the association started its steep decline, a total of 707 claimants had won $10.26 million. A year later, even though the group was now in free-fall decline, the number receiving compensation had risen to 1,047 and the total compensation to $14.5 million (BLA Papers, N.C. Industrial Commission reports).

The question of "apportionment" created a major legal complexity that reduced the dollar amount of awards in both Carolinas. Apportionment refers to a situation in which a worker's disability or disease is only partly work related. Insurance companies often argued that some percentage of a claimant's lung disability had been caused by smoking or by some disease not peculiar to the mill environment; therefore, the company should pay only for the remaining portion. In *Morrison v. Burlington* (1980) the North Carolina Court of Appeals rejected apportioned settlement, concluding that state law "does not contemplate that the commission shall act as a board of medical inquiry, assigning or proportioning a worker's incapacity to work to other discernible infirmities." This ruling seemed consistent with workers' compensation laws elsewhere (Singletary and Hammer 1980, 4). The state Supreme Court reversed the lower court, however, and ruled that apportionment was allowable under North Carolina law. The chair of the Industrial Commission lamented that this ruling would make its work nearly impossible: "What does the Commission do when the doctor states unequivocally that a portion of the disability preexisted and was not aggravated by the occupational disease, but cannot state what portion preexisted and what portion was aggravated by the occupational disease?" (Stephenson 1982).

Relatively speaking, the textile industry was politically more powerful in South Carolina with its less diverse economy. Consequently, the legal barriers facing the Brown Lung Association and potential claimants there were considerably more difficult to surmount. By early 1978, claimants in North Carolina had won a significant number of awards, but no one had won a byssinosis award from the South Carolina Industrial Commission, and there had been very few settlements outside the award process (Stucker 1978; BLA Papers). There had been two major stumbling blocks. First, the state required that the claimant be diagnosed by members of a medical advisory panel whose findings were binding on the board; they could not be cross-examined by the plaintiff's lawyer, nor could the plaintiff offer alternative expert medical testimony. Second, a two-year statute of limitations began running when the person became disabled, even if the victim did not know the cause of her or his illness.

In 1978, however, South Carolina made the medical board advisory in nature and allowed the commission to listen to medical evidence presented by claimants. The legislature changed the two-year statute of limitations so that it began running when the claimant was told he or she had byssinosis. Persuading the General Assembly to remove these two legal obstacles was the single most significant legislative accomplishment of the Brown Lung Association in the Palmetto State—whose state motto is "While I breathe, I hope."

In addition to hoping, members had been lobbying the legislature for several years for these and other changes. In late 1976, the year after the group formed, members testified about their complaints before a joint legislative study committee. Their testimony helped persuade the chair of the committee, Senator Isadore Lourie, to promise to offer reform legislation in 1977 (Mauldin 1976; Lourie 1991). This was Lourie's first contact with the association. He was impressed by the members' expression of their "real human needs" that industry had ignored. For the next several years Lourie, a lawyer who considers himself a Harry Truman–style liberal Democrat, was one of the group's staunchest allies in working for legislative change (Lourie 1991).

The following year, members again trooped to the legislature to tell their stories and to confront textile lobbyists in demonstrations outside their Columbia office (Stucker 1977). Although the textile industry strongly opposed change, the legislature did make some modest changes in 1977 (allowing compensation for partial disability and allowing lifetime medical benefits) and more significant changes in 1978. Senator Lourie (1991) remembers these demonstrations as quite effective in creating a public climate that supported change as well as in persuading legislators that a real need existed. He describes them as dignified, peaceful demonstrations by honest, hard-working people who were obviously sick and in need of help. Lourie gives much of the credit for continually dramatizing these needs and capturing public attention to one of the association's founding organizers, Frank Blechman, whom he saw as a brilliant young man with a strong sense of social justice.

Two factors explain why the legislature took action. The most significant was the threat of federal intervention. After association members offered effective personal testimony at national hearings for both the House and Senate, the possibility of a federal takeover of the workers' compensation system seemed a distinct possibility. The South Carolina Brown Lung Association chapters were more interested in a federal program than were North Carolina chapters because the laws in South Carolina were seen as more difficult to reform (Judkins 1992). This different perspective caused a little internal friction about strategy at the governing board level (BLA Papers). South Carolina's two U.S. senators had cosponsored a bill to create a special federal program for byssinosis victims in January 1978 (Stucker 1978). Legislators were afraid that if the state did not make some reforms, they could lose control of the program. This was a long-standing fear and one of the factors that had led to the creation of a joint legislative committee in 1975 to study and review workers' compensation laws "in view of changing federal guidelines and making appropriate adjustments therein" (*South Carolina Legislative Manual* 1989, 501; Lourie 1991). According to Senator Lourie, at the end of the fights in 1977 and 1978, even the South Carolina Textile Manufacturer's Association and the state Chamber of Commerce supported the changes. They realized that modest reforms might forestall federal intervention and more dramatic change (Lourie 1991; Stucker 1978).

The second factor helped the association's legislative program in all states but had a relatively stronger impact in South Carolina, where lawyer legislators are allowed to practice law before state agencies and commissions. Having direct representation in the legislature is one of the hallmarks of interest-group power. Although no mill workers or byssinosis victims sat in the legislature, a number of the lawyers who represented them in workers' compensation cases did. For example, Senator Isadore Lourie, the most consistent and influential friend the Brown Lung Association had in the state legislature, represented the first claimant to win compensation from the South Carolina Industrial Commission in 1978 (*Brown Lung Reporter* 1, no. 1, 1978). To put it in the crassest possible terms, to the extent that compensation was made easier for claimants, Lourie and other lawyer legislators would benefit in collecting fees from successful clients. Was this a conflict in interest? It was not deemed so under South Carolina law. Ethically, it created no greater conflict for these lawyers than for the handful of mill executives who sat in the legislature and voted against any change in law that would benefit employees stricken with byssinosis. A less cynical analysis is that no one knew better about the unfairness of the compensation system to byssinosis claimants than lawyers. Senator Lourie, who still handles workers' compensation cases, strongly maintains that the financial motivation is much less important than the high sense of social conscience that most lawyers derive from their training in constitutional law and national ideals (1991).

In 1990, the only year for which figures are available, sixteen South Carolina lawyer legislators earned $492,000 in eighty-three workers' compensation cases (Scoppe 1991, 11A). Although this is a relatively small number of legislators in a body of 170 (124 in the House and 46 in the Senate), and although the number may well have been different in the late 1970s, it does suggest that there was a base of natural support on which to build.

Lawyer legislators dominated the coalitions that supported the easing of compensation restrictions. For example, a vote on July 3, 1979, in the state senate found Lourie leading a losing bloc of eleven, three-fourths of whom were lawyers, against twenty-seven senators on the other side (including two mill executives), less than half of whom were lawyers (*Journal of the Senate* 1979, 1679–80). Had not a significant portion of the legal profession taken an interest in helping the victims of byssinosis, whatever their reasons, the Brown Lung Association would not have won the victories it did.

As significant as these legislative victories were, the association failed to achieve other legal changes. They never came close in their efforts to gain "presumptive diagnosis," which would have shifted the burden of proof from the claimant to the mills, forcing them to demonstrate that cotton dust did not cause any breathing problems. Even the Brown Lung Association's lawyer friends in the legislature couldn't support this idea. Lourie describes himself as "not really a presumption man" (1991), and virtually all the other lawyers I spoke to in both Carolinas opposed presumption (Interviews). Presumptive diagnosis certainly was not in the self-interest of lawyers, because it would have eliminated their role in most cases.

In addition, the association failed to gain protection against mills that harassed or fired family members of those who failed claims. In 1986, after the Brown Lung Association was virtually nonexistent as an effective interest group, Senator Lourie held hearings on a bill that gave workers some modest protection (Shealy 1986; Lourie 1991). The bill was promoted by another grassroots group, the Workers' Rights Project, along with lawyers in the compensation area. Passed in May 1986, it allowed workers to sue for lost wages if they could prove they were fired for filing a claim (S.C. Code of Laws, 41-1-80). This provided very little protection for the worker and no protection for relatives. To quote one lawyer, "In South Carolina you can be fired if they don't like the way you part your hair" (Rudnick 1993).

The Brown Lung Association also wanted payment to begin when awards were first made, rather than be delayed while the company appealed. They wanted the doctors who consulted with mills to be excluded from testimony at hearings. They thought the mill should pay for the claimant's first medical examination (as was usually done in North Carolina). They wanted lawyers' fees to be added to the award, not taken from it. Finally, they wanted an end to the practice of apportioning benefits according to how much of the disability was due to byssinosis (BLA Papers).

None of these changes ever passed. According to Senator Lourie, the explanation for this lack of success was simple: the sad fact was that whenever both the Chamber of Commerce and the Textile Manufacturers Association were absolutely determined to stop a bill in South Carolina, it could not be passed. After allowing some modest reforms that they felt would forestall federal action, they were determined that there would be no further reforms (Lourie 1991).

The connection between lawyer legislator self-interest and workers' compensation laws is less clear in other states where prohibitions on lawyer legislators exist. Nevertheless, those who have represented compensation clients before coming to the legislature and those who may do so in the future are more likely to understand and sympathize with their plight. The Brown Lung Association deserves credit for making this link meaningful. Until its organizers located potential claimants and encouraged them to file their cases, lawyers who worked in the area of workers' compensation did not know about the problems faced by occupational disease claimants. The Brown Lung Association did a great deal to educate them in this area.[2]

The personal testimony of Georgia members played a significant role in persuading the Peach State to ease legal restrictions on byssinosis claims. Retired textile workers who were members of the Augusta Brown Lung Association chapter testified before a state legislative joint study committee in 1980 (Cook 1980) and continued presenting their own stories before the Industrial Relations subcommittee the next year (Munro 1981). They told legislators about the two major impediments in Georgia compensation laws. First, byssinosis was not listed among the diseases that could be considered compensable. Second, the statute of limitations ran out a year after retirement, regardless of whether the person knew that he or she had an occupational illness. By this time, compensation laws had been changed in both Carolinas, so interstate inequity became a major justification for change in the Peach State. In the words of one disabled retiree, "I do not think it is right that people like myself are denied the right to file for compensation in Georgia, when right across the river in South Carolina people who worked for the same company I did can file a claim and receive compensation" (quoted in Munro 1981).

In 1982 the Georgia General Assembly reduced these barriers, but not nearly as much as the association would have liked. They did add byssinosis to the list of occupational diseases, but they took a much more conservative position on the statute of limitations. Georgia started the statute's clock running at the time of last exposure and gave the claimant three years to become disabled and be diagnosed. In the Carolinas, the shorter statute of limitations did not begin to run until the diagnosis was made. Georgia did provide a window of opportunity for those who became disabled before the law was passed. Anyone who had been disabled before July 1979 was given until July 1983 to be diagnosed and until July 1984 to file a claim (Munro 1982). Unfortunately for anyone who fell into that category, the Brown Lung Association was so weak by this time that it was unable to sponsor many clinics to identify victims.

The number of cases filed with the help of the association brought pressure on the commissions to process these occupational disease cases more quickly. Most work-related accident cases are settled without formal hearings and litigation; strain on commission staff and hearing officers is minimal. In contrast, the textile companies and their insurance carriers contested virtually all byssinosis claims. The bureaucratic result was a much greater burden on staff and hearing officers, a backlog of cases, and delay. This was especially true in the Carolinas, where the Brown Lung Association instigated the filing of hundreds of cases in the late 1970s.

A 1979 study performed under contract with the U.S. Department of Labor by Brown Lung Association staffer Joseph "Chip"

Hughes found that those cases that had been settled had taken an average of twenty-five months. At that time 68 percent of the thousand claims that had been filed had not been settled, and the sample of those cases included in the study had been pending for an average of twenty-two months (Hughes 1979, 38). Even after both Carolinas had removed some legal obstacles to compensation, administrative and legal delay were major stumbling blocks. Insurance carriers used delay as a powerful bargaining tool to negotiate for lower settlements. Victims frequently said that time was something they didn't have. The study concluded that workers' compensation was failing to meet its most basic promise:

That workers' compensation is a "swift and adequate remedy" as promised by state statutes is highly dubious in light of overwhelming evidence to the contrary. The lack of administrative procedures for case processing, the absence of standardized medical criteria for meeting the burden of proof, and the lack of adequate benefits for totally and permanently disabled byssinosis claimants make it difficult to even call workers' compensation a "system" because of the haphazard and arbitrary nature of the case proceedings. [Hughes 1979, 38]

Armed with the data from this study and their own personal experiences, association members lobbied authorities to reduce the delay. In South Carolina, after many press conferences and much legislative testimony, members won a meeting with Governor Dick Riley in the fall of 1980 to voice their complaints. He gave them a sympathetic hearing and subsequently declared the week of October 5–12 "Brown Lung Week." The group had established enough legitimacy and sympathy in the eyes of the public that the governor had to give them at least symbolic recognition. Unfortunately, the group gained little more than symbolic support. Riley failed to name a panel to study the workers' compensation system, as the association had requested, but came up instead with a modest proposal of his own: to have the state provide a free examination of claimants by state medical school lung specialists (BLA Papers).

In North Carolina the Brown Lung Association gained some action in addition to symbolic support. Governor Jim Hunt also declared a "Brown Lung Week" at the same time as South Carolina's, but in December 1979 he also appointed a study committee to examine the claims process and make recommendations for administrative improvements. He named one member of the association and a lawyer who frequently represented byssinosis victims to the seven-member committee. The panel was chaired by Robert Byrd, a former dean of the law school and the University of North Carolina. It met for three months—hearing testimony from four members of the Brown Lung Association and from Joseph Hughes, the staff member who had performed the 1979 study—and issued its report on April 10, 1980. Florence Sandlin, the association member who sat on the committee, issued her own minority report at the same time. She remembers that the association staff gave her a great deal of help in writing her report (Sandlin 1991).

The governor's study committee did conclude that there was excessive delay. After a claim was filed, it took three to four months for the medical panel's examination to take place and another couple of months for the doctor to file a report; another two and a half months more elapsed before the Industrial Commission scheduled the first hearing. Further medical examinations were often necessary because about half the time the examining doctor failed to give any "statement of opinion on the causal connections between the claimant's disease and his occupational exposure." The panel also found that doctors on the state medical panel to whom claimants were assigned varied widely in the likelihood that they would diagnose byssinosis; the probability ranged from 20 to 91 percent. This variation and the disagreement among doctors about the standards by which byssinosis was to be diagnosed provided many opportunities for further legal appeal. The committee recommended twenty-five reforms in all, including standardization of diagnosis, additional staff, and a large number of procedural measures to reduce delay (Byrd et al. 1980, 3, 7, 10).

The minority report accepted nineteen of the majority's recommendations but had four major objections. First, it called for presumptive diagnosis, a long-time goal of the Brown Lung Association. Sandlin (1980, 2) argued that the majority had failed to recognize that this was the only way to end delaying tactics. Second, the majority had endorsed apportionment of settlements, whereas the Brown Lung Association had maintained for a long time that apportionment unfairly eroded the size of awards. Third, the committee had failed to attempt to resolve the medical questions concerning some standard way of diagnosing byssinosis; rather, it had recommended that another panel of pulmonary specialists be appointed to resolve these questions (Byrd et al. 1980, 9–11). Fourth, the committee did nothing about opening commission records to claimants' lawyers and the public. Closed files had made research on commission actions difficult for the Brown Lung Association staff (Hughes 1979, app. D).

There were several minor complaints as well. Sandlin wanted to strengthen the recommendation for choosing the medical panel in order to exclude doctors "who have an excessive income from textile mills or who have a large referral business from the mills" (1980, 4). The majority report did note that "the Commission should be aware of the extent of a panel physician's work for employers or industry and should consider the appropriateness of his continued service" but made no formal recommendation in this regard (Byrd et al. 1980, 17).

Despite the fact that the Brown Lung Association did not get everything it wanted, it had won on a significant number of points, as the minority report recognized before lodging its reservations: "The number and breadth of the recommendations affirms that the Industrial Commission's policies and procedures had many shortcomings. The Committee's recommendations touch on several of the areas in which improvement is desperately needed" (Sandlin 1980, 1). The association's newsletter claimed that twenty of the twenty-five recommendations were exactly what the association had long wanted, and that it had achieved six of its eight major desired changes ("North Carolina: BLA Reforms Adopted" 1980).

A week after the study committee filed its report, Governor Hunt announced that he was accepting the proposals ("North Carolina: BLA Reforms Adopted" 1980). He appointed an Implementation Review Subcommittee of three members on which the Brown Lung Association had indirect representation. In addition to Chairman Byrd, the subcommittee included Paul Michaels, a Raleigh lawyer who frequently represented byssinosis claimants. He was balanced by Ron Dilthey, who was employed by Liberty Mutual Insurance Company, the largest workers' compensation carrier for the mills (*Brown Lung Reporter* 2, no. 8, 1980). In its final report in April 1981, the subcommittee found that all the recommendations had been implemented save one that required legislative action (BLA Papers; commission report). Within two months the legislature enacted the last recommendation, that awards by the mills appealed accrue interest from their original date. Both Governor Hunt, who had made a personal commitment to the work of the study committee, and the Industrial Commission, which had been heavily pressured by Hunt, lobbied hard for passage. Brown Lung Association members also attended legislative committee meetings during key votes (*Brown Lung Reporter* 3, no. 4, 1981).

Although they fell short of what the Brown Lung Association would have liked, the reforms did have a significant impact on the processing of claims. In national congressional hearings a year later, Paul Michaels testified that the reforms had cut the time for a typical case by about a fourth, from two years to about a year and a half (U.S. Congress 1982a, 59). Nevertheless, the amount of

compensation collected was probably not sufficient by itself to affect the industry's attitudes toward dust control. Even using the
lowest estimates for the expense of dust control, compensation
awards were only a small fraction of what it would cost the mills to
comply with the regulations that they were still fighting. Mills paid
more than $10 million in compensation between 1971, when North
Carolina workers first filed for byssinosis compensation, and the
end of 1981. The $1 million a year compensation average was less
than .5 percent of the annual $206.1 million that OSHA estimated
would be required to meet the regulations ("Occupational Exposure" 1978, 27369). Clearly, it was not cheaper for the mills to clean
up than to pay workers' compensation.

The history of job accident cases reinforces the conclusion that
the strategy of forcing change in employer behavior by using workman's compensation awards is not effective. The National Commission on Workman's Compensation Laws concluded in its final
report in 1972 that accident rates were not necessarily lower where
payments were high (Shaffer 1978, 192). Other studies have drawn a
similar nondefinitive conclusion (Ellis 1976). Schroeder's examination (1986, 154, 157) of workers' compensation and occupational disease drew an even more negative conclusion: "For various reasons,
worker's compensation and tort remedies have not provided incentives to reduce toxic exposures. . . . Whatever the deficiencies of the
system for compensating injured workers may be, they pale in comparison to its treatment of workers disabled by disease."

ENFORCEMENT OF THE DUST STANDARDS

Another way the Brown Lung Association employed institutional
disruption was in its encouragement of strict enforcement of workplace regulations in the mills. Though members themselves had no
access to the workplace, OSHA inspectors did. To the extent that
the group could induce inspections, and to the extent that inspections disrupted normal work patterns, the Brown Lung Association
could make its presence felt indirectly.

The organization utilized several tactics in this regard. They vo-
cally criticized state OSHA programs for not inspecting properly or
frequently, and they filed complaints with the national OSHA. For
example, in March of 1980 the association filed a formal complaint
that South Carolina OSHA did not have enough inspectors. Federal
OSHA officials agreed with the complaint and ordered the South
Carolina Department of Labor to increase the size of its program

and perform more inspections (BLA Papers). By hiring a lawyer to help with processing violations and by performing more inspections, the South Carolina OSHA program did avoid a federal takeover (Covington and Dennis 1980, 7), despite continuing complaints from Brown Lung Association members.

Using inspection problems as a basis for complaint, members met with the governor and testified at legislative hearings in an unsuccessful attempt to prevent the renomination and confirmation of the South Carolina commissioner of labor, Edgar McGowan. His strongest support came from the textile manufacturers, who describe him as unusually fair, understanding of the industry perspective, and not as pro-labor as other labor commissioners (Interviews).

As part of their efforts to educate active workers, Brown Lung Association organizers and members encouraged those in the mills to call for inspections. Their leaflets explained workers' rights to do so without identifying themselves to management, buy they had very little success in persuading active workers to complain (Interviews; BLA Papers). Charlotte Brody (1991) thinks the major explanation for this failure was that the association really could not protect workers from employer retaliation, despite the protections that were written into the regulations. The organizers knew that. So did the workers. Even state OSHA officials were aware of this problem. They candidly admit that they can offer little protection to workers who are fired after making a complaint, because the company is almost always able to show that the dismissal is unrelated to the complaint ("Job Fear" 1992).

State OSHA inspections left much to be desired. The *Charlotte Observer* series that ran in February 1980 was extremely critical of state enforcement of OSHA regulations (Covington and Dennis 1980, 6–7). The newspaper's examination of state records found that only 297 of the 614 mills in both Carolinas had been inspected, that both states had allowed mills two or more years to end violations, that regulators failed to reinspect or took the mill's word that remedial action had been taken, and that officials had consistently levied minimal fines.[3]

The response of those in charge of state-run OSHA programs was twofold. First, they blamed the feds. Labor Commissioner Edgar McGowan complained that federal officials were constantly changing their view on what OSHA should accomplish: "There have been four assistant secretaries [since 1973], and every one had a different view of OSHA." Second, they defended their actions as the lesser of two evils. OSHA had never taken the ultimate step of trying to close a mill for failing to meet standards because state officials viewed the loss of jobs as a greater evil than the potential danger of byssinosis. A North Carolina OSHA official defended the practice of granting of nearly unlimited extensions for compliance by arguing that cotton dust did not place workers in immediate danger; state OSHA officials saw byssinosis as a long-term problem that developed over years. The fact that they were dealing with a temporary standard pending the industry's Supreme Court appeal of final OSHA standards provided another rationale for inaction. State officials argued that using their scarce resources to enforce a standard that was likely to be replaced shortly did not make sense when they would likely have to begin the costly process all over again (Covington and Dennis 1980, 7).

The four-year timetable for compliance with the final standards began running in March 1980. After several Reagan administration reviews and modifications to reduce the costs of compliance, the final standards went into full effect on 27 March 1984. The South Carolina Department of Labor announced that it would enforce them fully with inspections and the imposition of fines up to $1,000 for each violation ("State Will Enforce" 1984).

North Carolina's OSHA program made several hundred inspections in the early 1980s to determine initial compliance but has done few since then, according to a state spokesperson (Lewis 1991). South Carolina's OSHA program does continue to perform regular inspections but at a very slow pace with few follow-ups; between mid-1985 and January 1987, it made five inspections and one follow-up monitoring visit (Knight 1987). According to state-provided data, twenty-three inspections were performed over the four and a half years between 1987 and mid-1991 at eighteen different mills, a rate of about five inspections each year. Four of those twenty-three inspections found mills that had four or more apparently serious violations (such as dust exceeding permissible levels, lack of training, improper use of respirators, poor work practices). There was no record of any follow-up inspections in three of these mills. The other six mills with any violations seemed to have fewer and less serious violations (failure to post regulations properly, failure to monitor dust levels on each shift change).

The only effect the association has had on state inspections since the early 1980s has been to file a few complaints or pass on complaints from workers, without using the workers' names. Because these complaints do not come from active workers or from persons who are identified, neither the South Carolina nor North Carolina OSHA takes them very seriously. As "informal" or "anonymous" complaints, they are usually handled by correspondence with the mill in question rather than actual on-site inspections (Lewis 1991; Lybrand 1991).

The changing political environment prevented the Brown Lung Association from sustaining any of its pressure tactics. Funding cut-offs made it impossible to continue the screening clinics that were vital for locating and identifying victims. With fewer claims being filed, there was no way to put further pressure on agencies administering workers' compensation. The Reagan administration's de-emphasis of OSHA's regulatory activities undercut efforts to pressure the mills through potentially punitive inspections. Given the association's failure to recruit active workers who could force more inspections and tight state budgets that couldn't support many inspections, mills had little to fear. In addition, the managers of modernized mills that survived foreign competition felt that they were generally in compliance and no longer worried about most of the details of the regulations (Interviews).

All the Brown Lung Association's energies became focused on protecting the dust standard from any weakening revision under the new administration and on its own financial survival. Before we turn to that struggle for survival and the last years of the group, we need to examine the conflict from the perspective of the textile industry.

7

THE TEXTILE
INDUSTRY RESPONSE

It should have been the mother of all political mismatches. Poor, uneducated, sick, retired mill workers should have been no more than a minor irritant to King Cotton and the mills of the New South. Indeed, until the birth of the Brown Lung Association, that's the way it was. The issue of occupational disease was exiled to the silent realm of nonissues. It was not on anyone's political agenda in the South. It was one of those dangerous class-based issues that could potentially endanger the rule of those who owned the lands that grew cotton and those who owned the mills that processed it. Most disabled workers didn't know what was wrong with them. Those few who may have known didn't participate in politics. Mill owners and state health officials, who should have known—and maybe did know—had a self-interest in not finding out.

DENIAL (PRE-1970)

The response of the textile industry to byssinosis can be divided into three rough stages: denial and neglect, resistance and delay, and minimizing risks and costs. Prior to 1970 the industry was able to neglect the problem by simply denying that the disease existed and ignoring challenges to that position. It held enough political power to keep the issue off the political agenda and prevent action.

Beardsley's important study of the neglect of mill workers' health care through 1970 describes what happened—or rather, what mostly did not happen. When it did happen, it was for reasons other than the paternalistic ideal of concern for workers. Owners "were far less interested in maintaining a healthy work force than in maintaining high profits, whatever their pronouncements. . . . In the area of workplace health, improvements were primarily tied to production techniques . . . undertaken for the most part in the interests of greater efficiency and greater profits . . . workers, not owners, bore the cost of waiting. And for byssinosis victims the cost of delay was high indeed." Beardsley found another shortfall—between the rhetoric and the actions of state agencies, which "had frequently proclaimed their intention to secure the well-being of workers. But the close alliance between government and industry rendered agency promises meaningless. As one South Carolina labor department chief actually admitted, 'our people' were the owners of textile mills, not their employees" (1987, 313).

Warnings had been sounded that mills certainly should have heard. In 1940 M. F. Trice, an industrial hygienist for the North Carolina Industrial Commission and the State Board of Health, wrote an article in *Textile World* titled "Card Room Fever: Strict Control of Dust Will Eliminate Health Hazard from Low-Grade Cotton." He warned that "there is a specific agent in cotton dust capable of producing the observed symptoms and ultimately the pathological changes in the lungs which cause complete disablement in a number of workers exposed to cotton dust for a long time" (1940, 68). He went on to recommend that high-pressure air hoses be eliminated in favor of vacuums for cleaning equipment and even going so far as enclosing the carding machines to eliminate worker contact. His warning was ignored.

When Arend Bouhuys attempted to gain the cooperation of Georgia mills in performing a federally funded survey of their workers in 1964, the state textile association actively opposed him. Executive Vice-President T. M. Forbes of the Georgia Textile Manufacturers Association sent a confidential letter to all member mills dated 4 June (copy in BLA Papers). He recommended that they put pressure on Emory University, where Bouhuys was a faculty member at the time, on the grounds that it was supporting a study he considered a waste of taxpayer money. "If you are acquainted with any of the trustees of Emory University you may consider it desirable to talk with them about the health of your own employees and about what your company has done to provide safe, healthful and comfortable working conditions in your plants." He closed the letter by reminding members that they did not have to cooperate in the study.

The implications were clear. Forbes and the Georgia Textile Manufacturers Association were trying to frustrate the study of a disease by preventing cooperation and by bringing political pressure to bear on a professor through the university's board of trustees. Attached to the letter was a copy of Forbes's 2 June 1964 letter to the president of Emory, stating his objections and charging that the "Georgia textile manufacturing industry has been damaged" by the very announcement of the study. Forbes described byssinosis as a disease "whose existence has never been proven," for which "there is no factual basis for claiming that there is a high incidence, or even a slight existence," and "about which those who have spent their lives in the industry do not know."

One of the last clear and extreme expressions of this position appeared in the July 1969 issue of *America's Textile Reporter.* An unsigned editorial titled "It All Depends" drew a contrast between the southern version of free market capitalism, called "our Old American Capitalistic idea," and what it saw as the radical socialistic ideas of northern congressmen, who hypocritically engaged in South-bashing while ignoring the problems of their own region. Unintentionally, it revealed the xenophobia and incredible insensitivity of some southern economic leaders.

The Hon. James G. O'Hara from Michigan had made up his mind to champion the TWUA's somewhat tawdry insistence that our textile mills are sinkholes of sin and dens of iniquity [by supporting] "Federal standards for industrial health and safety." . . . we are thinking of Congressman O'Hara's concern about people far away from his rotten boroughs, we remind ourselves that his constituents die more from lead poisoning, lose more fingers and hands from trip hammers and forging machines, and as a matter of fact kill each other more often than do our Southern cotton mill people. . . . We are particularly intrigued by the term "Byssinosis," a thing thought up by venal doctors who attended last year's ILO [International Labor Organization] meetings in Africa where inferior races are bound to be afflicted by new diseases more superior people defeated years ago. As a matter of fact, we referred to the "Cotton Fever" earlier, when we pointed out that a good chaw of B. L. dark would take care of it. . . . Well, we would want to tell Mr. O'Hara that, and for all of our life, we have hated federal interference in our lives and businesses. . . . In our opinion, Congressman O'Hara is typical of the lousy representation we get from time-serving Northern Democrats who sell their souls to the venal labor leaders." ["It All Depends" 1969, 1, 27]

Such racist and insensitive rhetoric provided reformers with additional evidence that federal action was needed. With these attitudes, the South would never attend to its own problems.

RESISTANCE AND DELAY (1970–EARLY 1980s)

The issue of byssinosis began to get on the political agenda after 1970 for a reason that should be quite familiar to students of southern politics: federal intervention. Following the creation of OSHA in 1970, with its mandate to enact cotton dust regulations, the industry found it harder to neglect and ignore the issue. The industry was split on the question of what to do. Some continued to deny that the problem existed and resist as best they could—a time-honored southern tradition from other areas of political life, such as civil rights. The majority acknowledged that there was a problem but made efforts to minimize its importance and delay remedial action.

Understanding the importance of implementation in the policy process, Ralph Nader's consumer groups worked diligently to ensure that OSHA would carry out its mandate to protect workers. One of Nader's groups, Public Citizen, used the Freedom of Information Act to obtain OSHA documents showing that some southern members of Congress had successfully exerted pressure on the agency to exempt some parts of the cotton industry from even the weak standards that existed at the time.

Another document, which came out of the Watergate hearings, revealed clearer corruption. The Nixon administration had used promises to go easy on setting dust standards and inspections as a means to generate campaign contributions from the textile industry in the 1972 presidential campaign. George Guenther, the assistant secretary of labor who oversaw OSHA, wrote a memo stating that "the great potential of OSHA as a sales point for fund-raiding and general support by employers, I do not believe . . . is fully recognized. . . . While promulgation and modification activity must continue, no highly controversial standards (i.e. cotton dust, etc.) will be proposed by OSHA or NIOSH." This kind of attitude helped generate about a million dollars in contributions from the textile industry (quoted in Kotz 1978, B4). Milton Corn, who directed OSHA when the Ford administration finally issued proposals for standards just before Carter took office, described what he found in reviewing the records from the aborted Nixon presidency: "I came across so many wild things that I didn't have the time to figure out the 'whys' of them. The pressures from industry were extreme" (quoted in Kotz 1978, B4).

Industry reaction to OSHA's adoption of dust standards in 1978 ran the full range from warning of impending doom through trivializing the problem to taking a positive approach. In July 1978 *Textile World* led its story on the dust standards with the announcement of a death sentence: "On Friday, June 23, the world ended for some U.S. textile firms" ("Can Marginal Mills Endure" 1978, 23). The next month *America's Textile Reporter Bulletin* interviewed the president of the American Textile Manufacturers Institute, Robert Small, who likened the problem to "an allergy. If you are exposed to cotton dust and develop any kind of respiratory problem, it can be corrected providing you have not been exposed for a very very long period" ("OSHA Cotton Dust Standards" 1978, 18). Several months later, in the most upbeat advice offered in industry publications of the period, *Textile World* advised companies to "take the positive approach." Quoting Belmont Heritage Corporation's Jim Gentry, the short piece stressed that "you stand to gain a bonus in employee morale with positive action. . . . Your main object is showing your employees that management cares . . . you should not take a 'this is the law' or 'the costs will put us out of business' attitude" ("Don't Get Lulled" 1978, 58).

The industry followed a five-pronged approach during this period of delay and resistance to federal regulation. Initially, it used political connections and Nixon campaign contributions to stymie any attempt even to propose regulations.

Next, when it could no longer stop regulations from being adopted, the textile industry utilized every possible means of judicial appeal to delay their enforcement, even though—as industry trade publications warned—such appeals would do little more than "give mills some breathing room" ("Don't Get Lulled" 1978, 55). The principal legal ground for appeal was the question of what Congress had intended when it used the term "feasible" in the 1970 Occupational Safety and Health Act. Did it mean technologically feasible or financially feasible? If financially feasible, did that require a cost-benefit analysis? The industry wanted a full cost-benefit analysis performed before any regulations were put into place. That complex, lengthy, and highly subjective kind of process would buy them time and would perhaps weaken the final standards. Ultimately, after several appeals, the Supreme Court rejected their legal claim in June 1981. Although they lost the appeal, their efforts had won them an additional nineteen months. The original four-year timetable for full compliance had been scheduled to begin on September 4, 1978 ("Occupational Exposure" 1978, 27394). Legal appeals delayed that beginning until March 25, 1980.

A third element in the industry's tactics during this period of resistance and delay entailed the use of research to raise questions about the cause and extent of byssinosis. The complex scientific and medical questions surrounding the disease made it easy to produce research that muddied other findings. The industry was also in an excellent position to fund research: it had the resources and, equally important, the easiest access to mill workers. If one study was discredited, another could be produced.

A number of studies that did undercut the efforts of the Brown Lung Association were used initially to argue against the need for any cotton dust standards and later to justify minimal regulation. For example, Dr. Mario Battigelli, who testified on behalf of the American Textile Manufacturers Institute (ATMI) at the dust standard hearings in 1977, claimed that the levels of chronic bronchitis in the general population were high enough to explain problems among mill workers and that smoking was a much more important variable than cotton dust in causing lung problems. (Dr. Harold Imbus, Burlington's director of health and safety, made a similar claim in an article for the *Charlotte Observer* series; 1980, 23.) Dr. Russell Harley, also testifying on behalf of the ATMI, argued that the disease was reversible if affected workers were removed from dusty areas. OSHA rejected these arguments in favor of stronger empirical studies concluding that chronic obstructive lung disease was significantly higher among textile workers exposed to cotton dust, regardless of whether they smoked, and that the effects were usually not reversible ("Occupational Exposure" 1978, 27353–54).

Industry studies often found a link between cotton dust exposure and byssinosis but emphasized the low rates of the disease rather than the link. For example, in one of the largest studies ever done, Burlington examined more than 10,000 of its workers (Imbus and Suh 1973). It found the same significant relationship between byssinosis symptoms and lung function loss that was cited by other researchers as evidence for a causal link (Beck and Schachter 1983, 406). Yet in subsequent discussions of this work, Dr. Harold Imbus, the medical director in charge of the project, stressed the low overall rates of byssinosis among all textile employees (4.5 percent). He ignored the link between symptoms and reduced lung capacity and the much higher rate of byssinosis symptoms (18 percent) among workers in early preparation areas of production ("Burlington's Byssinosis Testing Program" 1977, 62; U.S. Congress 1979, 224; Imbus 1980, 23). A 1976 study performed by Dr. Charles Martin, the Cone Mills medical director, concluded that the rate of byssinosis was less than 1 percent among the 6,631 workers who were analyzed. Unfortunately for the textile industry's cause, however, Martin was able to find a statistically significant relationship between byssinosis and smoking in only one of six subgroups (Martin and Higgins 1976, 459–61).

Of course, virtually all studies depended on workers to give their own medical histories and report symptoms they had suffered. Critics of industry studies would point out that histories taken by company medical personnel were biased because many workers feared they would lose their jobs if they admitted any problems (Bronstein 1984, 1134). Nevertheless, regulatory relief was a cornerstone of the Reagan administration; therefore, Reagan's OSHA was quite willing to accept the results of industry studies that justified easing regulations. In January 1982, ATMI released a survey of about 400,000 workers who had been screened by their companies. The industry group reported a byssinosis incidence rate of four-tenths of 1 percent ("Industry Says Few Workers Get Brown Lung" 1982). The Reagan administration immediately seized this report as an opportunity to review the standards, even though the National Institute for Occupational Safety and Health (NIOSH) requested that OSHA disregard the conclusions. NIOSH said the study "violates many basic premises of the study of diseases" (McInnis 1982).

It is easier to win delays in enforcement if public sympathy can be aroused; hence, building a positive public image was a fourth important part of the strategy of delay. The industry employed several tactics to this end. One was the attempt to displace as much blame as possible. Industry publications, press releases, and public statements frequently pointed out that the causal agent seemed to be something that came to the mill from the farmers, not anything that was produced in the processing. In testimony before congressional committees textile spokespersons called for Department of Agriculture research to find ways of removing the offending agent from the cotton ("Textile Industry Profile" 1977, 52; Martin 1980; U.S. Congress 1979, 202; 1980, 526–27).

Displacing blame had some risks. The industry ran into political problems with another powerful southern economic interest group when they attempted to blame all breathing problems on smoking. In 1980 the North Carolina Textile Manufacturers Association ran an ad in newspapers across the state. Headlined "One out of five adult Americans has a chronic lung condition," it went on to attack the idea of presumptive diagnosis for byssinosis, asking whether it was fair to force textile companies to pay for breathing problems just because some of these people happened to work in a mill. The line that angered tobacco interests declared: "Doctors know that the majority of lung diseases are related to smoking." R. J. Reynolds responded that the ads were "erroneous and inflammatory," and a state agriculture official in charge of tobacco affairs asserted: "It's been well established that a certain amount of dust from textile manufacturing has contributed to the brown lung problem" ("Tobacco and Textile Companies Battle" 1980). The ensuing public relations battle between the two major economic interests in North Carolina prompted a *Durham Morning Herald* political cartoon captioned "A Brown Study." It depicted two darkened, diseased lungs glaring at each other, one labeled "tobacco" and the other labeled "textiles" (Rogers 1980). The textile industry withdrew its ads.

The "one out of five adult Americans" rate for lung problems was used for a number of years by textile interests in arguing that byssinosis rates could be largely explained by lung problems among the general population. This claim, which had been rejected by OSHA in the cotton dust hearings ("Occupational Exposure" 1978, 27353), was based on a study of one little town in Colorado. The Brown Lung Association asked the American Lung Association how it was possible to arrive at such a high figure. The American Lung Association responded that "the only way to get 20 percent is to include everybody with problems like hayfever and sinusitis" ("True or False" 1980).

The public image the industry attempted to project emphasized low profits and a good overall safety and health record. Its reported profit rate after taxes was 2.4 percent between 1972 and 1977, compared with a 5 percent rate for other manufacturing. Industry spokespersons touted an overall lower-than-average rate of illness and injury as evidence that "this industry has taken and continues to take a positive approach toward occupational safety and health" (U.S. Congress 1979, 202; 1980, 526)

Cotton Incorporated, an industry trade group, did spend a considerable amount of money on cotton dust research—and publicized its efforts in order to build the industry's image. Nevertheless, its record is noteworthy. Between 1971 and 1980 Cotton Incorporated spent nearly $8 million on sponsored research, the greatest yearly amounts in 1974–78, when the dust regulations were being seriously considered. Between 1977 and 1980, Cotton Inc. gave financial support to a majority of the papers delivered at annual cotton dust conferences sponsored by two other trade groups, the National Cotton Council and the Cotton Foundation (BLA Papers, Cotton Inc. memo). The conferences, which began in 1977, continue into the 1990s under the sponsorship of the National Cotton Council (Jacobs et al. 1990).

The public relations campaign had a negative side as well. When the industry could no longer ignore the Brown Lung Association, it began to attack. In a feature on Burlington's byssinosis testing program, *America's Textile Reporter Bulletin* charged that the Brown Lung Association was irresponsible in making superficial diagnoses of byssinosis at its temporary clinics ("Burlington's Byssinosis Testing Program 1977, 64–65). Dr. Imbus (1980), Burlington's medical director, charged that the clinics, "which have gained widespread publicity, have not been the public services they are purported to be. The association has distorted the facts, giving the public the impression that all breathing problems in textile plants are caused by the work environment. Indeed, they have led many workers who suffer conditions such as heart disease to believe their condition was caused by cotton dust. . . . The Brown Lung Association has managed to obtain a great deal of misguided sympathy from much of the media and the federal government." It was clear that the association had become powerful enough to gain the industry's attention.

The mills used the battle over protective masks as a weapon. The object was to turn active workers, who generally did not like wearing masks, against the Brown Lung Association. The dust standards required that employers provide workers with respirators in areas that did not meet the standards. OSHA did not intend this to be a permanent solution, though mills had argued in the hearings that respirators were a more cost-effective way to meet the standards. Personal respirators were to be used only until mechanical means could be installed and in special situations, such as maintenance and repair, where the mechanical controls were not working. If the dust level was less than five times the permissible levels, single-use disposable face masks could be worn; higher levels mandated the use of mechanical masks. Moreover, if a physician found that an employee could not wear a respirator, that employee had the right to be transferred to a different job with no loss in earnings ("Occupational Exposure" 1978, 27396).

As soon as the standard went into effect in March 1980, the battle began. Wearing a mask in a hot, humid, and dusty workplace is not easy or pleasant. OSHA had anticipated in writing the standards that "worker resistance to wearing respirators can be great" because of facial irritation, loss of vision, hearing, mobility, and breathing resistance. OSHA tried to deal with these problems by requiring proper training on how to wear the mask and educating employees as to why it was needed; allowing them to choose their masks, to decide when filters needed to be changed, and when the masks needed to be cleaned; and, ultimately, guaranteeing transfer with no loss in wages if all this failed ("Occupational Exposure" 1978, 29384–87). How well this worked depended on how well employers lived up to the spirit as well as the letter of the requirements.

Employers knew about employee resistance. Under the older standard employees had resisted when asked to wear masks. Before the new standards went into effect, Robert Timmerman, chief executive of Graniteville Mills, using the language of the paternalistic mill culture, said that his company did not require employees to use masks, even where they were needed: "Our people put it on and our people almost had a revolt. Our people said, 'Mr. Timmerman, we can't breathe with these, they're trying to kill us' " (Covington et al. 1980a, 4). In view of this knowledge, the mills' desire to meet standards through the use of respirators alone was somewhat hypocritical, to say the least.

When employees were required to wear masks and complained, they were frequently told that it was the fault of OSHA and the Brown Lung Association. The association responded with a torrent of flyers handed out to active workers at gates of the mills. The message was that the mills were at fault for not cleaning up and that workers had a number of important rights with respect to masks. One such flyer was headed "Dear Brown Lung Answer Person." It was modeled after a "Dear Abby" column and began with a question from "Fussin' and Fumin',": "My company says that it's OSHA's fault that I have to wear a mask. I already have a breathing problem and this mask is more than I can stand. What can I do?" The association printed this and other flyers under their Department of Labor grant for the education of active workers. Although the mills complained about these grants, such education may have been necessary, given the unwillingness of many companies to live up to the regulations.

Workers lodged so many complaints about how the mills were implementing the respirator provisions that OSHA stayed the effective date of those requirements for seventy-five days (OSHA 1980). Eric Frumin (1980), the safety and health director of the Amalgamated Clothing and Textile Workers Union, charged that mills had "solicited these complaints in order to attack OSHA." The Brown Lung Association made some of the complaints. A letter to OSHA director Eula Bingham from the chair of the association's standing committee on OSHA leveled eight different complaints. Specific evidence from four plants, along with more general evidence, supported the complaints. For example, the letter charged that "we have not yet found a mill which offers powered air purifying respirators to their workers. Most don't even tell their workers about any masks other then the 3-M dust mask or a canister-filter quartermask" (BLA Papers).

The respirator provisions had been scheduled to go into full effect in September 1980, five months after the standards went into effect and after all mills had been given time to measure dust levels. OSHA Director Bingham announced: "There is widespread misunderstanding in the textile industry of how an effective respirator program should work. As a result, many workers are being burdened with requirements that may not be necessary under the standard, while others may not be fully protected against the dangers of cotton dust. To help correct this situation, we will meet with representatives of the cotton textile industry, workers and their unions and the National Institute for Occupational Safety and Health as soon as possible to develop guidelines for proper training and use of respirators" (OSHA 1980).

On the day that the postponed respirator provisions were to go into effect, in December 1980, OSHA announced another thirty-day stay. Mill officials charged that this last stay was politically motivated to pass the responsibility over to the Reagan administration ("Flip-flop On Dust Mask Rule" 1980). The respirator regulations did not finally go into effect until January 19, 1981.

The fifth part of the textile companies' strategy of resistance and delay was to appeal all fines that followed inspections, so as to gain as much time as possible to meet the standards. Appealing and even paying fines may have been the rational course of action from an economic point of view because good faith efforts to meet temporary standards could be self-defeating. During the four-year grace period before the final standards were to take effect, mills were to be held responsible for meeting the older air standards of 1 milligram. The engineering technology required to meet these temporary standards was different from that needed to meet the standards that were finally adopted (0.2 milligrams in yarn production areas, 0.75 in slashing and weaving, and 0.5 in other areas). Because of lax enforcement, many mills had not met the temporary standards when the countdown for the permanent ones went into effect in March 1980. Those mills that had not done so now had an economic advantage because they would have to make only the one investment, whereas the mills that had acted more responsibly might lose all the money they had spent up to that point. One mill owner, who had spent half the company's net worth to meet the temporary standard between 1976 and 1980, made the point: "It's conceivable that some of our competitors might be just as well off not to have spent anything until the new standards are adopted and then try to meet them" (Ellis 1980).

Hermitage Mills was one that did not spend anything; it represents the extreme of resistance in both word and deed. A 450-employee mill in Camden, South Carolina, more than eighty years old, Hermitage was initially inspected in 1974. The inspection revealed that the air was six to seven times the relatively high dust standards in place at that time. After six years of delay and appeal, owner William Pitts told a state judge: "Nobody has proven cotton dust is a source of disease. . . . In forty years, we've not had one single employee in either department [carding and picking] disabled because of a respiratory problem" (Dennis 1980, 8).

Pitts (1980, 24) saw the struggle as one between hard-working builders of prosperity and power-hungry bureaucrats looking to take away basic property rights: "This fight is as old as civilization: the unending war of a free people with inalienable rights granted by God, against those tyrannical power-hungry politicians intent on the establishment of a totalitarian government." He pictured those who claimed to be suffering from byssinosis as lazy people who were too sorry to take care of themselves, violating the southern mandate of self-reliance. "It is sickening to see the gutless minions of the news media siding with those few crybaby Americans who obviously are looking for a handout from the very hand that fed and clothed their families." Finally, he pictured the mill owners in the New South tradition as saviors of the South. "Without these owners and the splendor of the cotton textile industry, the South would perhaps still be groveling in the ashes of the Civil War." Two years later William Pitts sold his outdated mill. He never had installed any dust control equipment, and the new owners decided it might be cheaper to close the old mill and build a new one to meet the standards (Ellis and Dennis 1983).

Beardsley's examination of the neglect of the problem before 1970 laid the blame squarely on the shoulders of mill owners and state agencies. Between 1970 and the early 1980s, much of the blame for the slow adoption of protective measures and the failure to compensate disabled workers can also be placed on mill owners and state agencies. Although they were losing some of their political clout as the southern economy diversified, textile owners were still powerful enough to fight a delaying rearguard action. Even then, the case can be made that improvements came as much from economic necessity to modernize as from government mandate. As in the past, state agencies worried at least as much about protecting the mills from fines and economic hardship as about worker health.

COST AND RISK MINIMIZATION (EARLY 1980s–)

Following the realization that the standards would actually go into effect with no major modifications by the Reagan administration, virtually all members of the industry who had not already done so began pursuing a strategy of cost and risk minimization. The idea was to eliminate future problems by screening employees to make sure that no one who was predisposed to contract byssinosis would be placed at risk. Many companies were using screening of job applicants to eliminate those who had lower-than-expected lung capacity (Bronstein 1984, 1135). Typically, prospective employees who have less than 80 percent of "normal" lung capacity are rejected for jobs in dusty areas. Employers feel that with preemployment screening and ongoing medical surveillance, no one will ever reach the state of irreversible chronic byssinosis (Interviews).

Burlington, which liked to regard itself as the leader in taking responsible action, was the pioneer in risk reduction. In 1969, even before federal legislation was passed, the company began studying the problem among its own workers with the help of the state and Duke Medical School. When the completed study found significant rates of byssinosis symptoms among cardroom workers, Burlington officials admitted the dust problem and began routine medical surveillance. Beardsley (1987, 239) attributes these actions to a concern with the negative image that the industry was suffering. It was affecting all aspects of business, including recruiting top-quality personnel and professionals.

A 1977 article in *America's Textile Reporter Bulletin* featuring Burlington's byssinosis program claimed that the company was "assisting employees in filing for compensation where disability has developed" ("Burlington's Byssinosis Testing Program" 1977, 64). In his article for the 1980 *Charlotte Observer* series on byssinosis, Burlington's director of health and safety, Dr. Harold Imbus, made a similar claim: "We keep our employees informed about where we stand on dust matters. We discuss their breathing tests with them. We publish information about byssinosis in our company newspaper, and we use videotapes to explain the problem. We care about our employees and we believe they know that" (1980, 23).

Unfortunately, action again failed to match rhetoric. The company failed to make clear to all its workers with breathing problems that they had the symptoms of byssinosis. In April 1980 the North Carolina Industrial Commission cited Burlington for withholding this information ("Burlington Caught Hiding Evidence" 1980). The company was a leader in minimizing costs more than in helping disabled workers.

The key question in determining whether mills could use surveillance to minimize costs was who would control the surveillance programs. The industry won a clear victory in this complex area. The explanation of this victory requires that we trace the history of the surveillance issue from the initial proposed standards to the final resolution in late 1986.

When OSHA held hearings on the proposed standards in 1977, the Brown Lung Association and its supporters had hoped to have medical surveillance of employees performed by an independent entity, just as had been done in the black lung surveillance program for coal miners (Bronstein 1984, 1134). This would protect the confidentiality of records. The fear was that the mills would intimidate employees to suppress any problems and that problems they did identify would be diagnosed to minimize liability. The mills clearly won on this issue. The standards issued in 1978 made them responsible for performing the examinations on a yearly basis. About the only guarantee the employees won was the right of access to these records, either for themselves or by some designated representative ("Occupational Exposure" 1978, 27397–98).

The right to be transferred to some less dusty job with no loss in wages if they should be unable to wear respirators ("Occupational Exposure" 1978, 27396) was a short-lived victory: the Supreme Court struck down that particular provision in the June 1981 decision that otherwise went against the textile industry (*American Textile Manufacturers Institute, Inc. et al. v Donovan et al.*, 452 U.S. 490). The Court ruled that the provision was not justified because OSHA had not shown a clear health-related need for it. Although the point was not widely regarded as significant at the time and received little attention in news coverage, it was an important victory for the industry. Rather than complain about difficulties with the masks and run the risk of a loss in wages, workers simply might not wear the masks unless forced to do so. Then, if they refused, they could be fired. In short, mills were handed the means to pressure workers who might be developing lung problems out of the mill.

By 1980 it was clear to the Brown Lung Association that medical surveillance issues were extremely important. In a letter to OSHA Director Eula Bingham in August, the association complained that mills were using preemployment screening tests to exclude prospective workers who scored below 75 percent of expected lung capacity. Many of these people, who had spent all their lives in textile employment and who were looking for better jobs or who had been laid off in economic downturns, were caught in a catch-22 situation. Unless their lung function was less than 60 percent of expected capacity, they didn't qualify for workers' compensation or Social Security disability payments. They were judged too sick to be hired by the companies but too healthy to qualify for government programs. In addition, the association charged that mills sold to new owners were treating all the old workers like new hires. A mill in Bladenboro, North Carolina, had discharged all existing workers who scored less than 75 percent after new owners took over. The Brown Lung Association pleaded with OSHA to make sure "that employers will not be able to use this standard, designed to protect workers, to further their own ends at the expense of the workers" (BLA Papers).

Using data from the surveillance programs they had been running, the industry pressed its advantage with the Reagan administration in February 1982. Having lost in the Supreme Court eight months earlier on the question of whether a cost-benefit analysis had to be done, Reagan's OSHA announced that in view of the new data the existing standards would be reviewed for "cost-effectiveness" (OSHA 1982) rather than for cost-benefit reasons. Although the terms sound similar, they differ conceptually. Cost-benefit analysis focuses on comparing expected costs with expected benefits. Cost-effectiveness refers to finding the least expensive means of achieving the same effectiveness. The question was whether the Reagan administration would use this seemingly legitimate approach to accomplish what it had tried to do with cost-benefit analysis: weaken and possibly eliminate the regulations that were nearly in place.

In August and September 1982 the House Subcommittee on Investigation and Oversight of the Committee on Science and Technology, chaired by Tennessee's Albert Gore, Jr., held two sets of hearings in direct response to OSHA's announced review. Gore set the tone of the hearings when he scheduled as the first witness a byssinosis victim who was having trouble getting compensation. After Roy Dowdy, a Brown Lung Association member from Danville, Virginia, told his story, Gore invited him to "stay here to give a practical human dimension to the problem" and to feel free to comment as he wished (U.S. Congress 1982a, 11).

Although Dowdy was the only worker to testify, workers' experiences were the driving force behind the hearings. Paul Michaels, the Raleigh lawyer who had represented many byssinosis claimants and who had been a member of Governor Hunt's commission to study North Carolina's workers' compensation procedures, provided much of the testimony. He revealed that the surveillance regulations in conjunction with the respirator provisions were being used by the mills to their own advantage. The provisions create

hardships on individual workers because OSHA also requires that once you recognize this person is a reactor, they send them to the doctor. That presents a problem because then the doctor might diagnose it and say he is a reactor and send him back to the mill. He either has to be taken out of the exposure or given a nondusty job or they give him a respirator. When they give a person a respirator in a mill, they are basically telling them goodbye. It is a terrible situation. It is a large helmet that basically does not work. It gives them headaches and they become ostracized from other workers. In most cases when I have represented clients who have had this situation, they are gone from the mill within a year's time because they have not been given a nondusty job; the respirator alternative is really nonexistent.

Gore closed the portion of the hearings pertaining to byssinosis by ridiculing OSHA for reopening the standards for review and then wished Dowdy the best of luck in winning long overdue compensation (U.S. Congress, 1982a, 63–64, 67–68).

The second set of hearings focused more directly on the OSHA review. Gore opened the hearings by quoting Roy Dowdy's previous testimony, giving a personal tone to the complex scientific questions he was about to explore. Then Gore laid out the purpose of the inquiry: "In February 1982 OSHA again announced its intention to review the cotton dust standard" citing new health data. "What was this 'new data?' How credible is it? What have OSHA and NIOSH scientific staff and others in the scientific community said about this new health data? How was the data reviewed within OSHA?" (U.S. Congress, 1982b, 1–2).

Although the problems of Roy Dowdy and his fellow workers cast a shadow over questions about control groups, causality, and the like, the Brown Lung Association provided no testimony in the hearing. The only direct spokesperson for the workers was a representative of the Amalgamated Clothing and Textile Workers Union, who charged that the textile industry was submitting "spurious studies" to help "President Reagan and Mr. Auchter [the new director of OSHA] to accomplish what they have promised—the deregulation of American industry." Gore challenged the industry researchers on many counts and concluded that "the weight of the scientific evidence clearly supports the current standard on cotton dust exposure. The industry does not like the current standard and has fought it vigorously. Having lost on economic grounds in the Supreme Court, they turned to an effort to reopen the scientific argument that supported the current standard. . . . OSHA, at the behest of industry, has reopened the scientific debate because they knew of this study underway in industry, selected by the industry, and summarized by the industry, without any peer review, without any openness as to raw data, and on that basis, OSHA is now discussing changing the standard" (U.S. Congress 1982b, 247, 106).

OSHA published its proposed amendments to the standards in June 1983 and held hearings over the next several months. A month prior to their publication the administration did an about-face in its position on the use of engineering controls on cotton dust. In May it announced while other cost-effectiveness measures would be considered, it would not question the requirement that mills use mechanical means to meet the standards as originally set out in 1978.

One explanation for this turnabout was that by 1983 the horrors of misregulation in the Environmental Protection Agency had become a public relations disaster for the administration. Ann Burford, the head of the EPA, had been forced out of office. OSHA appeared to be the next possible target. An unnamed source at OSHA told the press that "what's going on here is just as bad as what happened at EPA. For the first two years we've done nothing but reconsider standards that were already promulgated under the previous administration" (Arthur 1983). Congress was using its powers of investigation and oversight in hearings in five different committees—like those chaired by Albert Gore—to put OSHA under the legislative microscope. The White House may have been looking for an example to prove that it cared about health protection and stop criticism. The OSHA source told the press, "I don't think it takes too many brains to figure this one out." Promising to keep the engineering controls in place would serve that cause.

In addition, by 1983 it was becoming clear that most mills, especially the larger ones, were meeting the standards without suffering any reduction in profit. In fact, they were doing a little better than the overall industry average, possibly because·meeting the standards helped encourage modernization (Ellis 1983). Hence, the announcement did not appear to bother the larger mills, which virtually all claimed to be meeting the dust standards anyway. Congressman Carroll Campbell, who represented South Carolina's Greenville area and was regarded as the congressional spokesperson for the industry, said "I don't think that the industry is too upset," because most mills had already met the standard. The only cries of anguish came from the smaller mills that had been unable to make the necessary capital investments (Ellis and Dennis 1983) and were now running out of time to meet the standard. At this point, closing these mills was to the economic advantage of the larger mills.

OSHA held hearings in September and October 1983 and took post-hearings comments until nearly the end of the year ("Occupational Exposure" 1985, 51225). By this time, industry was much better prepared for any testimony the now dying Brown Lung Association could muster. The American Textile Manufacturers In--stitute hired a lawyer experienced in compensation proceedings to challenge the testimony of the few association members who showed up at the hearings in Columbia in October 1983. A sympathetic observer described the hearings as resembling a court of law (Judkins 1986, 163).

The Brown Lung Association's strongest testimony came on the wage retention provisions and on exempting washed cotton. These were the only two areas in which OSHA acknowledged the group's participation in the final regulations ("Occupational Exposure" 1985, 51155, 51162). On wage retention, Brown Lung spokespersons argued that many workers would not complain about their breathing problems because they feared being transferred to lower-paying jobs. This made the question of wage retention a health issue. On washed cotton, association spokespersons argued against expanding the definition. Along with the ACTWU, they believed that any such expansion would be premature because a great deal of research was still under way.

In December 1985 OSHA finally acted, but not before taking one last look at the regulations—on the grounds of cost. This time the reexamination was at the behest of the White House Budget Office, not OSHA, which is within the Department of Labor. Labor Secretary Bill Brock had worked out an agreement between the textile industry and the union on the medical surveillance program. Ultimately, labor won on most of the points in this internal executive branch battle.

When the final revisions were announced, there were very few surprises. OSHA retained the requirements for engineering controls and dust level standards as promised in May 1983. A number of cost-saving modifications were added, however. For example, dust monitoring in areas that were meeting the standard was reduced from a one- to a two-year requirement. The definition of washed cotton was expanded against the wishes of the union and the Brown Lung Association. The new standard exempted most cotton industries that were not engaged in yarn production (knitting, warehousing, cotton seed processing). It weakened medical surveillance requirements even further, using the concept of "action levels": if a mill had achieved dust levels of one-half the required limits or lower, it would need to perform medical examinations only every two years, not every year. A guarantee of current wages for workers transferred to other jobs because they couldn't wear masks was the only positive for the Brown Lung Association—and even that guarantee applied only if an alternative job was available ("Occupational Exposure" 1985, 5122). One could argue that this limit rendered the protection meaningless for all practical purposes. If no other job was available, the worker would be forced to endure wearing a mask indefinitely—or quit.

Although the Brown Lung Association and its allies had been able to protect the basic requirements of the cotton dust standard, they were not the real issue at this point. That battle had been won once the large mills had made the necessary investments and modernized in the early 1980s. The important issue was worker rights in medical surveillance programs. With the exception of a weak right to wage retention, the mills had won an almost total victory here. They retained control over the medical testing and control over the information thus acquired, although the worker was to be given the test results. Moreover, they were able to lower costs by lowering the frequency of both medical monitoring and dust monitoring. These victories would enable the mills to minimize future costs of dust regulation, very possibly at the expense of workers who were denied jobs or forced to wear masks. Even giving in on wage retention was not a significant concession. OSHA, using industry data, concluded that because engineering controls were taking care of most of the problem and because "relatively few employees are unable to wear respirators . . . a wage retention provision will not create major costs" ("Occupational Exposure" 1985, 51155).

The Amalgamated Clothing and Textile Workers' Union, not the Brown Lung Association, was the major player on the workers' side in negotiating the final standards. To the delight of Secretary of Labor Brock and OSHA, the union and the textile industry had engaged in extensive negotiation between the end of the hearings and the final announcement. The most important tradeoff was that the union gave in on action levels, and industry gave in on wage retention guarantees.

While implementing screening and surveillance programs to minimize risk, the industry continued to fight the compensation of disabled workers, appealing awards in nearly all cases in an effort to force lower settlements. Even though the Brown Lung Association had succeeded in gaining North Carolina Governor Hunt's help in streamlining the compensation process, the industry had better contact with the Industrial Commission that actually decided cases. In early 1981 the North Carolina Textile Manufacturers Association put together its own twenty-minute film giving the industry position on a number of issues relating to compensation. It succeeded in getting the entire state Industrial Commission together in Raleigh to view the film, including the deputy commissioners who held initial hearings. The Brown Lung Association complained, stating that its representatives had been denied the right to talk to the entire commission and that the chair of the commission had been refusing to meet with them. Chairman Stephenson explained that the film had not involved controversial legal questions such as apportionment—but the executive director of the

Textile Manufacturers Association later said that it did include the industry position on "nonapportionment" (BLA Papers, undated news clippings). Stephenson was caught trying to obfuscate the impropriety of commission actions on a grammatical technicality.

THE PERSPECTIVE OF MANAGEMENT

Two days after the final standards went into full effect on March 27, 1984, M. L. Cates, Jr., ex-chair of the American Textile Manufacturers' health and safety committee and a key industry spokesperson, announced what sounded like acceptance: "People have disagreed with the standards, but the period of opposition is over" ("State Will Enforce" 1984). This was however, a different textile industry than had existed when the standards were originally proposed in the early 1970s. Many of the less modern plants, unable to compete with foreign imports, had closed down; they had also been the dustiest. Those that had modernized were using new, inherently cleaner, and less labor-intensive processes. Although Cates and other industry leaders still blamed the standard for mill closings, the more important change agent was foreign competition. The same mills that had the capital and foresight to modernize in order to meet the competition had been able to build in dust controls in the process.[1] Although the dust standards required that the mills spend additional money on modernization, the modernization alone would have gone a long way in reducing dust. High-quality yarn cannot be made at high speed if there is a lot of dust present, and dust can also interfere with computer control and the monitoring of machines (Interviews).

In the 1990s most surviving mills have accepted the standards and no longer see them as controversial. They are now much more preoccupied with economic competition with imports. In fact, some mill owners and engineers feel that the standards had a side benefit of forcing them to modernize a bit faster and more comprehensively. They have found that yarn quality is improved with a less dusty manufacturing environment (Interviews). Moreover, employees seem to be more productive because they are happier working in a cleaner environment (Castellan 1991). Others feel that regulation-induced modernization took place in areas where modernization was not as badly needed (Interviews).

Thinking back on the long struggle, mill executives and managers now grudgingly admit that there was a problem, though they rarely say it directly. When asked for an interview on cotton dust regulations, one mill president's first response was "we've got it all under control now," an indirect acknowledgement that something once was not under control (Interviews). In a speech on his mill's safety record, another said that fear of being hurt by working in mills used to dominate their public image, but that efforts in recent years had changed that image (Lord 1991a). A few even admit that the government probably should have forced the mills to clean up faster than they did (Interviews).

When asked whether, with the benefit of hindsight, they would change their strategy in dealing with cotton dust, mill officials' generally focus on several related points. The answer most frequently heard is that they should not have been held responsible for the problem; rather, the blame and responsibility should have been placed on farmers and ginners who delivered the cotton to the mills with some unknown causative agent. They argue that it would have been more logical to go after the source than after them. Some think that farmers avoided the responsibility because they had more political clout than did mills. (Interviews). Of course, this is another indirect admission that there was a problem, and it ignores the reality that it was their employees who were most affected, not those who harvested the cotton.

A second line of defense is that more research was needed before great expenditures were justified, that it is only logical to nail down the cause before spending great sums of money on preventive measures. Ideally, that indeed would be the case. But in the meantime, workers were getting sick and dying, and enough was known about how to prevent the disease to justify action. Of course, one can sympathize with the economic situation faced by mills. Their profit margins were not large, and no one knew precisely how much it would cost to make the necessary changes, despite the many estimates that were floating around. Competing mills in Third World countries were not having to make these expenditures. Officials felt they might be choosing between jobs and uncertain but costly methods of preventing an illness that nobody completely understood. Whether justified or not, when some mills did go out of business, officials were quick to blame the regulations. Some unemployed workers also blamed the regulations, according to surviving Brown Lung Association members who felt the sting of their former colleagues' accusations (Interviews).

Although research fairly clearly demonstrates otherwise, mill officials find comfort in claiming that not all the cases in their own mills were really byssinosis cases, or at least not "pure" byssinosis cases. Some maintain that cotton dust at worst only slightly aggravated problems that were already present because of smoking or allergies. They say that the Brown Lung Association did retired workers an injustice raising their hopes for workers' compensation claims to which they were not really entitled. They charge that the association, along with greedy lawyers, shopped around for doctors who were willing to make a diagnosis of byssinosis that was not justified medically (Interviews). Of course, they and their lawyers also sought second opinions if they disagreed with the initial one. Because of differing scientific studies, mill officials could argue to the public and convince themselves that the size of the problem was vastly overstated. They can now argue that there was a real problem only in the smaller, dirtier mills, now gone, and that as soon as they themselves learned of it, they began taking care of it through medical programs.

When mill management learned of the problem is another point of contention. Some officials maintain that they did not hear of byssinosis until the late 1960s, let alone know anything about how to prevent it. They explain delay in terms of "the learning curve" and argue that it took time to figure out what to do and technologically how to do it. (Interviews).

Finally, officials often argue that the government forced them to spend more money than necessary to achieve the needed results. Many feel that preemployment screening and medical surveillance would have been adequate, although a few concede that making the workplace less unpleasant had the side benefit of making it easier to attract new workers (Interviews).

Those officials I interviewed in a very unscientific small sample were divided in their overall evaluation of the effectiveness of the Brown Lung Association. A few credited the group with bringing attention to the problem and forcing a faster cleanup. A few more credit the association only with waging a very effective public relations campaign. The rest give the group little credit, arguing that it misled disabled workers and did nothing to pay for the research needed to solve the problem (Interviews).

With our own benefit of hindsight, it is easy to conclude that the mills should have recognized the problem earlier and should have spent more money on solving it and less on fighting the regulations and appealing awards. It seems clear that they did rationalize their positions—and certainly their memories—in terms of economic self-interest. Had they been operating a more profitable industry with less pressure from foreign competition, it might have been easier for them to do the "right" thing. But they too were humans whose position was determined by where they sat. And they sat in a region that had taught them to distrust government and to survive by paying labor as little as possible.

8

SUFFOCATION

The election of Ronald Reagan in November 1980 spelled doom for the Brown Lung Association. When Reagan and his advisers put his administration in place in early 1981, one of the first orders of business was to cut the federal programs that were the lifeblood of the fledgling grassroots interest group. If cutting was not enough, the administration went on the attack. It challenged the association's past use of funds, demanding that money be returned. It even started a criminal investigation into the possible misuse of grant monies. Within a few years, little of the Brown Lung Association was left.

In March 1981, only two months after entering office, new OSHA director Thorne Auchter ordered the destruction of 135,000 booklets with a photo of Louis Harrell on the cover. Although the picture had been taken while Harrell was still working in the mill, his somber, sad face with doleful yet clear eyes looking up toward the heavens seemed to foretell what was written behind the cover: "Louis Harrell worked 44 years in the cotton industry [for J. P. Stevens in Roanoke Rapids]. He died of brown lung in 1978." Harrell had been an early member of the association, attending such formative meetings as the one in July 1976 when Michael Szpak announced that he was leaving the group.

OSHA also ordered the withdrawal of three films, two slide presentations, and a poster that took a pro-worker point of view on occupational health. Auchter's spokesperson at the Department of Labor justified the actions in terms of fairness and balance. The pamphlets were destroyed because they were "too sympathetic" to byssinosis victims. Harrell was "obviously ill" and that "makes a statement that takes a side"; moreover, industry had complained of bias (*Brown Lung Reporter* 3, no. 3, March–April 1981, N.C. ed.).

Harrell's widow, Lillian Harrell, told reporters that "my husband was not an enemy of the U.S. Government. He was just a sick man."

The normal upper-class bias in interest-group organization was reinstated. Uneducated, old, and sick textile workers would no longer pose a significant threat to powerful regional economic interests, even if those interests had been weakened by a diversifying southern economy and by foreign imports.

LOSSES IN FUNDING AND STAFF

Funding had always been a pressing problem for the association. The group depended on three major sources: grassroots money raised by members in a wide variety of activities, foundation grants, and government grants.

The potential for grassroots money was fairly low. The relative poverty of most members and potential members mandated low dues, typically two or three dollars each year. In most cases dues were simply considered donations. No one was ever ejected for not paying. Dues rarely generated enough income to pay for printing costs of the chapter newsletters. Because the group was usually located in low-income mill village settings, friends and neighbors were poor prospects for donations. Mass mail solicitations raised some money, but never a significant part of the group's budget (BLA Papers).

As we saw in examining the birth of the Brown Lung Association, foundation grants provided its original lifeblood. Foundation grants continued to be the most significant funding for the group's activities at its peak and even during its long decline. Together with monies from religious groups, private foundation grants provided about half of the $300,000 budget in 1981. Staff members spent a very significant part of their time pursuing foundation money. In 1979, they reported to the governing board that they had applied for sixty grants. Members and staff made a number of fund-raising trips to New York and Washington to explore possible grant applications. In September of 1977, for example, they visited eleven funding sources and got leads on twenty-five others during a five-day trip to New York (BLA Papers). Most applications did not bring results. Over the years they received the most money from the Catholic Church's Campaign for Human Development—more than $310,000 between the birth of the group and mid-1982 (Dennis 1982), including a grant of $37,000 in 1979 to begin expanding into Georgia and

Virginia. Grants for expansion continued into the 1980s, even after older chapters with no more grant money began to fold (BLA Papers).

The federal government provided about a third of the association's operating monies in its peak years. VISTA began funding twenty staff positions in July 1978 (BLA Papers). This income was lost in July 1981. Organizers were not surprised. Charlotte Brody (1991) remembers that even before the Reagan administration took office, a person designated to become an official in the new administration—a protégé of Jesse Helms—told one of the Brown Lung Association organizers in North Carolina that cutting off their VISTA-paid positions and other grants would be a first order of business.

In 1978 OSHA had awarded the group a four-year grant valued at just over $320,000 for the purpose of educating active workers, the "New Directions" program. That too ended in 1981 when the Reagan administration canceled the last year of the grant, valued at $93,000 (Dennis 1982). After 1981, there were no more government monies.

The group received a small portion of its funding from other sources. In-kind contributions were particularly important. The Aiken chapter obtained the free use of facilities for meetings, clinics, and fund-raising activities. For example, the local Catholic Church allowed its meeting hall to be used for the making of family portraits by a photographic studio that gave the chapter a percentage of the profits. Volunteers and college interns such as those from the University of North Carolina School of Public Health, and law students in special summer programs such as one run by the Southern Poverty Law Center filled a number of staff positions (BLA Papers). A great many of these efforts never appeared in the budget of the association.

In 1978 the association attempted to tap more traditional charitable funding sources by requesting $27,000 and $37,000 from the United Way campaigns in North and South Carolina respectively. Both requests were rejected. When the United Way in Roanoke Rapids explained that the group was too controversial, several Brown Lung chapters picketed mills asking employees to make donations to them instead of to United Way. Shortly thereafter, organizer Frank Blechman founded a fund-raising agency for nonestablishment groups to counter the United Way in the Carolinas. It was appropriately labeled "the Other Way." Frank and his brother-in-law Mike Russell, another association organizer, dreamed up this approach on a family beach trip in the fall of 1978 (Blechman 1991). In 1981 a less confrontational label was coined, Human Endeavor. Much of Human Endeavor's energy focused on pressuring employers to allow workplace giving campaigns and payroll deductions. This effort generated some publicity but little money (Drogin 1980a); it never raised more than a few thousand dollars for the association (Blechman 1991). In 1982 South Carolina did allow Human Endeavor to solicit state payroll deductions, but only after the Brown Lung Association was removed from the list of charities it would fund (Mauldin 1982).

Actual revenues rarely met budget projections. For example, in October 1977 staff projected a 1978 budget of $492,641. However, by the end of the year actual revenues were under $200,000. In November the board voted to cut staff monthly salaries from $625 to $500. The next month staff discussed the possibility of cutting the number of staff positions from twenty-five to eighteen as a cost-saving measure. In 1981, revenues covered only $220,000 of the projected $300,000 budget (BLA Papers). After that the budget and revenues fell dramatically. The Brown Lung Association was just one of many groups that had lost government support, so competition for private foundation monies became even more fierce. By 1986 the budget was down to $24,000 (Dennis 1982). Since then the group has languished on just enough money to keep a few offices open.

The budget cuts of the Reagan administration that eliminated the twenty VISTA positions in July 1981 reduced staff jobs from their peak of thirty-five and a half to fifteen and a half.[1] Soon thereafter, when OSHA canceled the remainder of the New Directions grant, six more positions were lost.

The first positions eliminated were the staff assigned to existing chapters. The hope was that these chapters were now strong enough to stand on their own. The few staffers that remained concentrated on new chapter development in Georgia and in Virginia, as well as on associationwide matters such as legal affairs and securing new grants.

By the end of 1981 the staff was down to less than ten (BLA Papers). Six months later there were only five staffers (Dennis 1982), and those didn't last much longer. The last paid full-time staff member left in 1982 (Brody 1991). By the mid-1980s the organization was operating with only a couple of volunteer part-time staff advisers and the energies of a few dedicated remaining members. In 1991, the organization listed only three volunteer advisers on its letterhead.[2]

Without the guiding suggestions of organizers, and the energy and skills of regular staff, the Brown Lung Association quickly fell into disarray.[3] The culture of powerlessness that had isolated and separated southern workers for generations overpowered any lessons learned about the need for unity and sacrifice for the whole.

The traditional political imbalance was restored. Only the rugged stubbornness of a few key members kept any chapters alive.

THE OSHA AUDIT

After the initial cancellation of federal grants, remaining staff and members found themselves engaged in an eight-year battle with the Reagan and Bush administrations. In 1982 OSHA charged that the association had misspent the more than $220,000 it had received in the three years of the New Directions grant before it was canceled in 1981. OSHA alleged that money had been improperly spent on lobbying and demanded the funds back. Staff had to gather books from the remaining chapters and try to track down the books of those that had closed. Many could not be found. One chapter office in North Carolina had burned down. The Spartenburg chapter had stored its records in a building with water leaks; when the materials became waterlogged, they were discarded (Warren 1991).

By January 1984 what had seemed a minor irritant, compared with the actual loss of the grant monies, had become a disaster. OSHA disallowed almost all the money that had been spent under the grant and demanded the return of $228,783 (Warren 1991). Ben Judkins, who was voluntarily helping the group at the time, had the impression that "the Reagan administration really did not expect the money; they just wanted to discredit and immobilize the association. I don't think they realized how destroyed it already was" (Judkins 1992).

The association appealed OSHA's 1984 ruling, but the appeal was delayed pending the outcome of a criminal investigation of the association's grant activities by the inspector general of the Department of Labor. Charlotte Brody was interviewed by an investigator and answered written questions. It seemed to her that the main thrust of the questions was to see whether organizers had any ties with the Communist party or other radical groups. She had no such ties (Brody 1991). OSHA dropped that witch hunt in mid-1987 but then proceeded to demand that more records be sent for a complete audit. In February 1988 the association sent the agency six boxes of records.

On 7 December 1988, forty-seven years after Pearl Harbor, OSHA dropped its bomb on Lamar Case, who had been president of the association since 1984, when the previous president had resigned following the first OSHA attack. A letter from R. Davis Lane, regional administrator of OSHA, told Case that the "final determination" of this audit allowed $8,628.86 of the monies the association had spend and disallowed the rest, $222,094.38: "You are hereby requested to pay this amount by sending a cashier's check payable to the 'U.S. Department of Labor—OSHA' " (Warren 1991).

At this point the association had only a few thousand dollars in assets and no staff. Case and his few loyal supporters, vowing to fight rather than dissolve the organization, called on Bob Warren, an independent civil rights lawyer recommended by a former organizer. Warren recommended that they attempt to gather further materials upon which to base an appeal. A desperate plea to all former members turned up some additional records. In January 1989 Warren requested the first of two extensions to prepare the materials.

The hang-up was the Department of Labor's insistence that the materials be organized in auditable form. In the words of John Pendergrass, assistant secretary for OSHA: "The documentation as well as any other information provided in support of your appeal, must be clearly referenced to the audit report findings and page numbers." Unfortunately, the group could not afford an audit. They did hire the firm that had prepared audits and tax returns while the grant was in place to do spot checks and estimate costs for full preparation. The firm estimated that it would cost between $5,000 and $8,000 to reply to all of the 1,700 individual exceptions OSHA had listed. The Brown Lung Association could not afford even that (Warren 1991).

As a desperate last attempt to answer the charges, Warren sent OSHA the materials, not yet in auditable form, along with a statement by the accounting firm. He also tried to gain some political leverage by raising questions about OSHA's policies.

By insisting upon unreasonable requirements from a poor organization, you have denied the Brown Lung Association due process and have insured that this organization will be found *not to have complied with OSHA regulations in spite of the fact that the records showing its compliance have been furnished.* The Brown Lung Association protests this inherently unfair treatment and desires a hearing before an impartial Administrative Law Judge if you do not alter your position.

He went on to point out that there had been no problems in the quarterly audits performed during the time of the grant and that the group, having no money, had complied the best it could with the audit request. At this point most of OSHA's objection was that auditable records were not provided to verify expenses. Given the spot checks that had been made, Warren was confident that if the records could be audited, the expenditures would be allowed. He hoped to raise the issue of whether it was fair for the government to prosecute groups for failing to perform audits for which they could not pay. That was a policy question the government did not wish to raise. It might lead to government funding for audits (Warren 1991).

On July 7, 1989, OSHA once again ruled against the association, rejecting the new records because they were not in auditable form. Once again they requested a cashier's check for $222,094.38. They ended the letter by threatening interest "at the U.S. Treasury rate" if the debt was not paid within thirty-one days, and "additional collection actions" after ninety days (Warren 1991).

For the next eight months Warren lobbied to convince the Department of Labor that it was not in the government's interest to pursue the matter. He received some help from a new and friendlier congressional representative for the Greenville area. When Carroll Campbell became governor of South Carolina in 1986, Democrat Elizabeth Patterson won his old congressional seat. She was the daughter of the late Governor Olin Johnston, who had been one of the state's few politicians genuinely sympathetic to the plight of factory workers. Patterson, despite a very conservative voting record, inherited some of her father's populist leanings. She intervened with the new secretary of labor, Elizabeth Dole, on behalf of the Brown Lung Association (Warren 1991; Case 1991).

In early spring of 1990 OSHA gave in to the logic of the situation and possibly to Warren's threats to raise an uncomfortable policy issue. In any case, the battle was over. If the government wanted to destroy the association, there was not much left to destroy. No money could be recovered because the association had no assets; the struggling group had spent about $4,000 fighting the charges (Case 1991). A one-paragraph letter dated April 5 advised Warren "that the Occupational Safety and Health Administration (OSHA) has received Department of Justice concurrence in terminating debt collection" (Warren 1991).

The battle had a devastating effect on the Brown Lung Association, especially following OSHA's initial ruling in early 1984. It diverted the group's already scarce resources to things that were irrelevant to the goals of the organization. It frightened members and volunteers, scaring some away. Ex-staffers such as Charlotte Brody, who had been helping on a voluntary basis, became discouraged and quit. One president resigned when OSHA demanded money, and the next president found himself forced to remain in office because no one was willing to succeed him. In a typed statement of late 1988 or early 1989, an obviously frightened Lamar Case (n.d.) spoke of fears that he was being made a "scapegoat." Writing association members two days after OSHA had demanded a check for more than $222,000, President Case fearfully warned members that the association's president and executive board would be held responsible, along with staff, for the money (Case 1988).

The atmosphere during those eight years was one of growing panic bordering on hysteria. Association members, who had enough problems with poor health and subsistence incomes, now felt that the entire federal government was trying to destroy them. They were frightened, confused, overwhelmed, and even sometimes ashamed about rumors that their group had misused taxpayer money. It is a wonder that any remained loyal. Spending their time in gathering and organizing fragmentary old records was far removed from the exciting confrontations with textile mills and legislative lobbying of days past.

Available evidence strongly suggests that other than losing records, the group had done nothing wrong. In going through association files, volunteer attorney Bob Warren found a memo dated September 10, 1978, which stated that no money would be paid in advance to the association from the OSHA grant until after expense vouchers were received. Warren (1991) believed this meant that "OSHA was screening and pre-approving items for payment, therefore relieving the BLA from liability for spending grant money," and Frank Blechman (1991) confirmed that OSHA had approved vouchers. The agency never bothered to look at any of this. Its original findings were based on the fact that records were missing, and the later finding and appeal rejection on the fact that the records provided were not in auditable form (Layne 1988; McMillan 1989). Members of the Brown Lung Association had good reason to feel persecuted.

RAPID DECLINE

The contrast between the beginning and end of 1981 was dramatic. Early in the year the local chapters were functioning, holding regular meetings and turning in their activity reports to central staff. The reports reveal that attendance at monthly meetings averaged some fifteen people per chapter. Each chapter was still picking up several new members each month. Outreach efforts by telephone and by what organizers called "Fuller Brush" (door-to-door) work continued, with chapters making between five and twenty contacts each month (BLA Papers). But the six months following the loss of the VISTA slots and the OSHA grant positions were "a disaster," according to an internal budget memo (BLA Papers). The loss of staff was especially devastating to the chapters. When asked about what had happened to the Aiken chapter, the last president of the local group attributed its downfall to the departure of the VISTA worker.

The reason we aren't existing is because we couldn't get any help. We had three or four members like myself, and we were trying to keep the thing together without any help. We would go down [to the Aiken office] and stay part of the day, no way you can keep it going without keeping the office open. But after a while, we didn't have any money to do anything with, and you couldn't pay anybody, and you got rent to pay, and you got lights and water . . . and when you get our age, you're not able to have bake sales, and you can't get out and knock on doors. . . . As long as the government gave us money to pay a VISTA worker, we could keep one in the office. And they did lots of work. . . . You've got to have a leader . . . somebody who can get out and do things, not crippled and sick people like us. And that's why we had to close our chapter." [Interviews]

By the end of 1981 the association was making ends meet by not repaying the expenses of the remaining organizers and by borrowing money from the chapters and using the little grant money it had left. Few chapters were able to continue their newsletters, and those were only an occasional single sheet of paper published by new chapters in Georgia and at the state level. Soon they stopped as well. Other activities too declined dramatically, but not completely. The remaining staff did manage to hold some clinics and engage in lobbying efforts. The Greensboro, North Carolina, chapter sponsored two clinics in late 1981 and 1982 in nearby Lexington and Ashboro. Remaining organizers had hoped to form a new chapter in Ashboro, as well as in Greenwood, South Carolina (BLA Papers). The Greenwood chapter did get organized, mainly because the effort began in early 1981 when there were still plenty of organizers, but the Ashboro effort did not get off the ground. Other chapters, such as the longest surviving one in Greenville, gave breathing tests in its office on a walk-in basis.

In late 1981, members of the newly formed Brown Lung Association in Georgia testified at legislative hearings to change the restrictive statute of limitations so that those who were disabled could make successful claims (BLA Papers). The legislature changed the law in the spring of 1982. The amendment added byssinosis to the list of occupational diseases, increased weekly compensation benefits, and gave ex-workers a "grandfather clause": they had until July 1983 to be diagnosed and an additional year to file a claim. After that time, workers had to file their claims within one year after the last exposure to be eligible for workers' compensation. The association had hoped to have the limitation period begin running at the time of diagnosis rather than exposure, and they vowed to continue the fight. But as one member said, at least the new law gave "us old-timers a chance" (Munro 1982). The few remaining organizers had some significant success in Georgia, where they won a number of settlements for chapter members in Columbus, Griffin, and Augusta, but they did not have enough staff to move beyond these three chapters (Seymour 1991; Hudson 1991).

In Virginia, too, members lobbied to change restrictive state laws. The existing law made it very difficult to file a workers' compensation claim, especially for those who had been out of the mills for a long time. Claimants had to file within two years of diagnosis or five years of leaving the mill, whichever came first. Anyone who had smoked found it impossible to collect because the Virginia courts had interpreted the law to mean that the claimant must prove that exposure to cotton dust was the sole cause of her or his disability. Few doctors would testify that smoking did not contribute to the claimant's condition (*Brown Lung Reporter* 3, no. 5, July–August 1981). The remaining organizers helped members lobby for changes in 1981 and 1982, again by giving their personal stories at legislative hearings. In 1982 they were successful in gaining only a modest two-year extension in the statute of limitations, from five years after leaving the mill to seven years. This fell far short of the provisions in both North and South Carolina law that started the statute running only after the worker had been diagnosed as having byssinosis.

Ironically, the beginning of the association's steep decline came just when opportunities for growth and compensation were greatest. The group had won perhaps its greatest victory in the 1981 Supreme Court decision that upheld the dust standards. State laws and procedures were in place in the Carolinas and Georgia to allow easier compensation for retired disabled workers. North Carolina had begun penalizing mills that appealed awards by forcing them to pay interest if they lost the appeal. Significant change seemed possible in Virginia, if someone with knowledge, political skill, and energy could coordinate efforts—if for no other reason, because legislators might have been made to feel embarrassed that they were far less progressive than their two neighboring more "southern" states. By the end of 1981, however, the organization had begun to suffocate just as surely as the victims of byssinosis were suffocating.

The first chapter office to close was that of the Lincoln-Gaston chapter in Dallas, North Carolina, in March 1982 (Dennis 1982).

Most of the other offices followed within three years, but the formal closings came long after almost all significant activities had already stopped.

ATTEMPTS AT RESUSCITATION

In early 1982, faced with massive funding losses, the remaining staff tried to develop a new philosophy for the association. The key to this philosophy was the relationship of the chapters to the association as a whole. The proposals brought to the surface differences in how members and staff thought about the association. Staff attempted to convince members that they did not need offices and newsletters to have an association. A 1982 staff memo argued that though members saw offices as an ultimate goal, people and action were what really counted: "People make things happen. Members make phone calls, organize meetings, leaflet mills, testify at hearings. To the foundations, they judge us by what activities we can carry on, not by how many offices we keep open. . . . If all or most of the chapter's activities or energies are put into raising money for an office and not into other activities, then the office is dragging us down" (BLA Papers).

The problem was to convince members that actions were more important that offices. At a governing board meeting in February 1982, delegates promised staff that they would spend their energies raising money for the central fund. But a staff letter the next day expressed serious doubts that much would happen beyond this expression of "good intentions." Staff felt that members simply would not act responsibly: "Unless they get helped, urged, or reminded, [they] won't do anything to fundraise" (BLA Papers). The bottom line was that chapters never had become really self-reliant.

Another fear was that if members did keep promises to raise money, they "will be satisfied if they just raise enough to pay the rent, etc. [to keep their own office open] and not take the initiative to raise money to send in" (BLA Papers). To members, especially all of those who never went to association board meetings and whose only contact was through the office, the telephone, or the newsletter, the Brown Lung Association *was* their local chapter office. Most of the fights in which members did assert themselves involved questions of chapter independence and autonomy. The southern trait of localism dominated the lip service that was paid to association unity. When chapters raised money, they felt they were entitled to use it to support their offices. Ultimately, that is what happened. Those few chapters that had unique ways of raising a steady flow of money survived and kept their offices open. Those that could not raise money dissolved into little more than a local individual contact.

A fund-raising letter written in early 1982 laid out the ideal model the organization hoped to follow after the funding cuts. It represented the hopes of both members and remaining organizers, that they would still have both chapters and a strong association.

There was concern that the cuts in government funding of the Brown Lung Association through the Department of Labor's New Directions Grant and the Vista volunteer cuts would strain the association to the point where members would become discouraged. The results of the cuts were just the opposite. The members have responded to the cuts by increasing their contribution to the association. Now many of the Brown Lung offices are entirely member run. Members have taken on added responsibility for the planning of clinics and the consultation on compensation. The Association has found that a healthy byproduct of cuts in staff has been increased membership activity and responsibility. More than the nominal leaders of the association the members are now the organizers and the day in day out workers. For the first time many members are gaining the skills and the appreciation of what it takes to run a regional association of 7500 members and 15 chapters. This has allowed the remaining staff to concentrate in building in new areas, . . . legal coordination, the writing of materials, and the technical assistance to the membership. Chapters that need additional consultation from the professional staff are visited on a regular basis. . . . It is doubtful the association will return to the staff intensive model of organization. Although that intensity has paid dividends in the form of well educated capable members. [BLA Papers]

These brave words not only spelled out the hope for chapter survival but also admitted that the association had failed to realize its ideal of becoming a member-run organization. The letter went on to lay out goals for 1982. The key to achieving these goals was to be the learned skills and the initiative of members.

Growth is a top priority for the association in 1982. This growth should take two forms: increase in the number of chapters and members, and in the increased personal grown [sic] of the leadership and membership of the association. The growth will be aided by the number of large clinics planned in all states. . . . Development growth will result in the first Brown Lung state board in Virginia and the acceptance of the Opelika [Alabama] Brown Lung Association. In all chapters in all states, priority will be placed on the individual skills of the membership. If 1981 taught the association anything it was that the association's most valuable resource were its active members. At the end of 1982 all chapter newsletters will be totally member published and written. Members will do all the bookkeeping with the exception of the general ledger and payrole [sic] which will be contracted outside the association. An itenerant [sic] staff will provide the training along with experienced members. The association hopes to institutionalize this training within the chapters. Skilled members will train new members. [BLA Papers]

Members would solve the critical issue of funding by a combination of local efforts aimed at keeping the chapters alive and grants focused on specific outreach efforts. This way, members could keep the chapters they held so dear, and the organization could continue to perform the functions that defined it as an effective pressure group.

Local fundraising will play a larger role in the funding scheme for the association. This year the older chapter[s] will raise their entire overhead budget. Newer chapters are asked to raise half of their budgets and the newest chapters are attempting to include fundraising with some of their initial activities. This will increase the weaning for the association from the operational grant money. It will enable the association to request grant money only for specific program and growth projects. [BLA Papers]

Chapter fund-raising efforts never made up for the grant losses. Prior to the 1981 cuts, the central fund had given each chapter a $3,000 annual allotment for local operating expenses. In return, each chapter had agreed to send all the monies it raised over $1,000 to the central fund. Because most chapters were able to keep their doors open and telephones connected for a little over $300 each month, the annual allotment plus the little their variety of fund raisers brought in was sufficient. The monies they did send to the central fund accounted for only about $30,000 of the $300,000 association budget at its peak in 1981. In late September 1981 staff voted to reduce the chapter allotment to $2,000 (BLA Papers), but even that fallback position was abandoned by the end of 1981, when the association had to borrow from these chapter allotments to keep going. By 1982, the association could support only the new chapters. This placed all the burden on the established chapters to maintain themselves—something they had never done before. In addition, they were now expected to raise funds for the association.

The loyal core membership of many chapters certainly put forth a valiant effort, but there were too few members with too little energy to generate enough money to survive. For example, the Aiken chapter's fund-raising projects included selling plaques inscribed with various religious and secular homilies, cake and bake sales, a fish stew, gospel sings, barbecues, garage sales, printing and selling a cookbook, raffling everything from quilts to a woodburning stove, promoting family portraits for a photography studio, and sponsoring a weekly bingo game. The bingo game was their most promising and reliable source of income. Unfortunately for the chapter, the subcontractors who ran the game failed to pay their taxes. Since the contract made the chapter responsible for the taxes, members brought in another person to run the game an additional year in order to pay off the $10,000 tax debt (Seymour 1991). Disgusted and tired, the remaining members closed their office in March 1984 (Interviews).

Most chapters didn't last very long after staff left. Lamar Case, president of the remnants of the association from 1984 to 1991, succinctly described the sequence of events in a memo: "In 1982 and 1983 all the staff workers were let go and offices started closing" (Warren 1991). Greensboro, one of the original three chapters, closed in March 1984. Florence Sandlin (1991) remembers that there were only ten active members (including her husband, who had been on oxygen for several months) when she personally closed the office. The Anderson chapter hung on until 1987 or 1988 (Powell 1991).

The two South Carolina chapters that survived the longest, Columbia and Greenville, also relied heavily on proceeds from bingo games. In 1990, Columbia lost its bingo game when the operators were charged with failing to pay $5,000 in taxes. Unlike the Aiken subcontractors, the Columbia bingo operators were contractually responsible for this debt, so at least the chapter members didn't have to pay it. Nevertheless, the result was the same. Having lost their best source of steady income, they closed their doors in February 1990 (Pittman 1991).

Once the office doors closed, even those few members with the energy and skills to work on newsletters, keep books, train new members, or counsel claimants stopped working. For them, the closing of their chapter office meant that the organization was dead, that their job was over. There were no longer organizers to convince them that they did not need an office to do most of these things, to tell them how to do them, or to lead them in accomplishing them.

After sources of government funding were cut off in 1981, the association met with an adviser from the Catholic Campaign for Human Development at their May 1982 board meeting in an effort to find ways of generating a sustained income. Pat Speir advised them that they had depended too much on outside groups. He went on to suggest that their best hope was to work out an agreement with those whom they helped win compensation claims that the beneficiary would donate 5 percent of her or his award to the association.

For example, in North Carolina in April 1982, twenty-six victims received nearly $270,000. Had each of them donated 5 percent, more than $13,000 would have gone to the association (Dennis 1982). Such an arrangement would have provided a steady income to the association so long as it used the money to seek out more victims. To keep some pressure on industry and to replace sick and dying members, the association needed to recruit constantly. Receiving a cut from awards would have created an incentive to do so.

The governing board rejected their helpers' advice, however, and decided to try to survive with more cookbook sales and the like. The board did ask for a voluntary 2 percent contribution from those winning awards and settlements but argued that "most people getting this compensation [were] in debt" and would have little left over after paying their bills "with doctors, medicine, [and] hospitals" (Dennis 1982). The choice was characteristic of southern workers, who value individualism and volunteerism over almost all other values. As southerners have done for generations, they rejected external coercion, even when that coercion was a necessity for group survival. Group loyalty came second to individual autonomy.

Focusing the limited energy of members on fund raising created another problem for the struggling organization. There would be little time or energy left for the real work of the association: clinics, counseling, mass filings, complaints, lobbying, and protests. In 1982–83 the group tried to work around this problem by hiring canvassers to seek contributions door to door. They were successful in raising $100,000, but they ran afoul of state charity laws. Canvassers told potential donors that the money would go to the aid of byssinosis victims, whereas in reality well over half of it went to those running the canvassing operation and to pay the association's debts (such as money owed to former organizers and bookkeepers) of $35,000 (Dennis 1982). Canvassing operations stopped ("Byssinosis Group Spent No Money" 1983; "N.C. Bars Brown Lung Fundraising" 1983).

Despite the fact that the money enabled it to pay off debts, given the turmoil surrounding the charges, the project did the association far more harm than good. It created a great deal of negative publicity and animosity among members, judging from the angry letters and internal memos concerning who was responsible for mismanaging the canvassing effort (BLA Papers). The group lost some of the public legitimacy it had worked so long to build and found itself with no steady source of income, fewer members, and low morale.

With the association in decline as an independent entity, remaining organizers and members attempted to form coalitions with other groups. They joined the white lung (disabled asbestos workers) and black lung movements to create the Breath of Life Organizing Campaign (BLOC). The three groups of disabled workers and their advisers came together in a September 1982 congress in Durham, North Carolina, to form the coalition. The agenda focused on the problems of occupational lung disease victims. They announced plans to hold hearings on problems in gaining compensation, but without outside funding and outside help, little happened after the congress. Sharing headquarters with the Black Lung Association in Charleston, West Virginia, BLOC published its first newsletter in late 1985. BLOC's South Carolina headquarters are shared with the remnants of the Brown Lung Organization in Greenville. In 1985 the group also announced that it had written a national occupational disease compensation bill in the hope of reviving congressional efforts to reform workers' compensation laws, efforts that had failed during the latter years of the Carter administration. In the political environment of the Reagan and Bush administrations, little came of this endeavor beyond the introduction of some bills in Congress by sympathetic legislators (Judkins 1992).

Other coalition efforts also failed to yield any action to help the association. In a 1988 grant application for a single staff person to help run clinics, Lemar Case noted that the association had worked with the Workers' Rights Project in Greenville (later changed to the Carolina Alliance for Fair Employment), the Committee of Concerned Citizens in Augusta, and the Central Savannah Health Project in Aiken, South Carolina, as well as BLOC. Case had almost single-handedly kept the Greenville office functioning through most of the 1980s. He was the vice-president of the local White Lung Association as well as president of the remnants of the Brown Lung Association. Yet however his heroic efforts did little more than keep the organization alive in name only. With the exception of the Danville, Virginia, chapter, where a small group was still active in late 1991, the remaining contact people where chapter offices had been located all reported "no activities" (Interviews; Powell 1991; Sandlin 1991; Solomon 1991; Hudson 1991; Pittman 1991; Ford 1991). The combination of grant losses, staff losses, poor organizational decisions, and government harassment had been too much. All that was left was the shell of a once active organization.

Could the Brown Lung Association have survived as an active political force without staff and outside grant monies? Former staffers are split on the answer to this question. Some argue that it was a mistake to have become dependent on grants in the first place (Interviews). Others now conclude that the plan for a self-sustaining organization never was very realistic, no matter what vision they had at the time. The grants that funded organizer efforts allowed them to reach people that otherwise would have been untouched (Austin 1991; Hughes 1992). The imbalance of power and resources between disabled workers and the mills was too great for the workers without external help (K. Russell 1991; Stanley 1992). Looking back, Mike Russell (1992) concludes that the workers were more realistic about what they were up against than the young idealistic advisers who came from the outside.

9

CONCLUSIONS

The story of the Brown Lung Association may be worth telling in its own right, but the story becomes more valuable if we can learn some lessons from this effort to organize disabled southern workers. After a brief survey of the successes and failures in the struggle, we shall compare the efforts of this group with those of other grassroots movements to see what lessons can be learned.

SUCCESSES AND FAILURES

Many theoretical and practical issues complicate the evaluation of the success of interest groups in bringing about policy change. The definition of success and the difficulty in proving causality are central to these issues.

If success is measured simply in terms of change, we might conclude that the birth and growth of the Brown Lung Association was associated with change in the objective situation of textile workers. As of 1975, only a weak cotton dust standard was in effect, the Nixon administration had delayed setting stronger standards, and no workers had ever been awarded compensation for brown lung in the Carolinas. By the beginning of the decline of the group in mid-1981, relatively strict standards had been set and upheld by the Supreme Court. By September 1982, when the group was too weak to hold any more clinics and when most of the cases they had directly stimulated had worked their way through the compensation system, 2,295 cases had been filed in North Carolina, and 1,047 of them had won awards or settlements for a total of $14.5 million, according to North Carolina Industrial Commission figures. South Carolina's Industrial Commission does not break out byssinosis claims, but estimates from the Brown Lung Association papers indicate that of about 350 cases filed through 1982, some 180 won awards or settlements totaling about $3.5 million.

Legal changes in both Carolinas had eased the way for future claims. The group was beginning to move into Georgia, Virginia, and Alabama. Political leaders at both state and national levels recognized the association as a legitimate player in the policymaking process. For example, in 1981 the association played a significant role in successfully lobbying to change North Carolina law so that mills and their insurance companies had to pay interest on awards they appealed (*Brown Lung Reporter* 3, no. 3, May–June 1981). The Brown Lung Association had spent years fighting for this change. They enlisted the active support of Governor Hunt and the state Industrial Commission. The proposal came directly from the twelfth recommendation of Governor Hunt's Brown Lung Study Committee, which included an association representative among its members (Byrd et al. 1980, 7). They hoped this penalty would discourage the frivolous appeals that mills made in order to force lower cost settlements. On the national level, senatorial staff actively worked and competed to gain the support of the association for different versions of laws aimed at reforming national workers' compensation laws (BLA Papers).

However important these victories were, they were incomplete. Changes in the national political environment stymied the threat of federal intervention that had prompted states to change their laws. Legal changes to ease the way for successful compensation claims could not help retired workers with byssinosis if they were not identified and encouraged to file. Just after these legal changes were fully in place, the association lost the staff resources to locate potentially compensable victims of the disease. The association never again would come close to matching the 1,700 screenings performed in clinics in 1981 (BLA Papers).

Consequently, the decline of the group was associated with a marked decline in claims filed. In North Carolina the average number of monthly claims filed in 1981 was forty-eight. The next year the number dropped to twenty-five (Judkins 1986, 193). North Carolina stopped keeping separate figures in mid-1987 because of the drop in cases filed. Between 1982 and 1987 the average number of byssinosis cases filed fell to nineteen. Through June 1, 1987, a total of 3,416 cases had been filed with 1,835 of them winning awards or settlements totaling $30 million dollars. Officials estimate that in the late 1980s the number of cases filed each month in North Carolina was no more than ten or twelve (Hinton 1991). The average award or settlement in each successful case was $16,345. If we use this average and assume the same success rate for cases filed since 1987 (about 60 percent in North Carolina were compensable), then about $1.2 million in compensation has been awarded each year since 1987, bringing the total to about $35 million by mid-1991.

In South Carolina the number of claims was only eighteen in all of 1982. Only a few more than fifty claims have been filed since then, with just one in 1986 and only a trickle after that (Baker 1987; Interviews). No precise figures are available because the state's Workers' Compensation Commission does not break out byssinosis claims from other occupational lung disease claims (Research Department 1991). When asked why he had so few byssinosis cases, one lawyer candidly explained that it was because the Brown Lung Association was no longer sending him any (Interviews).

The roughly fifty percent success rate for filed claims in all states was not as high as the success rate for black lung claims in the mining industry (Judkins 1986, 193). Combining this fact with the high probability that many victims never filed, only a small fraction of those estimated to be partially or totally disabled from byssinosis ever received any compensation. Based on the work of Arend Bouhuys's group (1977), the most frequently cited number of workers disabled by byssinosis nationwide was 35,000 ("Occupational Exposure" 1978, 27353), including 18,000 in the Carolinas (Drogin 1980C, 2). Of these 18,000, we can estimate that about 2,500 (2,100 in North Carolina and 400 in South Carolina) received some compensation through mid-1991, or about 14 percent of those who suffered the disease. In other states where the laws were not significantly changed or where the association had a much lower profile, the success rate was much lower.

Until the association came into being, however, virtually no one had won compensation. The Brown Lung Association did have some short-term success in getting monetary help for a significant number of victims in at least one generation of mill workers. Without it, most of these victims would never have filed or won any compensation, because no one would have run the screening clinics that identified those with byssinosis among retired workers. Even though they represent but a small fraction of potential claimants, none of them would have been compensated had it not been for the Brown Lung Association's success in raising the consciousness of doctors, lawyers, and workers and in pressing for legal changes that made compensation possible.

Success was mixed with failure for even those who won compensation. Many, if not most, settled out of court under the threat of a lengthy appeal process. Those who settled received far less than those who had the physical and financial strength to wait out all the appeals. Here the association often had to do battle with the lawyers representing members as well as the mills and their lawyers. Association staff felt that lawyers representing members would often encourage settlement, because appeals meant much more legal work with little potential gain in fees. Settlements often dropped medical costs in favor of a lump-sum payment. If the lawyer's fee was based on a percentage of the cash award—as it almost always was—there was little self-interest in encouraging an appeal that would add only a marginal amount, if any, to the cash award (Interviews). It sometimes seemed to staff that the fees were all some of the lawyers cared about. One former volunteer vividly remembers visiting a victim's home while the lawyer was there to go over upcoming testimony. The juxtaposition of the lawyer's new BMW and the rundown milltown house created a lasting impression (Interviews).

The question of whether the Brown Lung Association had a significant causal impact on OSHA-enforced cotton dust regulations is a bit more problematic. Certainly the association actively produced input into all the political bodies that made policy decisions, from the Department of Labor's cotton dust hearings in the spring of 1977 to Senate and House hearings on workman's compensation reform in 1978, 1979, and 1980 and Al Gore's investigation of the dust standard review in 1982. Nearly all parties, including remaining Brown Lung Association members and textile spokespersons alike, agree that the mills are much cleaner than they once were (Noble 1986, 205; Baker 1987; Interviews).

Whether or not the mills are actually meeting cotton dust standards is open to question. Surviving Brown Lung Association members still complain that the inspections are less than thorough and that mills are given prior notice so that they can clean up beforehand (Interviews). Spokespersons for the OSHA programs in both Carolinas, however, deny that prior notice was ever given on inspection trips. Bill Lybrand (1991), who is responsible for enforcement in South Carolina's OSHA program, argues that workers often fail to distinguish between an announced consultation visit for advice and help in meeting requirements and an unannounced inspection visit. Mary Carol Lewis (1991) of the North Carolina OSHA thinks part of the explanation may be that when inspectors visit an area, they often inspect several mills to save travel costs, and word gets around pretty quickly. That aside, dust inspections have not been of high priority in recent years. South Carolina officials report that they still routinely do dust inspections and can document an average of about five each year since 1987. North Carolina, on the other hand, has not done many dust inspections since the several hundred performed in its early 1980s "emphasis program" to see whether the regulations were being met. The state plans another emphasis program in 1992–93. Both Carolinas have continuing problems in maintaining an adequate number of trained and experienced personnel to cover all the inspection areas for which they are responsible (Lybrand 1991; Lewis 1991).

Regulations require that mills take new dust measurements each time they change the blend of cotton for a new yarn style. Because modern mills run many styles at once and are always changing them in order to meet the precise needs of individual customers, this would necessitate taking new dust measurements on an almost continuing basis. Mill managers don't seem to worry about this requirement because they know that inspections are unlikely and because they believe they are taking care of the potential problems by preemployment screening and medical surveillance (Interviews).

Even if the mills are indeed meeting the dust standards, one cannot be certain how much the regulations contributed to any improvements. Textile spokespersons frequently claim that the modernization forced upon the industry by foreign competition has led to cleaner mills and fewer workers being exposed.[1] Others candidly admit that the regulations forced them to modernize more quickly and thoroughly than they otherwise would have done, at least in the dustiest processes such as opening and carding (Interviews). Perhaps the most accurate conclusion is that the Brown Lung Association was a necessary but not sufficient part of the complex political process that created the cotton dust standards. Once in existence, the standards encouraged more emphasis on cleanliness as the mills were modernizing.[2]

Those who organized the Brown Lung Association were interested in human goals that went beyond public policy. They wanted to help victimized workers gain a sense of personal power in their lives. The results are again mixed. Hundreds of individuals who felt alienated and powerless did gain some sense of community and empowerment in the waning years of lives that had been devoted to repetitive drudgery. The experience of those members who were most involved supports the assertion that actions are at least as important a measure of a changed consciousness as verbal expression (Judkins 1982a, 1982b; Fantasia 1988, 11). Even if members failed to sustain the association, it was a noble effort in the history of a region deeply marked by the tragedy of human waste and suffering. At the least, they claimed a measure of human dignity in the final years of lives spent in service to the low-wage industrial empire of the New South.

On the negative side, thousands were never touched by the movement; it never really penetrated the isolated loneliness of the mill villages in a large-scale way. The association failed to meet the tests laid out by Si Kahn, its intellectual founder: become free of dependence on organizers, take actions that involve risks, learn organizational skills, produce widely based indigenous leadership, involve a large number of people in projects that meet basic needs, exercise voting strength, gain positions of leadership in the power structure (1970, 116–19). Most of those who did gain a sense of power felt that power in a very individual and personal way. Once they extracted a small measure of what they thought was due them, most abandoned the larger cause of the group, never fully embracing the motto that was printed on much of their literature: "Single strands woven together make stronger cloth."

Certainly the group did not achieve all that its organizers wanted in changed compensation laws or in strictly enforced dust standards. They never got "presumption," their number one legislative goal, built into workers' compensation laws. Even some of their best friends in the legislature opposed the concept that the law should presume byssinosis for anyone who had worked in the mills for a given number of years and had breathing problems (Lourie 1991). Still, few groups, however powerful, get *all* they want. As already noted, it is remarkable that this one achieved any of its goals.

Of the policy areas where the association failed to achieve goals, one area stands out in particular: medical surveillance. Of all the many interrelated issues involved in the cotton dust standards, medical surveillance issues were those on which the Brown Lung Association had the least impact. Because mills won control of surveillance programs, present and future workers must depend on the good will of mills for their health and, should they lose their health, for protection of their employment (Bronstein 1984). One can only hope that the mills will show more good will than they did in earlier decades when they largely ignored health problems in the work force (Beardsley 1987). Nevertheless, even if mills just force out those who are developing breathing problems in order to avoid potential compensation costs later on, it may be an improvement on the past. It is better to lose a job before one becomes too sick to work at all than to keep that job and lose one's health in the bargain. Even in this worst-case scenario, the objective situation has markedly improved.

Perhaps the greatest failure of the Brown Lung Association was organizational. It failed to survive long enough to achieve more than a limited number of goals. It never achieved the necessary strength to provide the spark for a larger organizational movement among southern workers, as so many organizers initially hoped to do.[3] Its chapters were unable to sustain themselves without the organizer leadership and energy bought with external monies. Without organizers' help, their public image became badly tarnished, and they lost their status as legitimate recognized players in the political process. Butler Derrick, once one of the association's best friends in Congress, reevaluates it as having had no real grassroots support and being very unsophisticated (Derrick 1991). Although a few brave souls did the best they could to carry on, their efforts have been mostly ineffectual. Except for answering occasional questions from students, researchers, and a few people with breathing problems who seek them out, they have become invisible.

Looking back with the hindsight of twenty years, Si Kahn (1992) believes that he underestimated the problems posed by poor health, that he may have expected too much of people who were sick and dying. Sometimes it was hard even to conduct a meeting amid all the coughing. Both emotionally and organizationally, it was difficult to carry on when leaders were always dying; organizers had to train two or three times the number of leaders they would otherwise have needed. Because active workers never supported the group as they did the Black Lung Association, both leaders and followers had to be drawn from the old and sick. The inability to expand the base was critical.

The failure to build an ongoing organization posing a continued challenge to traditional southern powers supports Gaventa's conclusions about the obstacles that face the powerless (1980, 255–58). First, the powerless must overcome the strong sense of powerlessness that dominates their culture. With outside help, enough did overcome this obstacle to build an organization that faced the next obstacle: moving grievances to the issue agenda. The industry at first resisted by ignoring the Brown Lung Organization. When that didn't work, it brought to bear a wide range of powers to keep the issue of byssinosis off the political agenda: control over information, ties to local churches, implied threats of job loss and regional economic disaster, and exploitation of traditional fear and distrust of outsiders. When all of that seemed to be failing, the industry made minimal concessions, delaying as long as they could. Yet with help from the sympathetic Carter administration, the Brown Lung Association was able to engage in active conflict and win some significant regulatory and court victories on both national and state levels.

While this may sound like a victory for the ideal of political pluralism in the South, it was short-lived at best. As Gaventa argues, pluralism, especially on the local level, rarely ever develops fully, because the status quo is almost always too powerful (1980, 258). When outside support was cut off by hostile forces, the challenge ended in fairly short order. Some leaders were frightened away by the threats of government audits. Many members quit the group and went off on their own separate paths, encouraged to do so by the cultural value of exaggerated individualism—another reinforcing part of their culture of powerlessness.

One must be careful, as Gaventa points out, not to blame the victims of this culture (1980, 260). Though they were not without fault, the forces at play gave them very little chance for even the limited success they had. The South is still a long way from achieving a pluralist democracy in which the have-nots stand a reasonable chance of organizing and challenging the haves. The disparity in wealth and resources is too great.

COMPARISONS AND LESSONS

The life and death of the Brown Lung Association lends insight into the nature of grassroots movements when we compare it with other grassroots movements. Those who founded the Brown Lung Association self-consciously used earlier movements as models. Future movements will look as well to the successes and failures of the Brown Lung Association for guidance.

The Black Lung Association of disabled coal miners and their families offers the most obvious comparison. Beyond the similarity in name, the two organizations shared several characteristics. Both focused on the problems caused by an occupational disease. Both drew most of their members from retired and disabled workers. They had similar goals. Both strove to facilitate disabled workers' claims for workers' compensation. Both placed emphasis on preventive measures to ensure less risk to future workers. Both had the larger goals of community organization and the empowerment of the working classes. Both faced the difficult task of lobbying at the state as well as the national level to achieve their goals. Economic environmental forces beyond their control affected their fortunes by reducing the number of jobs in both occupations. Cheaper and cleaner sources of energy replaced coal, and foreign textile imports drove many textile mills out of business. As Judkins argues, both needed outside technical help in medical, legal, and organizational areas (1986, 187–88). Neither had membership with adequate skills in any of those areas. The two groups employed common tactics to achieve strategic goals. Both filed compensation claims en masse to generate publicity and to overwhelm an unresponsive system. Both used disabled workers as the central focus of demonstrations and testimony. And both attempted to increase their clout by forming coalitions with other groups.

Beyond these similarities, they shared common origins. Both movements grew out of the activist politics of the 1960s. Ralph Nader, a key figure in defining the nature of those times, wrote articles on both problems that served as catalysts for the beginning of both movements (Nader 1968, 1971). He brought national attention to the plight of both groups of workers and inspired young activists to become involved.

The Black Lung Association had a direct influence on the Brown Lung Association. By the time the retired textile workers were organizing in 1975, the miners' group had compiled six years of organizational experience. The initial brown lung organizers had worked with the United Mine Workers, whose leadership had come from the black lung movement. Brown lung organizers and members regularly talked to the black lung people about tactics and employed them as a kind of model (Smith 1984, 29; Blechman 1991; Brody 1991; Szpak 1991; Kahn 1992; BLA Papers). Thus, the similarities were no coincidence.

Finally, the movements were similar in that the election of Ronald Reagan in 1980 damaged them both. In a cost-saving measure the Reagan administration promoted a new law in late 1981 which undid many of the benefits that had existed in the federal black lung program (Judkins 1986, 106). By the mid-1980s the approval rate for black lung claims fell to 3 percent, the lowest they had ever been (Smith 1984, 29).

The differences between these two occupational health movements are more instructive than the similarities. Judkins (1986, 9–10) saw unionization as the major significant difference: "Coal miners have a history of relatively successful union experience, whereas southern textile workers do not." Even early organizers recognized that the black lung model had its limits. After noting similarities in a May 1975 letter, Frank Blechman noted the points where "the comparison falls apart: the industry is not unionized largely and hasn't been so that there is no tradition of militancy to draw upon" (BLA Papers).

The black lung movement cannot be separated from internal UMW politics. The initial black lung activists were local union activists who thought the UMW leadership was corrupt. Initial financial support for the Black Lung Association had come from a number of union locals (Smith 1984, 20–21). Black lung was an important workplace issue that they used, along with a disastrous explosion at a Farmington, West Virginia, mine (Judkins 1986, 66–67), to rally miners to challenge the UMW leadership of Tony Boyle in 1969 (Smith 1984, 23). One of the early leaders of the movement was Arnold Miller, a local union leader. His election as president of the UMW in 1972 marked the beginning of the decline of the Black Lung Association, as the union absorbed many of the movement's leaders and co-opted many of its goals (Smith 1984, 26; Judkins 1986, 102).

The relationship between the black lung movement and the UMW had profound implications for the life and decline of the Black Lung Association. The relationship between the textile union and the Brown Lung Association was different. As discussed in Chapter 4, the group would not have come into existence had it not been for union help, money, contacts, and retired workers with union ties. The group moved beyond its original union roots, however, to include nonunion areas and many nonunion members. Moreover, financial support from the union was relatively minor after the first year. The Brown Lung Association had to work much harder for financial support external to its own region. Although both groups had financial problems, dependency on support external to the South made the Brown Lung Association much more vulnerable to a cutoff in funding. As we have seen, that cutoff did occur, and it rendered the group nearly comatose.

The Black Lung Association could depend on a union base for virtually all its membership because of the high proportion of miners who had union experience. The Brown Lung Association's union base was very narrow because so few workers and retirees had had any positive union experience. Because the Brown Lung Association went well beyond a union base in membership, many of those who were recruited as members had fewer organizational skills and less understanding of how organizations work than did coal miners. Coal miners who joined the Black Lung Association were already activists with experience in union organizing, a history of participation in collective action, and collective ties to active workers through union membership. A key event in the early history of the black lung movement was the wildcat strike staged to pressure the West Virginia legislature into recognizing pneumoconiosis as an occupational disease (Smith 1984, 22–23). Within a week, some 30,000 active miners had walked off the job (Judkins 1986, 70). This kind of high-pressure collective action was totally beyond the experience or comprehension of most textile workers. Active workers never gave more than a few passing thoughts to the Brown Lung Association. They would not even join the group, let alone go on strike in support of legislation.

Union experience is certainly a profound major difference between the two movements, but it is actually the result of other underlying differences rather than the primary explanatory factor. The economic and cultural differences that affected the success of union efforts in these two very different geographical areas were the very same factors that affected the success of the two organizations.

How were the mill workers different from the miners who supported the Black Lung Association? The first important point is that the miners lived at the periphery of the South and developed a different culture because of different migration patterns, living patterns, and historical experience (Eller 1982, 7–12, 172–75). They were less southern than their blue-collar peers in the crescent of textile mills that spreads across the rolling hills of the heart of the South from southern Virginia into the red clay hills of Alabama. Thus the differences were largely a matter of degree. Textile workers were more thoroughly steeped in the southern culture of independent individualism. They believed that all collective efforts should be voluntary; they eschewed forced compliance of any kind. They were not natural joiners. They rationalized their disadvantages and risks. They feared retribution from those who ran the mills. Their strong sense of family loyalty prevented them from taking actions that might endanger the individual well-being of relatives. They had little patience with groups that couldn't help quickly and easily. As a result, they were often quickly disappointed when a short-term group effort did not bring quick results (Botsch 1981, 177–84). The culture of powerlessness that was such an important part of their history reinforced these tendencies (Gaventa 1980).

In addition, textile work presented a greater variation in health risks. Nearly all miners were subjected to a great deal of coal dust, but many textile workers labored in areas where there was relatively little cotton dust. These workers did not perceive any great risk and therefore had much less incentive to take any action. This meant that neighbors were less likely to share the same concerns than was the case with miners. Finding people with similar health concerns was more difficult.

Early brown lung organizers were aware of this difference. In a late 1974 report to Harold McIver of the Industrial Union Department, telling of his initial exploratory activities in South Carolina, Michael Szpak noted that the proportion of textile workers having byssinosis was not high enough to draw all workers to the group:

"Unlike black lung everybody ain't got it. That's a fact." But he thought there were at least enough to begin building a group, although he knew it would eventually have to include more than just those with breathing problems (Szpak 1991). The association never did get beyond this narrow base, which Frank Blechman now regards as a major mistake. He believes that organizers should have tried harder to involve more family members than the spouse; they should have created other units, such as auxiliaries of children, to perform well-defined functions (Blechman 1991).

John Kassell (1992), Mike Russell (1992), and Si Kahn (1992) all agree that failing to broaden the base was a major stumbling block. Kahn had hoped that the group could attract those who were just contracting the disease but still in the work force, as the black lung movement had done. Active workers could more easily have paid membership dues and would have provided longer-term leadership. Kahn and Russell argue that the organization should also have found ways to get lawyers more involved in helping to fund the association. Russell saw lawyers as often skimming off the best and easiest cases (those where smoking played little or no role) and avoiding the tougher cases.

If the Brown Lung Association had been able to win the political battle for presumption or even independent medical surveillance, it might have more easily persuaded active workers to join. With the textile industry maintaining control of medical testing and records, however, active workers were at the mercy of their employers. This dependence created a significant disincentive to join the Brown Lung Association, especially when workers knew how the mills felt about the group.

The physical and economic nature of the towns and cities in which mill operatives lived created relatively greater barriers for them either to unionize or to join the Brown Lung Association. After World War II the mill villages began to break up, and the economy of southern towns and cities began to diversify as textile jobs moved abroad. Miners were more likely to remain in the isolated single-industry coal mining towns of the Appalachians. Mill operatives were relatively more dispersed. Communication and meeting posed greater problems for them.

One of the most obvious differences lay in the accomplishments of the two groups. The miners were able to help bring about a federal black lung program and force reforms in its administration; disabled textile workers never got past first base in pursuing their own federal program. This comparison supports Piven and Cloward's famous thesis (1977, 24) that poor people's groups can achieve results only through forceful disruption. Retired and disabled miners could enlist the support of active miners in massive strikes, even when the union did not sanction those strikes. Disabled textile workers could offer no such threat.[4]

The lesson from these differences is that models of mass movements that work in one cultural setting may not work in another where power relationships and beliefs are different. The many cultural differences within the area known as the American South must be understood and considered in any attempt to plant the seeds of a popular grassroots movement. While the history of textile villages provides a few hopeful signs for those who would plant the seeds of protest, the cultural soil will support only stunted growth without massive doses of artificial nutrients—in this case, outside organizers and outside financial support.

In his comparative studies of the Brown Lung and Black Lung associations, Judkins (1982b, 1986) focuses on the important question of the relationship of organizers to members. Should a movement be led by a small cadre of disciplined and skilled professional organizers, or should it be democratically run by members themselves? McCarthy and Zald (1973, 20–22) argue that a small group of professionals can have greater impact on public opinion and policymakers in the modern media-dominated world. Organizers can use a relatively small group of members to create a paper organization and to act as props for media events. At the other extreme, Si Kahn argues for an open, democratic, member-run organization with as little hierarchy as possible, feeling that this will empower the lives of those in the group (1982, 10, 22, 32–39, 67, 148, 364–75).

Judkins argues that both the Black Lung and Brown Lung associations illustrate an important lesson on this critical relationship: a balance between outside professionals and inside grassroots members is needed for success. Outsiders provided resources and expertise that disabled workers did not have, including the ability to question the status quo in a social system that punished those who violated tradition; members "offered themselves as evidence" and put a very touching human face on often highly technical medical and scientific questions. Judkins charges that those who argue that the members should have been expected to do it all on their own are applying a double standard. Few expect those in business to survive without the assistance of hired professionals in technical matters (1986, 189, 176–83, 122).[5]

On the surface, the Brown Lung Association at its peak seemed to be a member-run group that received technical help from professional organizers and staff. As I argued in Chapter 5, however, the balance was in the direction of staff domination, even if it was hidden in friendly suggestions and advice. While the association appeared to fit Si Kahn's model of collective decision-making with little hierarchy and widely dispersed power (1982, 32–39, 148), or what Charlotte Brody (1991) labeled a feminist form of organization, in practice it was closer to the McCarthy-Zald (1973) model. Organizers were calling most of the shots even when they pretended they were not.

For Charlotte Brody, the lesson revolves around the notion of equality. Reflecting on the experience, Brody (1991) concludes that organizers were only fooling themselves by pretending equality among all organizers and members. They often wasted special skills by following the unwritten rule that "no one was allowed to have skills that no one else had" and handicapped themselves by pretending that no one person could do a given job better than another. It was counterproductive to pretend that everyone could do all jobs equally well. Those who were best at grant writing, for example, deserved recognition for that skill and should have been encouraged to apply it to their full ability. Instead, the practice of having everyone try nearly every job and of having multiple spokespersons represent the group often created problems in dealing with external groups, such as funding sources that preferred to deal with the same person on a long-term basis. Low organizer pay and high turnover only made the problem worse. In short, although members should be respected as valuable human beings and organizers should respect each other, a successful movement cannot equate moral equality with equality in leadership ability and skills.

If we extend the business analogy further than Judkins intended (1992), we gain additional insight into the nature of the balance between experts and members. Successful businesses must generate resources with which to purchase expert assistance. In the case of the Brown Lung Association, it was the experts who generated most of the resources to pay themselves for their help. When left on their own, members were unable to generate sufficient resources to continue to employ the needed experts over the long haul. Not enough members had enough commitment and skill to overcome the great physical, economic, and political obstacles they faced. Perhaps they were doomed to failure in any case, given the power of those who opposed them. Certainly, the great effort and great sacrifice on the part of many individuals did not create a self-reliant organization.[6] Throughout the 1980s nearly all available energy was expended on efforts to maintain the shell of an organization. Effective protest activities ended, and political decision-makers no longer recognized the association as a player in the interest-group arena.

The Brooklyn Welfare Action Council (B-WAC), a grassroots movement (1967–71) among women of color who were on welfare, provides a less obvious yet significant second comparison. B-WAC was the strongest and most well-known part of the larger Welfare Rights Movement. The cultural differences are obvious, yet links exist between this group and the two already discussed. The Brown Lung Association used the Black Lung Association as its model; the Black Lung Association used the tactics employed by the B-WAC activists as their own model (Smith 1984, 25). In addition, two important brown lung organizers were graduates of the Welfare Rights Movement in the rural South: Mike Szpak, one of the original founding organizers, and Dee Steele, who helped organize the Greensboro chapter in its early stages and was the association's administrator between 1976 and 1977 (BLA Papers). They had had previous experience in trying to transplant what was essentially a northern urban movement to a rural southern setting.

Providing tangible services was the central tactic employed by B-WAC to obtain members (Pope 1989, 35). The immediate need was to help welfare clients who were not receiving the benefits to which they were entitled because of a highly bureaucratic New York City Welfare Department. Organizers set up storefront offices all over Brooklyn to teach clients how to obtain those welfare benefits. They hit welfare offices with mass filings and overwhelmed the staff, refusing to leave until all their members had been served. The response of the welfare offices was to seek ways to relieve this stress by speeding up the provision of benefits. Each success brought new members anxious to get their share. Pope views all of these activities as fitting the Saul Alinsky style of organizing: mobilize, confront, and negotiate for change from your position of strength (1989, 46–47).

The problem was that B-WAC and all the associated storefront offices of Welfare Rights organizations never moved to the long-term problem of reforming the entire welfare system. They were too service oriented; the energies of leaders were spent on the short-term needs of members. They built a formidable member-run grassroots organization and called some public attention to the larger questions but had no energy left to promote broad social change (Pope 1989, 121–22). The Welfare Department co-opted some of the ideas of the group, such as having advocates working for clients and providing better information. It made changes that eliminated paperwork (and also some benefits) so as to reduce the ability of B-WAC to overwhelm its offices (Pope 1989, 57–59, 96).

B-WAC was dependent on too few funding sources and never established financial independence. It lacked enough professional staff help with broad questions of philosophy and strategy. Because protests could no longer bring quick tangible results to members, because staff could not make the transformation from a protest group to a more institutionalized organization, and because member-leaders were burned out, the Brooklyn Welfare Action Council folded in 1971 (Pope 1989, 122–23, 126).

Even this brief, simplified account reveals similarities to the Brown Lung Association. Both groups recruited members with a promise of helping to deliver tangible benefits. Information on how the system worked and institutional pressure on those that controlled the benefits were the means of delivery. But here the similarity ends. The welfare offices had the means to deliver the goods because they merely had to approve the paperwork under existing regulations. Reinforcement was almost immediate. There were quick successes to build upon. No adversary existed to appeal a positive decision.

In the case of the workers' compensation claims pressed by the Brown Lung Association, positive decisions were restricted first by state law. If that failed, decisions in the claimant's favor could be appealed in the courts—as they almost always were. This meant that the Brown Lung Association could not deliver tangible rewards to its members very quickly, if at all. The average person had more difficulty in seeing the connection between collective action and result. Because workers' compensation is highly legalistic and involves complex medical testimony, claimants had to be helped through the process by private lawyers and doctors, not by the Brown Lung Association. Identifying compensable victims, providing general information, giving advice on doctors and lawyers, and offering moral support added up to the most the group could ever do for the claimant. Persons who were successful in their claims might not give much credit to the Brown Lung Association for that success.

In short, if the balance of B-WAC was too far in the service-provision direction, the Brown Lung Association offered too few tangible services to attract many members. Appeals to active workers fell prey to the classic "free rider" problem (Olson 1965): if the group was able to improve workplace conditions, workers would benefit whether they participated or not. B-WAC stressed the immediate goal of helping individual members; the Brown Lung Association placed more emphasis on the general goals of reforming the workplace and federal workers' compensation standards.

Staff played different roles in these two organizations. Once B-WAC got started, staff were of minimal importance. It was truly a member-led organization—perhaps a little too much so in the view of Pope (1989, 132). In the Brown Lung Association, although members played important and necessary roles, they were much more dependent on staff than were members of B-WAC. Unlike the B-WAC staff, Brown Lung Association staff did discuss, debate, and plan the future (BLA Papers).[7] When staff left, the driving energy of the organization was gone.

The different energy levels of the members of the two groups explains much of their difference. Brown Lung Association organizers could not change this physical fact unless they could attract healthy active workers. Failing this, they were doomed to work with a literally dying membership who did well to make it to meetings, even when organizers picked them up and took them home. Leadership required philanthropically based motivation, energy, and skill—or at least a willingness to learn. The few retired workers who possessed this rare combination rarely survived more than a few years. Charlotte Brody, the organizer with the longest tenure, remembers feeling that it was time to leave the group in 1981 after she had outlived the entire original executive board (1991).

Public image was the one advantage the Brown Lung Association possessed over B-WAC. Middle-class taxpayers felt little sympathy for welfare mothers who demonstrated loudly for higher benefits—especially when those making the vehement demands were members of a minority and often "fat" (Pope 1989, 143). Brown Lung Association members protesting quietly in wheelchairs, sometimes equipped with oxygen tanks, evoked an infinitely greater measure of sympathy from middle-class citizens. The image was one of people who had worked hard all their lives, only to be cheated out of both their health and the financial means to survive. This was the most effective pressure the association could bring to bear on policymakers. Even so, it was rarely enough to match the arsenal of weapons at the disposal of lobbyists and insurance companies representing the mills.

Pope argues that B-WAC failed to transform itself from a disruptive institution demanding social change into a more formalized institution capable of negotiating with the establishment (1989, 132, 37, 42–43). This kind of negotiation should have been easier for the Brown Lung Association because staff played a larger role and because it had achieved greater community legitimacy. Yet Frank Blechman, a founding organizer who has given the fate of the group a great deal of thought, finds a similar fault with the Brown Lung Association. He argues that too often the group took an "all or nothing" approach with those in the political establishment—and got nothing. He and the others were never sophisticated enough to persuade legislative friends to set up behind-the-scenes bargaining sessions with their adversaries concerning changes in compensation laws (Blechman 1991). Perhaps the staffers were simply too young and having too much fun confronting older establishment types to think about serious negotiations. Fond memories of successful protests that generated positive media coverage for the group certainly came through in a number of staff interviews, as well as in the association papers. Compromise is a difficult value to teach to young idealists who think they will live forever. Whatever the reason for this failure, future organizers would be wise to give careful consideration to appropriate times for negotiation and consolidation of gains.

The Catholic Church provided both groups a great deal of support. It was the only church in the Valley area of South Carolina to sponsor Brown Lung Association meetings. The same was true in Danville, Virginia. Southerners traditionally view the Catholic Church with suspicion as an alien entity. Ironically, few, if any, Brown Lung Association members were members of the Catholic Church, the association's second most significant provider of income (after government sources). The local Protestant churches that workers and welfare mothers were most likely to attend lent little support in either case. Pope explains this lack of support for B-WAC in terms of its negative public image and some class differences (1989, 53). Many of the fundamentalist churches in southern milltowns are dependent on contributions from mills and from church members who are lower-level supervisory mill personnel. Thus, even though many ministers were at least sympathetic enough to be on the group's mailing lists, the risks of open support were too great.

Michael Szpak and David Dotson agree that the Brown Lung Association should have done more to try to establish links with local churches. Dotson feels that if successful, this would have reduced their reliance on the slow door-to-door method of recruitment. He is not sure it would have worked but regrets that he never really tried to develop such a link (Dotson 1991). In fact, coming from different cultures and religious experiences, few organizers would have been comfortable in trying to make this connection. Szpak, however, views religion as the most important community attachment that working-class southerners have. If they are to be drawn into any other organization, whether it be unions or a Brown Lung Association, the best place to start is in their churches. As of this writing, he is devoting his life to establishing this link: he is a fundamentalist minister working as an organizer for the AFL-CIO (Szpak 1991).

Mike Russell (1992), as a graduate of an Episcopal seminary, has a somewhat different perspective from that of fundamentalist Szpak. From early 1975 until mid-1978 he did try to build support in the church community in the Greenville area. He concludes that he and others underestimated the ability of ministers to engage in conflict avoidance. Local ministers, under cross-pressures from the varied interests of members, managed the balancing act by compartmentalizing their activities. They did sometimes allow the association to use their church halls for meetings and would say grace over the meals that were served: those were generic pastoral functions. But when meetings became recruitment drives in the form of clinics, they were less likely to cooperate, and they would not get involved in social protest actions. Mike Russell confronted one minister, who claimed that none of his congregation had byssinosis, with the fact that the association had screened two or three of his members as victims. Russell was asked to leave, and the relationship ended. The picture is reminiscent of that drawn by Liston Pope (1942) in the 1930s. Association members also compartmentalized their lives. Most didn't expect their ministers to go beyond the spiritual and get actively involved. Looking back, Russell believes that the members understood the power structure in the community much better than did the staff (1992).

The failure of either B-WAC or the Brown Lung Association to establish economic independence meant that both were dependent on the whims of outside funding agencies, and potentially vulnerable to manipulation and control by those groups. The Brown Lung Association found that it had to spend a great deal of time and energy on education programs for active workers because that is what was required by the OSHA New Directions grant. Although such programs had intrinsic merit from an occupational health point of view (Brody 1991), and education was one of the goals laid out by the association, the effort was almost worthless in terms of building the organization. It would have been better to shift staff to other activities, but the strings attached to the grant prevented that. When such funding sources dried up—either because of political and economic changes or because occupational health was no longer chic with foundations—both groups were in deep trouble. Organizations would do well to consider carefully before accepting funding for activities that may distract from their goals. They should certainly have plans for how to avoid the image of decline when that funding is lost.[8]

Finally, the members of both groups shared an ideological gap between the members on the one hand, and the theorists and organizers of populist grassroots movements on the other. Pope (1989,

142) notes that most B-WAC members were highly traditional in their views, unlike such theorists as Piven and Cloward. Brown Lung Association members were also traditional in their political orientation. Very few shared populist notions concerning the redistribution of wealth. Most accepted the traditional hierarchical social order. Most shared the feelings of other white members of the southern working class that the individual is more responsible for his own financial well-being than is the government (Black and Black 1987, 61). Their complaint was that too many of those at the top had failed to live up to their end of the bargain. They did not want the social contract changed so much as they wanted it enforced.

The Birmingham, Alabama, Citizen Participation Program (BCPP), established in the heart of the South and in an industrial setting, grew out of the political environment of the late 1960s and early 1970s just as did the other groups we have discussed. Yet it offers more contrasts than similarities, as Steven Haeberle's study (1989) reveals. The city fathers—not organizers or disgruntled citizens—began this network of neighborhood organizations in 1974, the year before the Brown Lung Association started. It was co-opted from the beginning—by definition. Because it was officially supported, funding was not a problem—as long as it served the interests of those who created it. The city had the means to keep it going with its own staff, even if citizens did not participate fully in all neighborhoods.

Citizen participation requirements for Community Development Block Grants helped drive this elite-led effort. Service oriented, much like B-WAC, the BCPP was intended to help city officials find out what citizens wanted and to provide feedback on the delivery of those services. That was its design. Its organizers and staff, unlike those of B-WAC or the Brown Lung Association, had no ambitions about expanding to broader social issues such as poverty. They limited the agenda to highly tangible physical goals that the city could accomplish: garbage collection, recreational facilities, zoning (Haerberle 1989, 12, 24–25, 122). These goals were much more likely to be realized, precisely because officials requested their articulation. In the other cases we have examined, officials would have preferred that the groups disappear.

The differing incentives for participation provide the most enlightening comparison. Haerberle (1989, 86–87) found that the free-rider problem was reduced by providing multiple opportunities for involvement. The organizational key was in using more board memberships, more advisory boards, and more committees, especially ad hoc committees to work on specific problems. Every person could find a niche. Meetings went beyond a passive audience listening to officers' reports; they broke up into small committee meetings in which everyone participated. These tactics helped members "understand a connection between their contribution . . . and whether the neighborhood organization succeeds with its mission." Haerberle also found that selective side benefits of honor and recognition helped in overcoming the free-rider problem.

B-WAC too employed the tactic of encouraging participation through multiple avenues of opportunity. Those who had won their claims were encouraged to help others fill out the forms, or run information tables, or prepare food and provide day care for members who were demonstrating. Pope saw the "ability to involve everyone in the group's activities, promote a sense of belonging, and instill confidence" as one of B-WAC's greatest strengths (1989, 69). Selective benefits, however, became an even greater factor here, as checks for clothing or furniture were given only to those who successfully completed difficult forms, and completing usually required B-WAC help. When B-WAC negotiated credit arrangements with a department store chain for its members, it added the stipulation that only members with at least three months active membership would qualify, thus denying those who would be free riders. (Pope 1989, 110). The problem that B-WAC had—unlike the Birmingham Citizen Participation Program—was keeping the benefits flowing.

The Brown Lung Association was at a severe disadvantage in providing either selective benefits or realistic opportunities for participation. Cleaning up the workplace would not help retired workers and would benefit all active workers equally, regardless of their own participation. Making workers' compensation easier to collect benefited members and nonmembers equally. People could go to the screening clinics and gain the necessary information about the process and about lawyers without actively joining and participating. Organizers were often reduced to pleading and begging people to participate in such actions as mass claim filings for altruistic reasons alone. Many claimants would have preferred to mail their claim forms to state officials (BLA Papers).

The Brown Lung Association certainly provided multiple opportunities for member involvement. Each chapter had fund-raising committees and various offices and board positions to fill. There were also newsletters to write, lay out, print, and mail, flowers to send to sick members, leaflets to hand out, letters to write to newspapers, door-to-door canvassing for possible victims, and telephones that needed to be answered. Nor was time a problem for members, since most were retired. Yet a number of obstacles prevented these opportunities from being utilized to the extent that they were in either Birmingham or Brooklyn.

The most obvious obstacle was physical frailty. Most members were unable to walk for any distance or even come to the office to work without considerable help. Educational limitations and a total lack of confidence in their ability to communicate prohibited many from writing letters or talking to officials on the phone. Those who did write letters needed extensive help in composing and printing or typing. A member would discuss his or her feelings, and then an organizer would write a more organized formulation on paper, asking if that sounded like what the member meant. Unfortunately, these day-to-day activities could create feelings of dependence as well as feelings of self-confidence. Even when self-confidence was the product, the communication process was time consuming and exhausting. Still, enough members found self-confidence to build a core of actively participating members. That active core was absolutely necessary for the success of the organization, and its importance should not be underestimated. But the rank and file found anything more than consenting to be driven to meetings and perhaps an occasional mass filing and demonstration to be beyond their abilities.[9]

Geography was a much greater problem for the Brown Lung Association than it was for the Birmingham Citizen Participation Program. Those suffering disabilities were spread over the southern piedmont, not concentrated in one neighborhood or one city. Associationwide meetings required five or six hours of driving. Even chapter meetings were difficult. Most members had no personal transportation, and many lived miles away from the office. One organizer could easily spend all morning ferrying people to a one- or two-hour midday meeting and then spend the rest of the afternoon taking them back home. Members spent considerable time sitting and waiting for other members to arrive or for their own rides.

The uncertain link between any of these activities and desirable outcomes greatly reduced any sense that individual efforts were meaningful. BCPP and B-WAC members could see fairly quick and tangible results; Brown Lung Association members rarely received reinforcement for their efforts. When victories did come, they were often symbolic and subject to further appeal. Between 1975 and 1978 the association members fought for the formulation of a cotton dust standard. When that was accomplished, they had to fight to see that it was not overturned through legal challenge. When the Supreme Court upheld the standard in 1981, they had to find ways to pressure the Reagan administration to stop additional review. After the standard went into effect in 1984, they had to apply pressure on state and federal officials to enforce it and to fight further review. That review continued until 1986, long after the organization had lost effectiveness. Winning compensation followed a similarly tortured pattern. There were almost infinite opportunities for their adversaries to appeal every victory. People who knew their time to fight was short faced delay after delay.

One might make a final brief comparison between the Brown Lung Association and a number of environmental grassroots movements. For example, the activities of the Love Canal Homeowners Association (LCHA), like the byssinosis controversy, pitted lay citizens against authorities and experts on difficult questions of scientific causality (Gibbs 1982). The question here was whether an abandoned chemical waste dump was adversely affecting the lives of those living in houses built where it once stood. The LCHA was relatively more successful than the Brown Lung Association because it had a number of relative advantages. Though both groups drew membership from the working classes, Love Canal residents were upper working class; they were much better educated and had much better connections. The brother-in-law of the housewife leader of the LCHA was a university professor who specialized in environmental problems. He connected the group with a variety of other scientists who had a professional interest in the problem (Gibbs 1982, 10, 16). Because it was an abandoned dump, the group's main adversary was unresponsive government. The Brown Lung Association faced an active industry with long-term profits at stake in addition to government. The concentration of the problem made communication much less difficult for the LCHA. Moreover, besides the possible health problems at stake for all those in the neighborhood, the danger destroyed the property values of all the homeowners. Their immediate self-interest was therefore more salient than that of textile workers.

Demographically, the citizens of the Southeast Branch of the United Neighborhood Organization in Chicago were much closer to the members of the Brown Lung Association. In 1982, led by Maria Elena Rodriguez-Montes, a remarkably energetic young woman whose parents were migrant workers, this neighborhood grassroots organization blocked the location of a proposed toxic waste landfill in the neighborhood (Terkel 1988). The key to its victory was not only energetic leadership, but mayoral politics. Harold Washington needed the Hispanic vote, and the group had enough clout to give or deny a significant number of votes. The Brown Lung Association never held such a pivotal position in an election of someone with the authority to give them what they wanted.

The experience of the Brown Lung Association compared with that of other grassroots groups suggests that any complete analysis must account for a wide variety of variables. The local culture in which potential members live is important. Exaggerated (and lonely) individualism combined with traditional values about the limited role of government and generations of acquiescence (or at least quiescent tolerance) to the social order does not make good soil in which to grow a movement that challenges the status quo.

Power relationships, which are often reinforced in the local culture, must be taken into account. A culture of powerlessness is difficult to overcome in any case; it is impossible without external resources and help. The promise that all classes can participate in the competition of democratic pluralism becomes a cruel hoax in the face of the kind of huge disparity in resources faced by the Brown Lung Association after 1981.

The skills and abilities of potential recruits are critical. More than a few must have the ability to do what is required. Otherwise, the organization will fall far short of becoming a member-run grassroots movement. Organizers should be willing to lead while maintaining respect for members. The other alternative is to try to force members to do more. That is difficult when limitations in skills and physical ability are as great as they were with disabled textile workers.

In deciding how far to push members, those who organized disabled textile workers into the Brown Lung Association were caught on the horns of a cultural dilemma. On the one hand, pushing them too hard would drive them away from membership. Organizational self-discipline was anathema to all but a notable few. Their culture taught them that the individual was more important than the group. Their culture also gave them so few skills and so little self-confidence that anyone who forced them to lead and make decisions to be imposed on the group was very likely to be spurned. On the other hand, a softer sell that attracted them would fail to give them the necessary skills and necessary sense of group discipline and loyalty. They would join and voluntarily cooperate when it suited them as individuals and quit when it did not. No organizer (at least within the white community) has ever solved this dilemma posed by southern working-class culture for more than a short period of time with more than a small number of people.[10]

Alinsky's dictum that mobilization must be aimed at quickly achievable goals finds some support in this story. The Brown Lung Association mobilized for long-term rather than quickly achievable goals, but such goals require an organization and membership that can survive for the long term. Attacking the regulatory process must be considered a long-term goal; the regulatory process is fraught with opportunity for appeal and delay. Ultimately, regulation is highly dependent on long-term implementation. That requires organizations with more staying power than the Brown Lung Association ever had.

The power that worked best for the Brown Lung Association was not the power that confronts and overwhelms, the kind of direct power that challenges the establishment at its greatest strength. The Brown Lung Association never had the votes to throw people out of office or the physical power to shut down places of work or government offices. Frank Blechman describes the association's most effective power as "delegitimizing" power, the ability to demonstrate in a dramatic way that those in charge have violated the social contract. He sees this approach as distinctly different from Alinsky's notion that power should be built to confront power. The power to delegitimize was built on the cultural strengths of the members as obviously hard-working, simple people who had not been treated fairly. When those in power saw that the public was losing faith in them and when they became uncomfortable about their own self-concept as moral and responsible civic-minded businesspersons, they were ready to make concessions to reduce their discomfort (Blechman 1991).[11]

In comparison with other movements, the Brown Lung Association certainly illustrates the importance of the free-rider problem. Unless benefits can be selectively limited to members, few will volunteer to become members. Anger based on altruistic values may have been enough for the few individuals who came to meetings regularly and helped the association survive as long as it did, but it does not build a very wide membership base.

One of the central questions that runs through the literature on grassroots movements is whether the poor should mobilize for protest demanding massive changes, or build formal organizations using more traditional lobbying methods for incremental change. While Piven and Cloward (1977) maintain that massive protest is the only real weapon the poor have, neither Pope (1989) nor Haerberle (1989) takes a strong position.[12] Pope comes closest in arguing that B-WAC members needed the formal organization to sustain them in their struggle and to protect members from potential organizer manipulation. She feels that massive protest had taken them as far as it could in the changing political environment of the Nixon presidency (1989, 94–95, 132).

The brown lung experience suggests that the answer to this question is the same answer we so often find in social science: it depends. It depends on the goals, members' capabilities, the nature of the opposition, the arena in which the policy conflict will take place, the local political and cultural environment, power relationships, and the larger political environment. No matter which path is chosen, it may depend ultimately on the unpredictable variable identified by Machiavelli, the greatest of all empirical political scientists—luck.

Even after a strategy is chosen and an arsenal of tactics selected, the environment can change, and gains may be lost. The change in the national political environment that took place in the presidential election of 1980 was paramount. Reagan was able to unite disparate groups in the belief that government was the problem (Schneider 1988, 57). For business groups, including the textile industry, this meant getting OSHA off their backs by cutting regulatory agency budgets and by appointing "administrators who were hostile to OSHA's primary goal, government efforts to promote worker safety and health" (Aberbach 1991, 240). Of course, the textile industry was selective in the regulations it opposed: it desperately wanted regulations to protect its mills from foreign competition, but it was less successful in this area because of the administration's general commitment to open markets.

The restraining power of the other branches of government prevented the Reagan administration's deregulatory efforts from being completely realized. But while the courts and the Congress prevented the cotton dust regulations from being taken off the books, they were unable to ensure strict enforcement. The administration put no real pressure on states to see that the rules were enforced.

More important to the life of the Brown Lung Association, the Reagan administration put an end to the experiment of using government grants to help realize democratic pluralism. It cut off the funding that had allowed the Brown Lung Association to join the competition among interest groups. It crippled what was left by demanding the return of previous grant monies. The association might have survived attacks on the regulations and the nonenforcement of those regulations; it was unable to survive direct attacks on itself. The bias of interest-group organization in favor of the wealthy was reestablished.

The story of the Brown Lung Association reveals something about the economics of deregulation. Prior to dust regulation, textile companies were able to survive by keeping the cost of labor quite low, at least the cost the mills actually paid. The hidden costs of ill health, lost human productive capacity, and social welfare were passed on to taxpayers (Hughes 1979). Supporters of the Reagan administration's goal of freeing industry from strangulating regulations rarely considered those hidden costs (or what economists call "externalities").

Had the administration succeeded in removing all the regulations, it is still doubtful that the old, labor-intensive textile industry could have survived. Even passing hidden costs on to taxpayers and relying on minimum-wage workers, the industry could not have competed with foreign mills that pay only a small fraction of the United States minimum wage. Savings on regulations would not have made up the difference. The only mills that could survive were those that went into high-tech production of high-quality goods: those that became capital intensive rather than labor intensive. From this perspective, the regulations hurried up an inevitable process. Now the hidden costs for cheap cotton goods are being paid by foreign workers. Whether they are better off risking their lungs at subsistence wages or being unemployed in abject poverty is a difficult moral dilemma.

One might argue that the Brown Lung Association took a very traditional political route for oppressed southern groups. It attempted to shift from a local to a national political arena where regionally powerful interests had less control over the political agenda. To the extent that state institutions changed sufficiently to make compensation at least possible, fear of federal intervention played a significant causal role. The link between compensation and the goal of cleaning up the mills was never really established, however. Compensation awards never totaled enough to make it cheaper for the mills to clean up, as had been envisioned in the original strategy laid out by Ralph Nader. Nevertheless, it is clear that the association played a major role in overcoming regional textile interests' efforts to prevent the establishment of national cotton dust standards. Once the regulations were in place, the Brown Lung Association was less successful in influencing implementation, largely because of its inability to penetrate the workplace and because textile interests were relatively so much more important at the state level, where responsibility for implementation rested.

The Brown Lung Association was spawned by the political climate of the 1960s and 1970s. It was an expression of young idealistic organizers' faith in Jeffersonian democracy, their belief that poor disabled retired workers could be organized into a democratic, self-run interest group in a region where the poor seldom played an active role in politics beyond occasionally answering the calls of demagogic leaders, who usually offered false hopes. For a short time, organizers and a few hundred active members met success. With the aid of grants from sympathetic foundations and a presidential administration that was sensitive to workers' problems, they captured media attention with their sad stories of exploitation, neglect, and betrayal. They played a necessary though not sufficient role in modestly, yet significantly, reforming state workers' compensation laws in the Carolinas and to a lesser extent in Georgia. They played an essential role in bringing about and protecting cotton dust standards that indirectly hurried the much-needed modernization of textile mills, thus doing the industry an unwanted favor.

In the final analysis, however, the balance and structure of political power in their communities and in the nation were too much against them. They suffered too many weaknesses to play a part in the drama of southern politics very long. They were too few, too old and sick, too spread out and isolated, too dependent on external grants that were available only because of unique historical conditions, and too southern. Because a culture of powerlessness had denied members the resources to maintain a viable organization, they were too dependent on the suggestions of the well-educated young organizers. Despite some collective experiences and collective victories, too few embraced a sense of collective good once their own personal good had been determined one way or another. Unwilling to relinquish their independence in voluntary personal action or the autonomy of their local chapters for the greater good of the association as a whole, they rejected mandatory plans that provided the only chance for organizational survival, small though it was.

After being temporarily upstaged, a traditional big-name actor in southern politics—textiles—seized the lead role. Consequently, the Brown Lung Association was written out of the script, and the play had a short run. Members were doomed to leave the stage of this tragic southern drama as yet another group of failed working-class heroes.

EPILOGUE

The view of the Dan River, as one comes down North Main Street in Danville, Virginia, is dominated by a huge neon sign proclaiming the city to be the home of Dan River Fabrics. The letters seemed to melt into the landscape through the moist air of the late spring 1991 evening at dusk. Because it was so familiar to them, the half-dozen members of the Danville Brown Lung Association who made it to their monthly meeting to meet the college professor who was writing a book may not have noticed this scene.

I had hoped to observe their meeting quietly and ask a few questions when it was over; instead, I found a hand-lettered sign on their storefront office saying "Welcome Dr. Botsch." Because the lawyer-legislator who was scheduled to speak to them about problems in the Virginia Workers' Compensation law had canceled, I was to be the centerpiece of their meeting. After I went through my usual questions about activities, membership, and fund raising, they asked me for advice on what they could do to accomplish their goals. I found myself playing the same role that organizers had played ten years earlier, offering friendly suggestions about how to locate and recruit new members and how to create favorable publicity. Through the thin wall came loud songs and cries of praise to God from a small group of fundamentalist Christians meeting next door. Their fervor was so great that at times we could hardly hear one another speak. The Brown Lung Association no longer has that kind of energy or fervor.

The Danville chapter, one of the two remaining chapters that still maintain an office (the other is in Greenville, South Carolina), resembles many of the other chapters that were formed in the late 1970s, except that it has survived. Its few members either have potential claims themselves or have spouses with breathing problems.

Alice Adkins, who replaced Lamar Case of Greenville as association
president in 1991, lost her husband to lung disease. He and a number of the other original members had been union supporters before
they became Brown Lung Association members. His claim of byssinosis was denied because he had been a heavy smoker for many
years. She stubbornly fights on in his memory, out of a deep sense
of personal anger that he was not treated fairly by the mill or by
the state.

The overall membership in Danville has dwindled from a peak
of fifty or sixty to little more than a dozen people in the area. Many
of those originally recruited by the organizers—who departed in
1982—became discouraged and left the association after their
claims were turned down. The chapter subsists on an annual dona-
tion from a mysterious stranger in New York who pays its $150-a-
month rent and utilities. The members send him thank you notes.
The effort of a handful of friends and volunteers keeps the phone answered and prints a short newsletter every few months, which is
sent to the roughly 300 people left on the entire association mailing
list. The chapter still sells cookbooks and holds bake sales, but
without the energy and knowledge of an organizer the members are
able to do little more than keep the office open and answer questions if someone should ask any.

Policy changes are still needed in Virginia. The state's compensation laws are so difficult that to the best of the members' knowledge, no one has ever won a claim there. The same tactics that
brought about policy change in the Carolinas might yet work in Virginia—if someone had the time, energy, and knowledge to locate
those who left the mills with breathing problems and organize them
into protest groups. That is unlikely to happen. The unique historical circumstances that linked organizers and resources with disabled workers no longer exist. There is no pressure at the national
level. Moreover, time is running out. Through surveillance programs, mills are greatly reducing, if not eliminating, the number of
people who leave the mills with potentially compensable lung problems. Workers who left in the 1970s are dead or dying.

Those who organized the association have moved to other activities that serve their strong notions of social justice. Frank Blechman works as an associate at the Conflict Clinic, a nonprofit
organization at George Mason University in Fairfax, Virginia, which
applies theoretical knowledge in helping people resolve disputes
both here and abroad. Charlotte Brody directs Planned Parenthood
in Charlotte, North Carolina. She feels that Planned Parenthood has
a great advantage over the Brown Lung Association in that it is not

overly dependent on the whims of foundations. It generates most of its own funding by providing quality services for which people are willing to pay. This allows her to fund community organizing around public health issues in a much more stable way than the Brown Lung Association could. Michael Szpak is an ordained minister who works for the AFL-CIO, trying to make the unlikely link between fundamentalist religious groups and union organization which he first envisioned when organizing in Greenville in 1975. Si Kahn continues to be involved in promoting community organization through the Grassroots Leadership Program out of Charlotte, North Carolina. Len Stanley and Dave Austin work together on a well-funded program to decrease smoking in ten communities across the nation. Chip Hughes spent seven years organizing migrant farm workers after leaving the Brown Lung Association in late 1979, and he currently trains those who work with hazardous wastes in a program supported by the Environmental Protection Agency's "superfund." Mike and Kathy Russell, who took turns working as organizers in western South Carolina from early 1976 until they left the area in early 1982, are both ministers at an Episcopal church in Maryland. David Dotson, who organized the Aiken chapter, now directs Catholic Charities in Knoxville, Tennessee. John Kassell, who came south from Washington, D.C., in early 1979, fell in love with South Carolina and earned his law degree there after leaving the association in late 1981 when funding went dry; he practices law in Columbia. Two of the last organizers, also went into law: Mary Lou Seymour works for Legal Services in Columbia, and Greg Campbell went on to law school.

The Brown Lung Association is nearly gone as a visible organization. There remain only a few faithful members such as Lamar Case and Alice Adkins, who do the best they can to keep the group alive. Although I certainly do not wish to exaggerate the reports of the death of the Brown Lung Association, barring some rejuvenating miracle the group soon will pass the way of most of its membership.

CHRONOLOGY

TIME LINE OF SIGNIFICANT EVENTS IN THE EVOLUTION OF COTTON DUST STANDARDS AND THE BROWN LUNG ASSOCIATION

1705: Ramazzini describes long-term and short-term symptoms of cotton dust–related lung disease in his study of mill workers.

1877: Adrien Proust names the disease "byssinosis."

1920s: A British study finds high rates of respiratory problems among textile workers.

1932: The U.S. Public Health Service performs a methodologically flawed study of one cotton mill and concludes that there is no problem in the United States.

1936: A mill worker in North Carolina files for workmen's compensation because of breathing problems. The state's Industrial Commission denies his claim.

1940: After a decade of study, the British Parliament makes compensation available to textile workers who have had at least twenty years of cotton dust exposure. It also identifies the classic symptoms of "Monday morning syndrome."

1947: The U.S. Public Health Service attempts to resolve conflicts by reviewing all research but reaches no definite conclusions.

1949: South Carolina allows compensation for occupational lung disease.

1950s: British doctor Richard Schilling derives a four-point grading system ($\frac{1}{2}$, 1, 2, 3) for the progressive stages of byssinosis, and identifies the causal agent as something in the boll of the cotton, not the cotton itself.

1960: Schilling is allowed to study workers in two American mills and finds high rates of symptoms, challenging the belief that byssinosis is not a problem in the United States.

1964: Dr. Arend Bouhuys performs studies (published in 1967 and 1969) of mill workers in the Atlanta federal penitentiary. His finding that one-third have byssinosis prompts intensive research by a wide variety of parties. The American Conference of Governmental Industrial Hygienists (ACGIH) lists cotton dust as potentially dangerous as a result of Schilling's work; two years later it recommends an exposure limit of 1 milligram per cubic meter of air.

1967: The North Carolina Board of Health performs the first state study of byssinosis and finds a 13 percent incidence among mill workers.

1968: The U.S. Labor Department adopts the 1 milligram standard as a regulation under the Walsh-Healey Act, which applies to all companies doing business with the government; this is the first official regulation in the United States.

1969: Burlington allows an epidemiological study of all its mill employees; it is concluded in 1971 with a finding of acute symptoms of byssinosis in nearly 40 percent of cardroom workers.

1970: Congress passes the Occupational Safety Health Act, which creates the Occupational Safety Health Administration (OSHA) and its research arm, the National Institute for Occupational Safety and Health (NIOSH). The bill also creates the National Commission on Workmen's Compensation to study the adequacy of existing state systems, and adopts 1 milligram as a temporary standard.

FEBRUARY. Burlington Industries allows Duke University and North Carolina Board of Health doctors to study its workers.

MAY. A national conference on cotton dust is held in Charlotte. Dr. James Merchant of the North Carolina Board of Health estimates that 25 percent of workers exposed to dust may develop byssinosis.

1971: Ralph Nader popularizes byssinosis as "brown lung" and lays out strategy for a grassroots movement. North Carolina amends its law to allow compensation for occupational diseases caused by the inhalation of dust, clearing the way for settlement of seventeen byssinosis claims in 1971–72.

1974: ACGIH recommends a standard of 0.2 milligram as measured by a "vertical elutriator," which soon becomes the standard instrument for measuring respirable dust.

JANUARY. The North Carolina OSHA makes its first mill inspection for cotton dust.

JUNE. The South Carolina OSHA makes its first mill inspection for cotton dust.

JULY. Young people interested in organizing around the issue of byssinosis meet at the Highlander School outside Knoxville, Tennessee.

AUGUST. The Brookside Mine strike in Kentucky ends, and those involved seek other issues around which to organize. Workers at the J.P. Stevens Mill in Roanoke Rapids, North Carolina, vote to be represented by the Textile Workers Union of America (TWUA).

SEPTEMBER. NIOSH recommends industrywide standards of a maximum of 0.2 milligram per cubic meter.

SEPTEMBER–DECEMBER. Mike Szpak develops preliminary plans for organizing disabled workers in Greenville, South Carolina.

DECEMBER. OSHA gives advance notice that it will soon begin considering a permanent dust standard and calls for interested parties to submit views. Those hearings do not take place for two more years. Mike Szpak, Si Kahn, Frank Blechman, Charlotte Brody, and others write grant proposals to fund their organizing efforts.

1975: The TWUA and Ralph Nader's Public Interest Research Group (PIRG) file a petition with the secretary of labor calling for a standard of 0.1 milligram. TWUA brings suit against OSHA to issue new standards.

MARCH. Szpak and Blechman form the Southern Institute for Occupational Health (SIOH).

APRIL. Because of problems in Greenville, organizers shift their initial organizing work to Columbia, South Carolina. On April 25 the first mass meeting of the Carolina Brown Lung Association (BLA) is held in Columbia. More than 125 people attend.

JUNE. In Greensboro, North Carolina, the association's first screening clinic is held; 100 people attend.

AUGUST. The Greensboro chapter is organized.

NOVEMBER. The Spartanburg, South Carolina, chapter is organized. Only 33 workers' compensation claims for byssinosis have been filed in North Carolina, and none in South Carolina until the first mass filing of claims is staged by twenty-seven members of the Columbia chapter.

1976: The Textile Workers Union of America (TWUA) and the Amalgamated Clothing Workers of America (ACWA) merge to form the Amalgamated Clothing and Textile Workers Union (ACTWU).

JANUARY–MARCH. The Greenville chapter is organized and later becomes one of the most active in protest activities. Chapters are organized in Roanoke Rapids and Erwin, North Carolina.

MAY. Youth Project threatens to cut off funding because of the split between two original organizers Frank Blechman and Mike Szpak.

JULY. The Blechman faction gains control, and Szpak announces his departure. A bi-state governing board is discussed.

AUGUST. The bi-state board is created.

SEPTEMBER. Youth Project reinstates its grants.

NOVEMBER. Jimmy Carter is elected president.

DECEMBER. The initial OSHA cotton dust proposal is published, calling for a standard of 0.2 milligram per cubic meter as measured by the vertical elutriator for all parts of the textile industry. ACTWU drops its suit after the proposed standards are published. By end of year, BLA up to six chapters.

1977: JANUARY. Carter takes office. BLA members confer at Highlander with Black Lung Association members.

FEBRUARY. The North Carolina OSHA director takes a job with the American Textile Manufacturers' Institute (ATMI) to help with the industry side of upcoming hearings.

APRIL–MAY. OSHA hearings on the proposed standards are held in Washington, D.C., Mississippi, and Texas; further comments are accepted until September. Brown Lung Association gains national media attention as fifty members testify at hearings.

MAY. South Carolina amends its workers' compensation law. Dr. Arendt Bouhuys and colleagues publish their estimate of 35,000 disabled active and retired workers among the total of 200,000 active and 235,000 retired workers. A NIOSH study finds an unusually high proportion of retired textile workers obtaining SSDI payments for respiratory problems. South Carolina BLA asks federal government to take over the state's OSHA program because of lax enforcement of dust regulations. The U.S. Department of Labor declines after the South Carolina OSHA steps up enforcement activities.

AUGUST. The Aiken, South Carolina, chapter is organized. The *Brown Lung Blues* begins publication.

SEPTEMBER. The Lincoln County, North Carolina, chapter (later Lincoln/Gaston) is organized.

NOVEMBER. The Rockingham, North Carolina, chapter (later Richmond/Scotland) is organized, and efforts begin in Eden and Reidsville (the latter never establishes a separate chapter).

DECEMBER. Senators Hollings and Thurmond hold hearings in Greenville at which BLA members effectively present criticisms of the workers' compensation system.

1978: JANUARY. Hollings and Thurmond introduce the Brown Lung Disease Act, a federal compensation bill modeled after the black lung program. It is reintroduced for several years but never passed.

FEBRUARY. A South Carolina claimant wins the first award from the state's Industrial Commission. It is appealed, and later a settlement is made.

MARCH. BLA files 129 new claims for byssinosis with the North Carolina Industrial Commission.

APRIL. BLA begins publishing North and South Carolina editions of the *Brown Lung Reporter,* a newsletter to help lawyers keep up with legal changes. An initial screening clinic is held to initiate a chapter in Stanly County, North Carolina.

MAY. South Carolina amends its occupational disease law to do away with mandatory medical board diagnosis that is binding on the Industrial Commission. It also changes statute of limitations so that the two-year limit begins running at the time of diagnosis rather than when the worker left the mill. These changes enable a significant number of byssinosis awards. There is internal debate within the Carter White House over the potential inflationary impact of proposed cotton dust standards. OSHA estimates the cost of compliance at $625 million; ATMI estimates $2.8 billion.

JUNE. OSHA publishes its "final mandatory occupational safety and health standards" for occupational exposure to cotton dust. Standards vary with the stage of the processing: 0.2 milligram per cubic meter for all yarn processing up to slashing or weaving; 0.75 milligram for slashing and weaving; 0.5 milligram for all other industries where workers are exposed to cotton dust, with one exception: for ginning (where seeds are removed) no numerical limit is set, but certain work practices and medical surveillance are required. ATMI goes to a U.S. Appeals Court to block the cotton dust standards and lobbies Congress to force additional study of costs and benefits. In October, the court issues a stay on the standards pending its hearing. Carolina BLA grows to twelve chapters with the addition of Anderson, S.C.

FALL. CBS's *60 Minutes* runs a segment on byssinosis, workers' difficulty in collecting compensation, and charges that companies withhold medical information.

1979: FEBRUARY. U.S. Appeals Court hears testimony on ATMI's appeal.

MAY. The U.S. Department of Labor completes a cost-benefit analysis and concludes that the variable 0.2 milligram standard is optimal. Members and staff meet at Highlander to discuss BLA's future directions.

JUNE. Joseph Hughes's study of retired textile workers applying for byssinosis compensation finds that few gain any appreciable award; most survive on SSDI and Medicare at about half their previous level of income. The association receives funding from the Campaign for Human Development to begin organizing in Georgia and Virginia and drops "Carolina" from its name.

OCTOBER. The U.S. Court of Appeals rejects the ATMI appeal and sets a date for the standard to go into effect. Industry appeals to the U.S. Supreme Court.

NOVEMBER. An editorial in *Textile World* condemns the decision and argues that an appeal to the U.S. Supreme Court will at least buy additional time.

DECEMBER. Governor Jim Hunt appoints a North Carolina commission to study delays in workers' compensation proceedings for byssinosis claims.

1980: JANUARY. Byssinosis awards and settlements in North Carolina total 286 and $3.76 million.

FEBRUARY. The *Charlotte Observer* runs a Pulitzer Prize–winning series on byssinosis, highly favorable to BLA positions.

MARCH. The cotton dust standard goes into effect, giving industry four years to meet the final dust level standards. Mills must work on a timetable for establishing medical surveillance, dust measurement, improved work practices, and the temporary use of respirators until mechanical dust controls are in place.

MAY–JUNE. Augusta, Georgia, chapter is organized. The Stanly County, North Carolina, chapter, moved to Concord to serve a three-county area, is renamed Ephraim Lowder Memorial Chapter in honor of its past president.

AUGUST. New chapters are organized in Danville and Martinsville, Virginia (Martinsville lasts only about a year).

SEPTEMBER. Requirements for respirators, scheduled to go into effect, are stayed for seventy-five days because of worker complaints.

OCTOBER. U.S. Supreme Court agrees to hear industry's appeal of the cotton dust regulations. The Columbus, Georgia, chapter is organized.

NOVEMBER. Ronald Reagan defeats incumbent president, Jimmy Carter.

DECEMBER. OSHA stays respirator requirements for another thirty days.

1981: JANUARY. Supreme Court hears the textile industry's appeal of the cotton dust standards, with Robert Bork presenting oral arguments for the industry. The respirator provisions go into effect.

FEBRUARY. Byssinosis awards and settlements in North Carolina total 543 and $8.01 million. South Carolina does not compile data.

MARCH. The Reagan White House requests that the Supreme Court refrain from issuing an opinion until the administration has reexamined the standards. A chapter is started in Greenwood, South Carolina, but meetings last only about a year and no office ever opens.

APRIL. Burlington is cited by the North Carolina Industrial Commission for withholding medical information from its employees.

JUNE. The U.S. Supreme Court rejects the Reagan administration's request for delay and the textile industry's appeal of the cotton dust standards on the grounds that Congress did not intend for OSHA to find expected benefits higher than costs before issuing a standard. The Court did take away the right of employees to have their wages protected if their inability to wear masks necessitates transfer to a different job.

JULY. BLA reaches its peak with seventeen chapters in four states, a legal office in Durham, North Carolina, a paid staff of 37.5, plus volunteers and interns. The Reagan administration cancels the association's VISTA workers program, and BLA loses twenty full-time staff.

The BLA legal office closes, moving its operation to a private home.

1982: The BROWN LUNG REPORTER ceases publication, and chapter office closings begin with Lincoln/Gaston and Ephraim Lowder Memorial in North Carolina. Within a few years all North Carolina chapters cease activity and close their offices. Greensboro lasts the longest. Most South Carolina chapters go on a little longer. A new chapter opened in Opelika, Alabama, holds on until the late 1980s.

JANUARY. ATMI claims that a study of 400,000 textile workers in 142 companies reveals only 0.4 percent with byssinosis. The findings are challenged by BLA and ACTWU.

FEBRUARY. OSHA announces that it will review the dust standards because of new data and try to find ways to improve cost-effectiveness.

MARCH. The National Academy of Science attempts to resolve byssinosis differences by reviewing research but divides on the question of whether there is sufficient scientific evidence to demonstrate that cotton dust is the cause. The World Health Organization responds that the evidence is conclusive.

APRIL. Georgia recognizes byssinosis as a compensable occupational disease and allows those with claims that do not meet the statute of limitations to be diagnosed by 1 July 1983 and file a claim by 1 July 1984.

SEPTEMBER. Byssinosis awards and settlements in North Carolina total 1,047 and $14.5 million. OSHA charges that BLA has misspent grant money and orders an audit.

1983: MAY. The Reagan administration announces that engineering controls will be retained in the dust standards.

JUNE. OSHA proposes amendments to standards to make them more cost-effective and schedules hearings.

SEPTEMBER–OCTOBER. OSHA hearings are held in Washington, Dallas, and Columbia, South Carolina. BLA members testify at Columbia hearings but are challenged on many points by an industry lawyer.

DECEMBER. ATMI and ACTWU begin negotiations on proposed modifications of standards. ACTWU and BLA both oppose deregulating washed cotton.

1984: A Griffin, Georgia, chapter is quickly organized for people trying to file claims before the July deadline, but it never opens a formal office.

JANUARY. The OSHA audit concludes that BLA owes the agency $228,783.

FEBRUARY. BLA appeals the audit, but appeal is delayed pending the outcome of a criminal investigation.

MARCH. The Aiken, South Carolina, and Greensboro, North Carolina, chapters close.

1985: Augusta, Columbus, and Griffin chapters close in Georgia.

DECEMBER. With ATMI and ACTWU agreement, the cotton dust standards are revised to require less frequent medical exams of workers in mills with low dust levels, to reduce frequency of dust monitoring in mills that have met the standard, to allow wage retention for workers who are transferred because of inability to wear respirators. In addition, regulations greatly reduce the application of regulations to industries outside textile yarn preparation and exempt a wide variety of washed cotton. OSHA notes that engineering compliance costs are half of 1978 estimates and therefore not an economic burden on industry.

1987: The criminal investigation against BLA is dropped. OSHA asks BLA to put records in auditable form. BLA submits six boxes of records.

1988: The Anderson, South Carolina, chapter closes. OSHA reviews BLA records, disallows $222,094, and demands repayment.

1989: JANUARY. BLA gathers additional records and appeals.

JULY. OSHA disallows appeal because records are not in auditable form and again demands repayment.

1990: FEBRUARY. The Columbia, South Carolina, chapter closes, leaving only two active chapters: Greenville, South Carolina, and Danville, Virginia.

APRIL. OSHA stops efforts to collect debts from BLA, which has no significant assets.

NOTES

INTRODUCTION. A SOUTHERN TRAGEDY

1. One such exception is an analysis of how the white downtown business interest and the black middle class bargained with each other in the southern urban setting of Atlanta (Stone 1989).

Chapter 1. THE CULTURAL AND POLITICAL SETTING

1. Dowd et al. (1987, 97, 99–100, 356–57) offer an interesting alternative to this hypothesis. They see rural values brought into the mill village and acknowledge that individualism impeded group action: "Workers felt free to complain about unjust treatment . . . individual negotiations [were] the norm. . . . Workers usually vented their anger in individual ways. . . . Personal strategies of resistance and accommodation defined the fabric of everyday life in the mills." But they also conclude that the rural values of community and neighborliness enabled workers sometimes to overcome these individual impulses and work together. Cooperation built on the communal rather than the individualistic side of mill village life is what enabled workers to join together in the great general textile strike of 1934. When the strike was finally crushed by the mill owners and their political allies, a new strategy of labor control evolved: divide and isolate workers by dismantling the villages and hiring workers from across the countryside. Thus, communal values would not get in the way of individualistic impulses. Those who came to form the Brown Lung Association were just entering the work force or were children when these changes were taking place. Many of them owned and lived in the old houses that once composed the mill villages, and many remembered and had taken sides in the great strike of 1934. Their experience in the Brown Lung Association illustrates both sets of values at work.

2. Zieger (1986, 9–12) offers an alternative analysis of immigrant labor. He argues that when faced with hard times, immigrants tended to turn

inward to family for support and survival. Those who had been here longer tended to choose more individual solutions, often pulling up their roots and moving in search of work. He argues that neither group was likely to choose the kind of collective or political action required for unions to thrive.

3. The propensity of southern workers—especially white southern workers—to be attracted to politicians who make promises couched in the rhetoric of individualism and volunteerism must be carefully weighed against the tendency of all Americans to be attracted to these themes. They are powerful themes for almost all working- and middle-class white Americans: witness the widespread disapproval of affirmative action programs that even imply quotas. But individualism has greater potential as a battle cry in southern politics, according to sociologist John Shelton Reed, who has practically made a career of exploring regional differences: "I believe that there is an individualistic ethic more common in the South than elsewhere, an ethic that says: in the last analysis, you (or at best you and your neighbors) are on your own" (1984, 6). Part of the appeal of the southern liberal and even radical politicians who found support among working-class southerners—and of some non-southern liberals such as Franklin Roosevelt—can be explained by the individualistic terms in which they expressed their message. Government programs were sold as self-help programs, not as socialism. Yet even those who promoted these programs were sometimes vulnerable to the charge that they violated the norm of individual self-reliance: witness Gene Talmadge's attacks on Roosevelt in the 1930s (Anderson 1975, 132–33). Black and Black (1987, 66) conclude that such attitudes explain " why most white and black voters have not continuously united around liberal—much less radical—goals and objectives and why conservative and moderate-to-conservative politicians have often won substantial majorities among working-class whites."

4. The "shotgun house" was the typical mill village dwelling, a long, narrow building with a narrow hall running down the middle or more often the side from the front door to the back door. Presumably, one could fire a shotgun in one door and the shots would come out the other. Physically, the house was also long and narrow, resembling the barrel of a shotgun, with the front being the narrow end. The design and term may also have African roots, possibly derived from the Yoruba *to-gun*, or place of assembly. Its physical configuration both inside and with respect to adjacent houses— front doors were usually within a few steps of each other—forces more social interaction among those who live in such houses, reflecting "a long evolution of an architecture of intimacy among black people." "By the middle of the nineteenth century the shotgun proved very popular for economic reasons . . . as a cheap rental house" (Vlach 1978, 131).

5. McLaurin (1971, 33, 37–80) argues that mill villages were initially built on the basis of keeping costs as low as possible. Later these mechanisms were added by the more enterprising owners to exercise better control. Kirby (1987, 296, 298–302), who paints a more positive picture of mill village life than most historians—stressing the social and sports opportunities provided in mill villages—admits that owners were more motivated by anti-unionism than by concern for the welfare of workers. Dowd et al.,

who stress the community and neighborly values brought from the country, also acknowledge that the goal, often frustrated by workers, was control (1987, 114).

6. See McLaurin 1971, xii, 53–59. Zieger's historiographical review of work on southern mill culture (1991, 35–59) asks whether the culture of southern cotton textile workers was distinctively anti-union. He concludes that a variety of factors explain the lack of union success in the mill regions of the South: the intense opposition and great power of those who ran the mills and the towns, economic forces that made significant wage concessions impossible, and the culture of the mill villages themselves. The cultural opposition, however, was not a clear anti-union tradition, as so many assume, but rather "the very qualities of egalitarianism and individualism that . . . militated against the ability to sustain the disciplined concerted action that alone might have successfully challenged . . . employers." Workers resisted and rejected all external authority, whether it came from owners or from would-be union leaders, preferring to rely primarily on their own efforts even when doing so was self-defeating.

Black and Black's important work on southern politics also offers a multicausal explanation for the lack of union success and includes individualism as a major factor: "Far from least important, southern unionization has been hampered by a tenacious strain of individualism that leads many workers to be inordinately skeptical of collective efforts to improve their economic standing" (1987, 65–66). Cooper and Terrill agree that among multiple factors explaining the lack of union success was "the cultural tradition of individualism and deference," but they argue that economics, the "highly competitive, labor intensive" nature of textiles, was paramount (1990, 679–80). A case can be made that the remarkable general strike of 1934 was the closest textile workers came to creating a sense of class solidarity. The failure of this effort reinforced the traditional notion that workers should depend on no one other than themselves (see Dowd et al. 1987, 353–54). My work supports the thesis of a multicausal explanation that includes cultural values—in particular, exaggerated individualism—as one of a number of significant impediments to effective organization. I do not try here to answer the methodologically thorny question of which factors have been most significant.

7. Paul Luebke (1990, 201–3) found that neither political party offers working-class citizens any alternatives to corporate power; the only question is which set of corporate interests will most benefit from government activities.

8. Lee Atwater used this term in an unpublished paper to describe the nature of the growing Republican base in South Carolina politics.

CHAPTER 2. COMPENSATING VICTIMS AND PROTECTING WORKERS

1. Despite these potential advantages, a federal system, unlikely as it is, might not be a panacea for disabled workers. Just as textile interests were able to delay and appeal the cotton dust standards for well over a decade,

they could appeal and delay the setting of compensation standards, especially those regarding medical standards of proof. Finding a funding formula that is fair and that satisfies all members of the textile industry would be difficult at best, politically impossible at worst. Mills that have invested in modernization, process less cotton, or engage in processes that are inherently less dusty would not want to subsidize those that are more likely to place workers at risk. Pooling costs would undermine one of the basic principles of workers' compensation: those who cause the problem should bear the burden. In addition, if the black lung program proved to be typical, costs would be much higher than original estimates. Moreover, the political nature of bureaucratic politics creates the risk that the administering body could be dominated by textile interests, who are certainly much more powerful than disabled workers. Administrative procedures might create new barriers and further delay. Finally, judging from other federal programs, litigation and delay would probably continue; the only differences would be that the litigation would take place in federal rather than state courts, and the issues would be different. The one way to minimize these problems might be to require companies that lose their appeals to pay claimants' attorney fees (Schroeder 1986, 168-71).

2. Robert Bork, whose later nomination to the Supreme Court by President Reagan was not confirmed, presented the textile industry's side. His argument rested on an economic definition of "feasible" and on industry estimates that economic costs would be six times government estimates. See "Textile Industry Fights Standards" (1981, 3B), which appeared in the *Augusta Chronicle* the day after Reagan's inauguration.

Chapter 3. WORKPLACE RISK AND SCIENTIFIC RESEARCH

1. This description is based on a number of sources, including my own knowledge of textile mills and discussions with workers. See also Hamby of the N.C. State School of Textiles (1986, 168-74); and Beardsley (1987, 63); both are excellent even though the latter was based on dated technologies.

2. A summary of the 1990 Cotton Dust Conference opens with a statement that seems to indicate great sensitivity on the part of conference officials—"Byssinosis is still a problem in United States textile mills. It appears that we are managing instead of solving the byssinosis problem"—and goes on to note that claims are still being filed and paid and that fines are still levied on mills for violations (see Jacobs, Wakelyn, and Domelsmith, 1990, 1). Most cases are those of people who worked in the mills before any safeguards were put in place in the late 1970s; even mill officials interviewed for this book admit that such cases will continue for the next decade or so. There are relatively few new claims being filed, in part because no one is going out and locating potential claimants, as the Brown Lung Association once did, but also because of generational replacement.

3. Because of the central role they are thought to play, most recent research focuses on endotoxins. Much of it utilizes animal studies, simply because one cannot use human subjects in studying the outbreak of chronic

disease under different conditions and different levels of exposure to different varieties of endotoxins (see Jacobs, Wakelyn, and Domelsmith, 1990). The emphasis suggests that perhaps what is needed is an endotoxin standard rather than a dust standard, especially since endotoxins can be present even when there is very little dust. Though research may eventually lead to that position, as of the early 1990s too much uncertainty still exists. Moreover, as yet there are no practical ways to monitor endotoxins in the mill environment, even though some genetics firms are using the findings of this research to set their own maximum endotoxin levels in genetic engineering, which routinely employs bacteria that produce endotoxins. Obviously, that is much more practical in a small laboratory environment than in a large manufacturing setting. Nevertheless, should current standards and employee monitoring prove insufficient in preventing chronic byssinosis, and should current research establish clearer causal links, new standards targeting endotoxins may again make questions of technological feasibility an issue between regulators and textile mills (Castellan 1991).

CHAPTER 4. THE BIRTH OF THE BROWN LUNG ASSOCIATION

1. Political science and sociology have developed several models to explain the development of social movements that attempt to enter the political arena and compete with more traditional economic interests. Doug McAdam (1982, chaps. 1–4) describes three general models, the first two of which he finds to have serious deficiencies. The pluralist model relegates those in social movements to the status of irrational citizens engaging in emotional outbursts. The resource mobilization model is a significant improvement in that it recognizes the lack of resources available to working- and lower-class citizens; however, it fails to give proper weight to the transformation of consciousness that is necessary for a protest to begin, even if all the other necessary resources are available. Finally, the political process model adds this crucial element. Judkins employs a similar modification of the resource mobilization model, although he gives it no new title and does not base his work on that of McAdam. Judkins argues (1986, 185) that the first actions taken by association members for very individualistic reasons had the potential of transforming their consciousness and enabling them to see wider public issues. The perspective of my work is similar to the McAdams-Judkins modification of the resource mobilization model. My major difference with Judkins is in the evaluation of the extent to which a change in consciousness took place within the Brown Lung Association (of course, I have the advantage of six more years of the group's history). Even though the consciousness of a few was changed, most retained their highly individualistic perspective, and the group failed to do what McAdam said was required: "For the movement to survive, insurgents must be able to create a more enduring organizational structure to sustain the insurgency. . . . [They] must be able to exploit initial successes . . . to mobilize those resources needed. . . . Failing this, movements are likely to die

aborning as the loosely structured groups previously guiding the protest campaign disband or gradually lapse into inactivity" (1982, 54).

2. See, e.g., "Brown Lung: A Case of Deadly Neglect" (1980).

3. Several studies have analyzed these well-known political and attitudinal attributes, including those cited in Chapter 1. Most of these attitudes as they relate to unions and class consciousness in a small Georgia textile community were touched upon by McDonald and Cleeland (1981); my own findings in examining a furniture and textile community in North Carolina were consistent with theirs (Botsch 1980).

4. Senate and House hearings on virtually identical bills to mandate uniform standards were held in 1978 and 1980 respectively (U.S. Congress 1978b, 1980). The specific problems and possible remedies for problems of income maintenance of those with occupational diseases are reviewed in U.S. Department of Labor (1980).

5. Judkins's (1986) comparison of the Brown Lung and Black Lung associations stressed the theme of worker participation, as seen in the book's subtitle: "Toward Worker Control of Occupational Health."

6. Bouhuys later became a member of the Brown Lung Association and gave it his full support until his death: for example, helping to obtain machines to perform breathing tests (BLA Papers).

7. Except where noted, the story of the founding of the group up through the struggle between Szpak and Blechman was pieced together from interviews with Frank Blechman (1991), Charlotte Brody (1991), Michael Szpak (1991), and Eleanor Stanley (1992), along with papers provided by Szpak.

8. For an excellent history of the Highlander school, see Glen 1988.

9. Brody (1991) went on to argue that a truly accurate history of the association would have to look at each of the chapters individually because of their relative autonomy and unique characteristics. My perspective is that the chapters had enough in common to justify a meaningful history of the association as a whole, even if some generalizations do not do complete justice to all chapters, and even if my familiarity with most chapters is based on papers and interviews. In either case, time and space preclude that more complete history for the present.

Chapter 5. ORGANIZATIONAL STRUCTURE AND LIFE

1. Judkins (1986, 182) noted that "less than 10 percent of total funding came from inside the organization." This referred to the organization as a whole, which was responsible for paying the salaries of chapter organizers. The chapters paid about half of their other operating expenses, such as rent, telephone, and newsletter costs.

Chapter 6. NOISE AND INSTITUTIONAL DISRUPTION

1. Bennett Judkins (1986) views this human evidence as the major con-

tribution of members of both Brown Lung and Black Lung associations and as their most effective tactic in arousing public concern and political action.

2. See, e.g., a three-page report written by the Brown Lung Association's legal staff member in South Carolina (Weimer 1981) which was the featured article in a publication of the South Carolina Bar Association; it was sent to all members of the bar's Insurance, Negligence, and Workman's Compensation Section.

3. The ability of state OSHAs to make regular inspections of industrial plants has not improved in recent years. In September 1991 a poultry plant fire in Hamlet, North Carolina, resulted in the deaths of twenty-five workers who could not escape because the exits had been locked. The plant had not been inspected. The dramatic nature of these deaths led the national office to threaten to take over North Carolina's OSHA program (see "U.S. Agency Orders N.C. To Improve Worker Safety" 1992, 3A). Deaths from byssinosis were much less dramatic, yet lack of proper inspections may have been just as much to blame.

CHAPTER 7. THE TEXTILE INDUSTRY RESPONSE

1. One plant I visited, built in the mid-1960s, had originally cost $50,000 per shift worker to equip fully. By 1991 the same plant had spent about $170,000 per shift worker in just the previous three years to modernize. Officials replaced more than 500 looms costing $2,400 each with less than half that many costing over $50,000 each (Interviews).

CHAPTER 8. SUFFOCATION

1. The Brown Lung Association papers never showed more than thirty-five and a half staff members. Newspaper reports of more than fifty in 1981 were counting unpaid interns and part-time volunteers (Blechman 1991; see Dennis 1982, 1-A).

2. One of these advisers was Mary Lou Seymour (1991), a former organizer who now has only infrequent contacts with the group. The second was Ben Judkins, who worked closely with the group in the mid-1980s while doing research for a book. When interviewed in the spring of 1991, he expressed surprise that he was listed as an adviser. The remaining members had asked him to become president in 1983 or 1984, but he turned them down on the grounds that it would fundamentally change the nature of the association. He felt they were simply looking for someone with energy and commitment after they had lost all their staff. He too reported only infrequent contacts with the group. The third was Bart Dredge, a doctoral candidate in sociology who is living in the Greenville mill village area while working on his dissertation and teaching at Furman University. He has retained the most contact with what remains of the association.

3. Judkins (1992) analyzed the relationship between the number of paid staff and the number of newspaper articles generated in the *Charlotte Observer* between January 1975 and June 1982. He found that relationship quite strong: the number of articles peaked in 1980 when paid staff peaked

and fell dramatically as staff dwindled in 1981–82. These data have never been published.

CHAPTER 9. CONCLUSIONS

1. See, e.g., the statement of Jerry Brooks, director of health and safety for J.P. Stevens (quoted in Baker 1987, 1A).

2. Judkins reached a similar conclusion (1986, 174).

3. Not all organizers would agree on this point, especially retrospectively. David Dotson (1991) argued that it was acceptable for this group to fade away, because not all groups or movements are meant to last. He thought its members had achieved some goals for themselves and left the legacy of a safer workplace for generations that followed. For him, that was enough. Charlotte Brody (1991) remembered seeing the movement in the beginning as a historical opportunity to inspire younger workers to stand up and fight the mills through example. Failing this, she agreed with Dotson.

4. According to Judkins and Dredge (1991, 134), the experience of the Brown Lung Association suggests that occupational health issues can be important tools for "linking active and retired workers." Though they concede that few active workers participated, they see the major obstacle as fear, not lack of interest. Fear was certainly a factor, but many organizers knew that they really had little to offer active workers that was of interest to them. The association never came up with an organizing model that could attract them. Most workers felt the same way about workplace health issues as they did about wearing seat belts: nothing was going to happen to *them*. The Brown Lung Association experience suggests some limiting conditions on using occupational health issues to link active and retired workers.

5. Judkins (1982a, 1986; Judkins and Dredge 1991) makes this argument within a framework called resources theory. The central idea is that the best way to understand a social movement is in terms of the requirements to bring together all the necessary resources. Members, leadership, legitimacy, media attention, and money are resources necessary for success.

6. Writing just after the organization began to decline Si Kahn (1982, 259–71) would also seem to fault the group for not becoming self-reliant enough; he suggested that assessing higher dues and charging for services are appropriate measures if groups are to avoid the danger of drastic cuts when the outside funds stop.

7. Frank Blechman (1991) argued that staff did not plan enough, especially about how to involve active workers. He felt that once the staff had dealt with all the day-to-day problems, they had too little time and energy left to make the necessary plans. This may be true, and perhaps staff should have placed a higher priority on recruiting active workers, but it is easy to blame failures on a lack of good planning. Numerous documents in the BLA Papers certainly show that efforts to plan did take place.

8. Kahn (1982, 259) makes a similar point in his work on grassroots organizing.

9. Judkins and Dredge (1991, 130) argue that the struggles with multiple targets (state governments, the national government, doctors, lawyers, and the textile industry) provided many opportunities for small successes that "created a subjective perception on the BLA membership of enhanced power to effect political change. . . . The experience of struggle transformed the consciousness of individuals." These continuing small victories and a transformed consciousness "contributed both to the recruitment into the movement and to the continuing participation of early members." Though it is true that all the many targets of action created many opportunities for small successes and publicity, it is also true that these efforts stretched already thin resources and added complexity that made the group all the more dependent on knowledgeable organizers. The more important point is that even though a few members at the core of the group had their consciousness changed through collective action, there were not enough of them to keep the movement going for long. My own estimate is a few hundred. Judkins (1982b, 65) estimated active membership at under a thousand. Blechman (1991) estimated that about 1,200 were quite active at some point in the life of the organization. Most of the others came for individual benefits and left when their cases were resolved. This was a common theme among those interviewed for this book. A few hundred to a thousand might have been enough had these been young people or if organizers had been able to continue to recruit and replace members as they grew too old and sick to remain active. But they were not young, and organizers lost the resources to replace them. A sense of collective empowerment was less important in the life and short-lived growth of the Brown Lung Association than the external resources that enabled organizers to locate and recruit members, the vast majority of whom never developed an interest beyond their own individual welfare.

10. Despite the dismal track record, a number of dedicated organizers persist in the belief that beneath the learned culture of powerlessness is a democratic culture of working together. Kahn (1982, 367–68) advises: "We need to encourage every group to rediscover its traditions and rely on those traditions for strength and unity." But the strongest tradition of most of these people is that of isolated individual action. The problem is not to rediscover but to create a more cooperative, group-oriented culture. That may be worth attempting, but it is a much more difficult task.

11. Doug Kingsmore, president and CEO of Graniteville, indirectly conceded this point in a 1991 newspaper interview when he said that the company had become dedicated to safe operation over the previous five years and that the textile industry was trying hard to remove people's fear about working in the mills, which was the dominant feeling a few years earlier (see Lord 1991a).

12. For an excellent review of Pope (1989) and Haeberle (1989), see Woliver 1990.

REFERENCES

Aberbach, Joel D. 1991. "The President and the Executive Branch." In *The Bush Presidency: First Appraisals,* ed. Colin Campbell, S.J., and Bert A. Rockman, 223–47. Chatham, N.J.: Chatham House.

Adams, Frank, with Myles Horton. 1975. *Unearthing Seeds of Fire: The Idea of Highlander.* Winston-Salem, N.C.: J.F. Blair.

Alinsky, Saul. 1971. *Rules for Radicals.* New York: Random House.

American Textile Manufacturers Institute, Inc. et al. v Donovan et al. 452 U.S. 490 (1981).

America's Textile Reporter 83, no. 28: (10 July 1969): 27.

Anderson, James E., David W. Brady, and Charles Bullock III. 1978. *Public Policy and Politics in America.* North Scituate, Mass.: Duxbury Press.

Anderson, William. 1975. *The Wild Man from Sugar Creek: The Political Career of Eugene Talmadge.* Baton Rouge: Louisiana State Univ. Press.

Arlidge, J.T. 1892. *The Hygiene Diseases and Mortality of Occupations.* London: Percival.

Arthur, Bill. 1983. "Some See EPA Follies as Key." *Charlotte Observer,* 21 May, pp. 1A, 4A.

Associated Press. 1990. "1990 A Bad Year; 1991 Looking No Better." *Aiken Standard,* 27 Dec., p. 1B.

Austin, David. 1992. Telephone interview with author, 20 Feb.

Bachrach, Peter, and Morton S. Baratz. 1962. "The Two Faces of Power." *American Political Science Review* 56: 947–52.

Baker, Bill. 1987. "Brown Lung Group Faces Funding Cuts, Fewer Cases." *Greenville News,* 18 Oct., p. 1A.

Beardsley, Edward H. 1987. *A History of Neglect: Health Care for Blacks and Mill Workers in the Twentieth-Century South.* Knoxville: Univ. of Tennessee Press.

Beck, Gerald J., and E. Neil Schachter. 1983. "The Evidence of Chronic Lung Disease in Textile Workers." *American Statistician* 37 (November): 404–11.

Beck, Gerald J., E. Neil Schachter, L.R. Maunder, and Arend Bouhuys. 1981. "The Relations of Lung Functions to Subsequent Employment Status and Mortality in Cotton Textile Workers." *Chest* 79: 26S–30S.

Berman, Daniel M. 1978. *Death on the Job: Occupational Health and Safety Struggles in the United States.* New York: Monthly Review Press.

Bethell, Tom. 1976. "1974: Contract at Brookside." *Southern Exposure* 4, no. 1–2: 114–18.

Billings, Dwight B., Jr. 1979. *Planters and the Making of the "New South."* Chapel Hill: Univ. of North Carolina Press.

BLA (Brown Lung Association) Papers. In the Southern Historical Collection, Southern Folklife Collection of the Manuscripts Department, University of North Carolina, Chapel Hill.

Black, Earl, and Merle Black. 1987. *Politics and Society in the South.* Cambridge, Mass.: Harvard Univ. Press.

Blechman, Frank. 1991. Telephone interview with author, 3 May.

Botsch, Robert E. 1980. *We Shall Not Overcome.* Chapel Hill: Univ. of North Carolina Press.

———. 1981. "You Can't Have It Both Ways: The Difficulties of Unionization in the South." In *Perspectives on the American South,* Merle Black and John Shelton Reed, 173–86. New York: Gordon and Breach.

———. 1982. "A Microanalytic Return to the Mind of the South." In *Contemporary Southern Political Attitudes and Behavior,* ed. Lawrence W. Moreland, Tod A. Baker, and Robert P. Steed, 24–47. New York: Praeger.

Bouhuys, Arend, et al. 1967. "Byssinosis in Cotton Textile Workers: A Respiratory Survey of a Mill with Rapid Labor Turnover." *Annals of Internal Medicine* 71: 257–69.

Bouhuys, Arend, Leo Heaphy, Jr., Richard F. Schilling, and J.W. Welborn. 1967. "Byssinosis in the United States." *New England Journal of Medicine* 277 (27 July): 170–75.

Bouhuys, Arend, J.B. Schoenberg, G.J. Beck, and R.S.F. Schilling. 1977. "Epidemiology of Chronic Lung Disease in a Cotton Mill Community," *Lung* 154: 167–86.

Bowen, Ben. 1991. Telephone interview with author, April.

Brody, Charlotte. 1991. Interview with author, 10 May.

Bronstein, Janet M. 1984. "The Effect of Public Controversy on Occupational Health Problems: Byssinoisis." *American Journal of Public Health* 74, no. 10: 1134–37.

"Brown Lung: A Case of Deadly Neglect." 1980. *Charlotte Observer,* 3–10 Feb.

"Brown Lung Protesters Get Union's Support." 1981. *Augusta Chronicle,* 5 May, p. B-2.

Brown Lung Blues. Newsletter of the Brown Lung Association, published periodically from Oct. 1977 through 1981.

Brown Lung Reporter. Bimonthly publication of the Brown Lung Association Legal Center, 1978–1982; in BLA Papers.

"Burlington Caught Hiding Evidence." 1980. *Brown Lung Blues* 2, no. 3.

"Burlington's Byssinosis Testing Program." 1977. *America's Textile Reporter Bulletin*, Sept., pp. 60–70.

"By-laws of the Board of the Brown Lung Association." 1979. 5 Dec.

"By-laws of the Brown Lung Association." 1986. 29 April.

Byrd, Robert, Ronald Dilthey, Ted R. Kunstling, Harry C. Martin, James Martin, Jr., Paul Michaels, and Florence Sandlin. 1980. "Report of the Brown Lung Study Committee to the Honorable James B. Hunt, Jr., Governor of North Carolina." Unpublished report, 10 April.

"Byssinosis Group Spent No Money to Aid Victims." 1983. *Charlotte Observer*, 14 Feb.

Caldwell, Erskine. 1933. *God's Little Acre*. New York: Grosset & Dunlap.

"Can Marginal Mills Endure the Cotton-Dust Standard?" 1978. *Textile World News*, July, pp. 23–24.

Carlton, David L. 1982. *Mill and Town in South Carolina*. Baton Rouge: Louisiana State Univ. Press.

"Carter Cutting Costs of Cotton Dust Rules." 1978. *Greensboro Daily News*, 7 June.

"Carter OKs Cotton Dust Rules." 1978. *Greensboro Daily News*, 8 June.

"Case, Lemar. N.d. Statement, copy in author's possession.

————. 1988. Letter of 9 December, copy in author's possession.

————. 1991. Telephone interview with author, 3 April.

Cash, W.J. 1941. *The Mind of the South*. New York: Knopf.

Castellan, Robert M. 1991. Telephone conversation with author, 21 February.

Castellan, Robert M., Stephen A. Olenchock, Kathleen B. Kinsley, and John Hankinson. 1987. "Inhaled Endotoxin and Decreased Spirometric Values." *New England Journal of Medicine* 317 (3 Sept.): 605–10.

Collis, E.L. 1915. "The Occurrence of an Unusual Cough among Weavers of Cotton Cloth." *Proceedings of the Royal Society of Medicine* (London Section, Epidemiology and State Medicine) 8: 108–12.

Committee on Byssinosis, National Research Council. 1982. *Byssinosis: Clinical and Research Issues*. Washington, D.C.: National Academy Press.

Conroy, Pat. 1974. "Horses Don't Eat Moonpies." In *Faces of South Carolina*, ed. Franklin Ashley, 47–56. Columbia, S.C. Commission on the Humanities.

Conway, Mimi. 1979. *Rise Gonna Rise: A Portrait of Southern Textile Workers*. Garden City, N.Y.: Anchor Press Doubleday.

Cook, Rhonda. 1980. "Brown Lung Disease Taking a Heavy Toll." *Augusta Chronicle, Augusta Herald*, 31 Aug., p. 4E.

Cooper William J., Jr., and Thomas E. Terrill. 1990. *The American South: A History*. New York: Knopf.

"Cotton Dust: Worker Health Alert." 1980. OSHA Booklet 3065. Washington, D.C.: USGPO.

Covington, Howard. 1980. "Dr. Burkhart: Found Less Byssinosis than He Expected." *Charlotte Observer*, 3–10 February, p. 12.

Covington, Howard, and Bob Dennis. 1980. "States Let Violators' Cases Gather Dust." *Charlotte Observer*, 3–10 February, pp. 6–7.

Covington, Howard, and Bob Drogin. 1980. "The Textile Industry Has Clout—and Knows How to Use it." *Charlotte Observer*, 3–10 February, p. 13.

Covington, Howard, Bob Dennis, Bob Drogin, and Marion A. Ellis. 1980a. "As Some in Industry Stall, the Victims Are Left Behind." *Charlotte Observer*," 3–10 Feb., pp. 2, 4–5.

———. 1980b. "Sometimes Death Is Victims' Only Compensation." *Charlotte Observer*, 3–10 Feb., pp. 9–10.

Crenson, Matthew A. 1971. *The Un-Politics of Air Pollution: A Study of Non–Decision Making in the Cities*. Baltimore, Md.: Johns Hopkins Univ. Press.

Dennis, Bob. 1980. "Mill Owner Spends 5½ Years Fighting Enforcement." *Charlotte Observer*, 3–10 Feb., p. 8.

———. 1982. "Brown Lung Group Struggles as Money Dries Up." *Charlotte Observer*, 24 May, pp. 1A, 4A.

Derrick, Butler. 1991. Telephone interview with author, 29 March.

Diem, J.E. 1983. "A Statistical Assessment of the Scientific Evidence Relating Cotton Dust Exposure to Chronic Lung Disease." *American Statistician* 37 (Nov.): 395–403.

"Don't Get Lulled by the Cotton Dust Stay." 1978. *Textile World*, pp. 55, 58.

Drogin, Bob. 1980a. "Does Group Help or Hurt the Cause?" *Charlotte Observer*, 3–10 Feb., pp. 17–18.

———. 1980b. "Even Friends of the Needy Turn Victims Away." *Charlotte Observer*, 3–10 Feb., p. 16.

———. 1980c. "A Story of Dust Delays—and Death." *Charlotte Observer*, 3–10 Feb., p. 2.

Dotson, David. 1991. Telephone interview with author, 6 May.

Dowd Hall, Jacquelyn, James Leloudis, Robert Korstad, Mary Murphy, Lu Ann Jones, Christopher B. Daly. 1987. *Like a Family: The Making of Southern Cotton Mill World*. Chapel Hill: Univ. of North Carolina Press.

"Eased Cotton Dust Standards Proposed." 1983. *The State*, 8 June, p. 3-A.

Eller, Ronald D. 1982. *Miners, Millhands, and Mountaineers*. Knoxville: Univ. of Tennessee Press.

Ellis, Lee. 1976. "Workman's Compensation and Occupational Safety." *Journal of Occupational Medicine*, June.

Ellis, Marion A. 1980. " . . . But Another Spends $3 Million for Cleaner Air." *Charlotte Observer*, 3–10 Feb., p. 8.

———. 1982. "Byssinosis Claims Fall: Cleaner Mills of Reticent Victoms." *Charlotte Observer*, 23 Jan.

———. 1983. "Cotton Dust Rules Help Industry, Union Study Says." *Charlotte Observer*, 18 March.

Ellis, Marion A., and Bob Dennis. 1983. "Mills Lament Ruling as Burden." *Charlotte Observer*, 21 May, pp. 1A, 8A.

Ellis, Marion A., and Robert Hodierne. 1980. "Where They Stand on Federal Program." *Charlotte Observer*, 3–10 Feb., p. 21.

Fantasia, Rick. 1988. *Cultures of Solidarity: Consciousness, Action, and Contemporary American Workers.* Berkeley: Univ. of California Press.

Finger, Bill. 1976. "Textile Men: Looms, Loans, and Lockouts." *Southern Exposure* 3, no. 4: 54–65.

"Flip-flop on Dust Mask Rule Angers Graniteville Officials." 1980. *Augusta Chronicle,* 17 Dec.

Ford, Betty, 1991. Telephone interview with author, 2 May.

Foster, Stephen William. 1988. *The Past Is Another Country: Representation, Historical Consciousness, and Resistance in the Blue Ridge.* Berkeley: Univ. of California Press.

Frumin, Eric. 1980. "Status of the OSHA Cotton Dust Standard." Memo from the Amalgamated Clothing and Textile Workers Union to all locals, 9 Oct.

———. 1991. Telephone interview with author, 30 April.

Gamson, William A. 1968. *Power and Discontent.* Homewood, Ill.: Dorsey Press, 1968.

Gaventa, John. 1980. *Power and Powerlessness: Quiescence and Rebellion in an Appalachian Valley.* Urbana: Univ. of Illinois Press.

Gibbs, Lois Marie, as told to Murray Levine. 1982. *Love Canal: My Story.* Albany: State Univ. of New York Press.

Glen, John M. 1988. *Highlander: No Ordinary School.* Lexington: Univ. Press of Kentucky, 1988.

Greenhouse, Linda. 1981a. "Court Goes Its Own Way on Key Regulation Cases." *New York Times,* 21 June, p. E-8.

———. 1981b. "U.S. Pulls a Switch on High Court." *New York Times,* 5 April, p. E-9.

Griffith, Barbara S. 1988. *The Crisis of American Labor: Operation Dixie and the Defeat of the CIO.* Philadelphia: Temple Univ. Press.

Haeberle, Steven H. 1989. *Planting the Grassroots: Structuring Citizen Participation.* New York: Praeger.

Hall, Bob. 1978. "The Brown Lung Controversy: How the Press, North and South, Handled a Story Involving the South's Largest Industry." *Columbia Journalism Review,* March–April, pp. 27–35.

Hall, Jacquelyn, et al. 1987. *Like a Family: The Making of a Southern Cotton Mill World.* Chapel Hill: Univ. of North Carolina Press.

Hamby, D.S. 1986. "Textile." *World Book Encyclopedia* 19: 168–74.

Harris, T. Reginald, James A. Merchant, Kay H. Kilburn, and John D. Hamilton. 1972. "Byssinosis and Respiratory Diseases of Cotton Mill Workers." *Journal of Occupational Medicine* (March): 199–206.

Heyden, Siegfried, and Philip Pratt. 1980. "Commentary: Exposure to Cotton Dust and Respiratory Disease. Textile Workers, 'Brown Lung,' and Lung Cancer." *Journal of the American Medical Association* 244 (17 Oct.): 1797–98.

Hinton, Nancy. 1991. Telephone interview with author, 28 May.

Hodges, James A. 1986. *New Deal Labor Policy and the Southern Cotton Textile Industry, 1933–1941.* Knoxville: Univ. of Tennessee Press.

Hodierne, Robert E. 1978. "Cotton Dust Standards for Textile Mills Still Not Ready." *Charlotte Observer,* 19 Feb.

Hrebenar, Ronald J., and Clive S. Thomas, eds. 1992. *Interest Group Politics in the Southern States.* Tuscaloosa: Univ. of Alabama Press.

Hudson, Charlotte. 1991. Telephone interview with author, 2 May.

Hughes, Joseph. 1979. "Brown Lung Disability: Costs, Compensation, and Controversy." U.S. Department of Labor Research Report, June.

——— . 1992. Telephone interview with author, 21 Feb.

Imbus, Harold R. 1980. "Burlington's Investments Minimize The Hazard." *Charlotte Observer,* 3–10 Feb., p. 23.

Imbus, Harold R., and M.W. Suh. 1973. "Byssinosis: A Study of 10,133 Textile Workers." *Archives of Environmental Health* 26: 183–91.

"Industry Says Few Workers Get Brown Lung." 1982. *Augusta Chronicle,* 20 Jan., 2A.

Interviews. Author's interviews with persons who wish to remain anonymous.

"It All Depends." 1969. *America's Textile Reporter* 83, no. 28: 1, 27–28.

"It's Time to Do the Obvious." 1980. *Charlotte Observer,* 3-10 Feb. 1980, 23.

Jacobs, Robert R. 1987. "Summary of the 1987 Beltwide Conference on Cotton Dust." In *Cotton Dust: Proceedings of the Eleventh Cotton Dust Conference,* ed. Robert R. Jacobs and P.J. Wakelyn, 1–2. Memphis, Tenn.: National Cotton Council.

Jacobs, Robert R., P.J. Wakelyn, and L.N. Domelsmith, eds. 1990. *Cotton Dust: Proceedings of the Fourteenth Cotton Dust Conference.* Memphis, Tenn.: National Cotton Council.

"Job Fear Keeps Many Whistle-Blowers Silent." 1992. *Aiken Standard,* 21 Jan., pp. 1A, 3A.

Journal of the Senate. 1979. Columbia, S.C., 3 July.

Judkins, Bennett M. 1982a. "Mobilization of Membership: The Black and Brown Lung Movements." In *Social Movements of the Sixties and Seventies,* ed. Jo Freeman, 35–51. New York: Longman.

——— . 1982b. "Occupational Health and the Developing Class Consciousness of Southern Textile Workers: The Case of the Brown Lung Association." *Maryland Historian,* Spring–Summer, pp. 55–71.

——— . 1986. *We Offer Ourselves as Evidence: Toward Workers' Control of Occupational Health.* New York: Greenwood Press.

——— . 1991. Telephone interview with author, 29 April.

——— . 1992. Letter to author, 16 March.

Judkins, Bennett M., and Bart Dredge. 1991. "The Brown Lung Association and Grass-Roots Organizing." In *Hanging by a Thread: Social Change in Southern Textiles,* ed. Jeffrey Leiter, Michael D. Schulman, and Rhonda Zingraff, 121–36. Ithaca, N.Y.: ILR Press, 1991.

Kahn, Si. 1970. *How People Get Power.* New York: McGraw-Hill.

——— . 1982. *Organizing: A Guide for Grassroots Leaders.* New York: McGraw-Hill.

——— . 1992. Telephone interview with author, 9 March.

Kassell, John. 1992. Telephone interview with author, 17 Feb.

Kay, J.P. 1831. "Trades Producing Phthisis." *North of England Medical and Surgical Journal* 1: 358–63.

Key, V.O., Jr. 1949. *Southern Politics in the State and Nation.* New York: Knopf.

———. 1961. *Public Opinion and American Democracy.* New York: Knopf.

Kilburn, Kaye H., Gerrie G. Kilburn, and James A. Merchant. 1973. "Byssinosis: Matter from Lint to Lungs." *American Journal of Nursing* 73, no. 11: 1952–56.

King, Wayne, 1977. "Cotton Mills Resist Cost of Curbing Dust." *New York Times,* 14 May, p. 21A.

Kirby, Jack Temple. 1987. *Rural Worlds Lost: The American South, 1920–1960.* Baton Rouge: Louisiana State Univ. Press.

Knight, James E. 1987. Letter to Lamar Case of the Brown Lung Association, 19 February. Copy in possession of author.

Kotz, Nick. 1978. "The Brown Lung Battle." *Washington Post,* 1 Jan., pp. B1, 4.

Larson, Arthur. 1978. *The Law of Workmen's Compensation.* New York: Matthew Bender.

Larson, L.W. 1979. *Analysis of Current Laws Reflecting Worker's Benefits for Occupational Diseases.* Washington, D.C.: U.S. Department of Labor.

Layne, R. Davis. 1988. Letter from OSHA Regional Administrator to Lamar Case, 7 December. Copy in author's possession.

Lemann, Nicholas. 1991. *The Promised Land: Black Migration and How It Changed America.* New York: Knopf, 1991.

Lewis, Mary Carol. 1991. Telephone interview with author, 30 April.

Lipsky, Michael. 1968. "Protest as a Political Resource." *American Political Science Review* 62 (Dec.).

Lord, Philip. 1991a. "Safety Truly Comes First: Graniteville Company Is Proud of Its Work Record." *Aiken Standard,* 12 May, p. 6c–7c.

———. 1991b. "Textile Plants Upgrade." *Aiken Standard,* 19 Dec., p. 1B.

Lourie, Isadore. 1991. Interview with author, 24 April.

Luebke, Paul. 1990. *Tar Heel Politics: Myths and Realities.* Chapel Hill: Univ. of North Carolina Press.

Lukes, Steven. 1974. *Power: A Radical View.* London: Macmillan.

Lybrand, Bill. 1991. Telephone interview with author, 6 May.

McAdam, Doug. 1982. *Political Process and the Development of Black Insurgency: 1930–1970.* Chicago: Univ. of Chicago Press.

McCarl, Bob. 1982. *While I Breathe, I Hope: Personal Accounts of Cotton Mill Workers with Brown Lung Disease.* A monograph published for the Brown Lung Association. N.Y.

McCarthy, John D., and Mayer Zald. 1973. *The Trends of Social Movements in America: Professionalization and Resource Mobilization.* Morristown, N.J.: General Learning Press.

McDonald, Joseph A., and Donald A. Cleeland. 1981. "Textile Workers and Unionization: A Community Study." Paper presented to meeting of the Southern Sociological Society.

McInnis, Doug. 1982. "The Cotton Dust Storm Returns." *New York Times,* 8 Aug.

McLaurin, Melton Alonza. 1971. *Paternalism and Protest: Southern Cotton Mill Workers and Organized Labor, 1875–1905.* Westport, Conn.: Greenwood Press.

McMillan, Alan C. 1989. Letter from Acting Assistant Secretary of OSHA to Lamar Case, 7 July. Copy in author's possession.

"Marshall Fighting Enforcement Delay." 1978. *Greensboro Daily News,* 1 June.

Martin, Charles F., M.D., and James E. Higgins, M.S. 1976. "Byssinosis and Other Respiratory Ailments: A Survey of 6,631 Cotton Textile Employees." *Journal of Occupational Medicine* 18, no. 7: 455–62.

Martin, James H. 1980. "Industry Alone Can't Stop Brown Lung." *Charlotte Observer,* 3–10 February, p. 23.

Martin, Randolph C. 1988. "Background Paper: Economic Opportunities for the People of South Carolina." *Background Papers for the Assembly on the Future of South Carolina.* Columbia: South Carolina Commission of the Future.

Matusow, Allen J. 1984. *The Unraveling of America: A History of Liberalism in the 1960s.* New York: Harper & Row.

Mauldin, Douglas. 1976. "Pay for Brown Lung, Lawyers Urge Panel." *The State,* 8 Dec., pp. 1-B, 8-B.

———. 1982. "State OKs 17 Charities for Payroll Deductions." *The State,* 1 Sept., p. 5-C.

Merchant, James A. 1983. "Byssinosis: Progress in Prevention." *American Journal of Public Health* 73 (Feb.: 137–38.

Milby, Thomas H. 1964. "Pneumoconioses." In *Occupational Diseases: A Guide to Their Recognition,* ed. W.M. Gafafer, 45–57. Washington, D.C.: U.S. Government Printing Office.

Morehouse, Sarah McCally. 1981. *State Politics, Parties, and Policy.* New York: Holt, Rinehart & Winston.

Munro, Jenny. 1981. "Workers to Request Law Changes." *Augusta Chronicle,* 6 November, p. 4-B.

———. 1982. "Workers Bill Signed." *Augusta Chronicle,* 23 April, p. B1.

Nader, Ralph. 1968. "They're Still Breathing." *New Republic* 158 (3 Feb.): 15.

———. 1971. Brown Lung: The Cotton Mill Killer." *The Nation* 212 (15 March): 335–37.

———. 1991. Telephone interview with author, 7 Oct.

"N.C. Bars Brown Lung Fundraising." 1983. *Charlotte Observer,* 29 Oct.

Neal, P.A., R. Schneiter, and B.H. Cominita. 1942. "Report on Acute Illness among Rural Mattress-makers Using Low-grade, Stained Cotton." *Journal of the American Medical Association* 119: 1074–82.

Newby, I.A. 1989. *Plain Folk in the New South: Social Change and Cultural Persistence, 1880–1915.* Baton Rouge: Louisiana State Univ. Press.

Noble, Charles. 1986. *Liberalism at Work: The Rise and Fall of OSHA.* Philadelphia: Temple University Press.

"North Carolina: BLA Reforms Adopted." 1980. *Brown Lung Blues* 5, no. 2.

"Occupational Exposure to Cotton Dust: Final Mandatory Safety and Health Standards." 1978. *Federal Register* 43, no. 122, pt. 3:27349–463.

"Occupational Exposure to Cotton Dust." 1982. *Federal Register* 47, no. 27: 5906–10.

"Occupational Exposure to Cotton Dust: Proposed Rule." 1983. *Federal Register* 48, no. 113: 26962–84.

"Occupational Exposure to Cotton Dust." 1985. *Federal Register* 50, no. 240: 51120–78.

O'Conner, John J. 1980. "TV: 'The Islamic Bomb' and 'Song of the Canary.' *New York Times*, 5 Nov.

Olson, Mancur. 1965. *The Logic of Collective Action*. New York: Schocken Books.

Oppel, Rich. 1980. "Reading This Series May Make You Angry." *Charlotte Observer*, 3–10 Feb., p. 2.

OSHA (Occupational Safety and Health Administration). 1980. "OSHA Stays Cotton Dust Respirator Provisions for 75 Days." News release, 26 Sept.

———. 1982. "Advanced Notice of Proposed Rulemaking." 9 Feb.

"The OSHA Cotton Dust Standards." 1978. *America's Textile Reporter Bulletin*, August, pp. 14–61.

Parks, Blair. 1981. "Work Diary of a Brown Lung Association College Intern." In possession of author.

Pittman, Daisy. 1991. Telephone interview with author, 30 April.

Pitts, William B. 1980. "A Mill Owner." *Charlotte Observer*, 3–10 Feb., p. 24.

Piven, Francis Fox, and Richard A. Cloward. 1977. *Poor People's Movements: Why They Succeed, How They Fail*. New York: Pantheon Books.

Pope, Jacqueline. 1989. *Biting the Hand That Feeds Them: Organizing Women on Welfare at the Grass Roots Level*. New York: Praeger.

Pope, Liston. 1942. *Millhands and Preachers: A Study of Gastonia*. New Haven, Conn.: Yale Univ. Press.

Powell, Robert. 1991. Telephone interview with author, 2 May.

Proust, A.A. 1877. *Traité d'hygiene publique et privée*. Paris: G. Mason.

Reed, John Shelton. 1984. "The Prevailing South?" *National Humanities Newsletter* 5 (Summer).

Report, National Commission on State Workmen's Compensation Laws. 1972. Report 64–65.

Report to the President and Congress of the Policy Group of the Interdepartmental Workers' Compensation Task Force. 1977. Washington, D.C.: U.S. Government Printing Office.

Research Department of the South Carolina Workers' Compensation Commission. 1991. Telephone interview with author, 3 April.

"Respiratory Disorders among Textile Workers." 1967. *New England Journal of Medicine* 277 (27 July): 209–10.

"Revised Standards for Dust and Formaldehyde." 1986. *Textile World* 136 (Jan.): 26.

Roberts, Rebecca. 1981a. "Brown Lung Group Explains Protest." *Aiken Standard*, 11 May, p. A-7.

————. 1981b. "Clara Lewis: Brown Lung Victim Plans to Keep on Fighting." *Aiken Standard*, 3 April, pp. A-1, 2.

————. 1981c. "Graniteville Agrees to Pay Clara Lewis." *Aiken Standard*, 13 April, p. A-1.

Rogers, V.C. 1980. "A Brown Lung Study." Political cartoon. *Durham Morning Herald*, 14 May.

Rook, G.B., A.N. Dempsey, V.F. Hillier, and J. Jeacock. 1987. "Further Observations on Byssinotics Diagnosed in Great Britain." In *Cotton Dust: Proceedings of the Eleventh Cotton Dust Conference*, ed. R.R. Jacobs and P.J. Wakelyn, 5–8. Memphis, Tenn.: National Cotton Council.

Rudnick, Irene. 1992. Telephone interview with author, 2 October.

"Ruling Cuts Funds for United Way, Human Endeavor." 1981. *Aiken Standard*, 3 Sept., p. A-4.

Russell, Kathleen. 1992. Telephone interview with author, 17 Feb.

Russell, Michael. 1992. Telephone interview with author, 17 Feb.

Sandlin, Florence. 1980. "Minority Report of the Governor's Brown Lung Study Committee." 10 April.

————. 1991. Telephone interview with author, 2 May.

Schilling, Richard S.F. 1959. "Epidemiology of Byssinosis." *Journal of Occupational Medicine* 1: 36–37.

Schneider, William. 1988. "The Political Legacy of the Reagan Years." In *The Reagan Legacy*, ed. Sidney Blumenthal and Thomas Byrne Edsall, 51–98. New York: Pantheon Books.

Schroeder, Elinor P. 1986. "Legislative and Judicial Responses to the Inadequacy of Compensation for Occupational Disease." *Law and Contemporary Problems* 49, no. 4: 151–82.

Scoppe, Cindi Ross. 1991. "Lawmakers Profit from Injury Cases." *The State*, 8 March, pp. 1A, 11A.

Seymour, Mary Lou. 1991. Telephone interview with author, 30 April.

Shabecoff, Philip. 1982. "Safety Agencies Find Their Common Ground Eroding." *New York Times*, 28 Nov. p. E-8.

Shaffer, Helen B. 1978. "Job Health and Safety." In *Consumer Protection: Gains and Setbacks*, 191–92. Washington, D.C.: Congressional Quarterly Editorial Research Reports.

Shealy, H. Jane. 1986. "Public Hearing Probes Reaction to Worker's Compensation Bill." *Charleston New & Courier*, 31 Jan., 2B.

Shingles, Richard D. 1981. "Black Consciousness and Political Participation: The Missing Link." *American Political Science Review* 75 (March): 76–91.

Singletary, Howard Earl, and Stanley Hammer. 1980. "Recent Decisions Clarify Law on 'Brown Lung' Disability." *Campbell Law Observer*, 25 July, pp. 2, 4.

Smith, Barbara Ellen. 1984. "Too Sick to Work, Too Young to Die." *Southern Exposure* 12 (May–June): 19–29.

"Smokers Shouldn't Work In Yarn Mills, Study Finds." 1991. *The State*, 16 December, p. 3B.

Solomon, Lib. 1991. Telephone interview with author, 2 May.

South Carolina Workers' Compensation Commission: Annual Report, 1989–1990. 1990. Columbia, S.C.

Stanley, Eleanor. 1992. Telephone interview with author, 20 Feb.

"State Will Enforce Cotton Dust Rule." 1984. *The State*, 29 March, p. 9C.

Stephenson, William H. 1982. "Workers' Compensation Act: Occupational Disease Policy Establishment." Paper delivered to Charlotte Conference on the Cotton Dust Standard, 18 Sept.

Stone, Clarence N. 1989. *Regime Politics: Governing Atlanta, 1946–1988.* Lawrence: Univ. Press of Kansas, 1989.

Stucker, Jan. 1975. "Brown Lung Compensation: Carolinas Group Seeks Aid for Cotton Mill Workers." *Washington Post*, 8 June, p. A3.

———. 1977. "Textile Interests Vow to Fight Brown Lung Bill." *Columbia Record*, 18 Feb.

———. 1978. "Law Changes May Make Brown Lung Compensation Possible." *Columbia Record*, 1 Feb.

Szpak, Michael. 1991. Interviews with author, 7 and 12 May.

Taylor v. J.P. Stevens. 1980. 300 N.C. 94.

Terkel, Studs. 1988. *The Great Divide*. New York: Random House.

Terrill, Tom E., and Gerald Hirsch, eds. 1978. *Such As Us: Southern Voices of the Thirties.* Chapel Hill: Univ. of North Carolina Press.

"Textile Industry Fights Standards." 1981. *Augusta Chronicle*, 22 Jan., 3B.

"Tighter Cotton Dust Standards Required." 1978. *Greensboro Daily News*, 20 June.

"Tobacco and Textile Companies Battle over 'Brown Lung' Liability." 1980. *New York Times*, 14 Dec.

Trice, M.F. 1940. "Card Room Fever: Strict Control of Dust Will Eliminate Health Hazard from Low-Grade Cotton." *Textile World*, March, p. 68.

"True or False." 1980. *Brown Lung Blues* 2, no. 3.

Tullos, Allen, 1989. *Habits of Industry: White Culture and the Transformation of the Carolina Piedmont.* Chapel Hill: Univ. of North Carolina Press.

"U.S. Agency Orders N.C. To Improve Worker Safety." 1992. *The State*, 9 Jan., p. 3A.

U.S. Congress. 1978a. Senate. Committee on Appropriations. *Brown Lung: Hearings.* 95th Cong., 1st sess.

———. 1978b. Senate. Subcommittee on Labor of Committee on Human Resources. *Hearings on S. 3060.* 95th Cong., 2d sess.

———. 1979. House. Subcommittee on Labor Standards of Committee on Education and Labor. *Hearings.* 96th Cong., 1st sess.

———. 1980. House. Subcommittee on Labor Standards of Committee on Education and Labor. *Hearings on H.R. 5482.* 96th Cong., 2d sess.

———. 1982a. House. Subcommittee on Investigation and Oversight of Committee on Science and Technology. *Compensation for Exposure To Hazardous Substances.* 97th Cong., 2d sess. (12 Aug.), No. 151.

——. 1982b. House. Investigation and Oversight of Committee on Science and Technology. *Byssinosis: An Evaluation of Scientific and Technological Issues.* 97th Cong. 2d sess. (22 Sept.), No. 166.

U.S. Department of Labor. 1979. *Report to Congress. Cotton Dust: Review of Alternative Technical Standards and Control Technologies.* 14 May. Washington, D.C.: U.S. Government Printing Office.

——. 1980. *An Interim Report to Congress On Occupational Diseases.*

USCA Survey Research Services. 1989. *Public Opinion in the Greater Aiken Area: 1980–1988.* Aiken, S.C.: USCA Survey Research Services, 1989, 56–57.

Vahradian, Scott. 1981. "Industry Attacks Cotton Dust Standard." *Mountain Life and Work,* May: 12–14.

Vlach, John Michael. 1978. *The Afro-American Tradition in Decorative Arts: Catalogue of an Exhibition at the Cleveland Museum of Art.* Cleveland, Ohio: Cleveland Museum of Art.

Warren, Bob. 1991. Telephone interview with author, 30 April 1991, and copies of correspondence from his files.

Wegman, David H., Charles Levenstein, and Ian A. Greaves. 1983. "Commentary: Byssinosis: A Role for Public Health In the Face of Scientific Uncertainty." *American Journal of Public Health* 73 (Feb.): 188–92.

Weimer, Deborah. 1981. "A Report on Compensation for Disabled Textile Workers." *The Insurance, Negligence and Workman's Compensation Report* 4, no. 1 (May): 1–4.

"WHO Disputes Academy Report On Brown Lung." 1982. *Aiken Standard,* 15 March, p. 5A.

Williams, Charles D., Jr., David E. Shanks, Robert Heyer, Edward Landis, Jr., Arnold Frazier, Tim E. Cooper, William C. Sugg, Jr., William C. Whiteside, and John E. Gardella. 1980. "Doctors Look at Byssinosis." *Charlotte Observer,* 21 June, p. 15A.

Woliver, Laura. 1990. "Book Reviews: American Politics." *American Political Science Review* 84 (Dec.): 1405–6.

Wood v. J.P. Stevens. 1979. 297 N.C. 636.

Woodward, C. Vann. 1960. *The Burden of Southern History.* Baton Rouge: Louisiana State Univ. Press.

Wyatt-Brown, Bertram. 1986. *Honor and Violence in the Old South.* New York: Oxford Univ. Press.

Zieger, Robert H. 1986. *American Workers, American Unions, 1920–1985.* Baltimore, Md.: Johns Hopkins Univ. Press.

——, ed. 1991. *Organized Labor in the Twentieth-Century South.* Knoxville: Univ. of Tennessee Press.

INDEX